# Scenic
# Driving

# BRITISH
# COLUMBIA

**Scott Pick**

Published in Canada
by
Thomas Allen & Son Limited

FALCON®

**_A_FALCON**GUISE®

Falcon® is continually expanding its list of recreational guidebooks. All books include detailed descriptions, accurate maps, and all the information necessary for enjoyable trips. You can order extra copies of this book and get information and prices for other Falcon® guidebooks by writing Falcon, P.O. Box 1718, Helena, MT 59624 or calling toll-free 1-800-582-2665. Please ask for a free copy of our current catalog. Visit our website at www.Falcon.com or contact us via e-mail at falcon@falcon.com.

**Published in Canada by:**
**Thomas Allen & Son Limited**
390 Steelcase Road East
Markham, Ontario L3R 1G2
Telephone: (905) 475-9126
Fax: (905) 475-6747
E-mail: info@t-allen.com.

Cover photo and all interior photos by Scott Pick.

Cataloging-in-Publication Data is on file at the Library of Congress.

CAUTION
All participants in the recreational activities suggested by this book must assume responsibility for their own actions and safety. The information contained in this guidebook cannot replace sound judgment and good decision-making skills, which help reduce risk exposure; nor does the scope of this book allow for disclosure of all the potential hazards and risks involved in such activities.

Learn as much as possible about the recreational activities in which you participate, prepare for the unexpected, and be cautious. The reward will be a safer and more enjoyable experience.

 Text pages printed on recycled paper.

# Contents

# Map Legend

| | | | | |
|---|---|---|---|---|
| Scenic Drive (paved) | ▬▬▬▬▬ | Provincial Highway | ㊼ ⑲⓪ | |
| Scenic Drive (gravel) | ▬ ▬ ▬▬ ▬ | Mine | ⚒ | |
| Scenic Side Trip (paved) | ▬▬▬ | City | ▦ | |
| Scenic Side Trip (gravel) | ▬ ▬ ▬▬ ▬ | Town | ○ | |
| Other Roads (paved) | ─────── | Pass | ) ( | |
| Other Roads (gravel) | - - - - - - | Peak and Elevation | ⛰ *9,782 ft.* | |
| Junction | □ | Glaciers and Icecaps | | |
| Bridge | ‿ | | | |
| Building | ■ | Wilderness Area, National/Provincial Park | **PARK** | |
| Point of Interest | ◻ | Provincial/International Boundary | A L B E R T A | |
| Campground | ▲ | | | |
| Hiking Trail | ·········· | Map Orientation | N ↕ | |
| River/Creek | ∿ | Scale of Kilometers | 0  5  10 Kilometers | |
| Waterfall | ∿ | | | |
| Lake | ▬ | Scenic Drive Location | ★ | |
| Marsh | ⁂ | | | |

v

# Locator Map

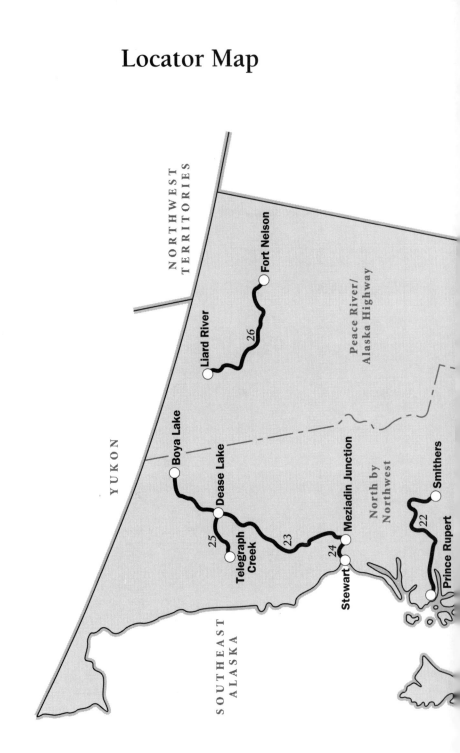

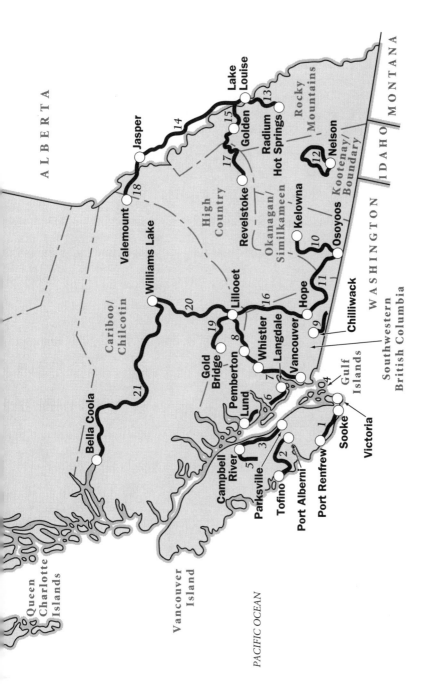

# Land and Sea Circle Tours Map

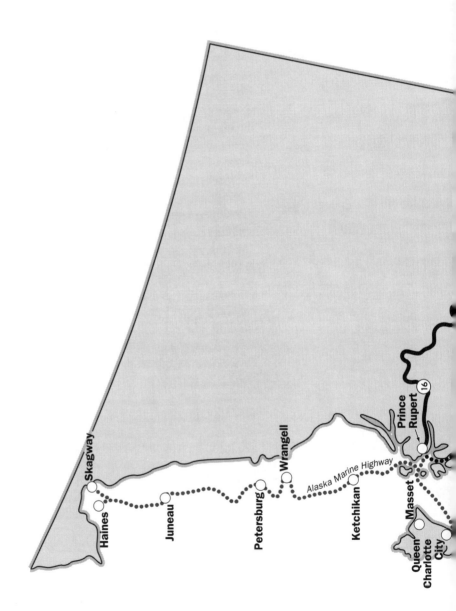

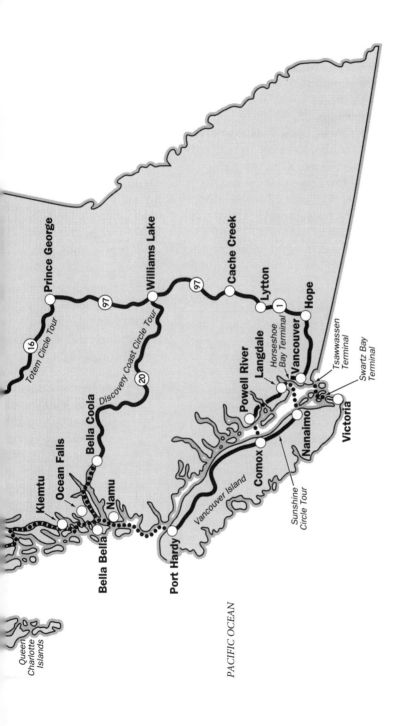

# Acknowledgments

Many thanks are owed to Falcon Publishing for expanding their Scenic Driving series north into Canada and for entrusting me with this much-needed book. An anonymous thank-you goes to all of the park rangers, forest service personnel, and others I met and questioned along my travels to research the drives in this book. To all of you I met along the way who wished me "good luck" on the book, I say thanks and hope I have produced a work that will help to further increase tourism in BC and make for a more sustainable future. I'd also like to acknowledge my hard-working truck and hiking boots that have allowed me to see so much of this magnificent corner of the world. Of course, if it wasn't for the support of my family for my adventurous ways over the years, I wouldn't have accumulated the knowledge of BC needed to do it justice. Most of all I want to give thanks to whoever created beautiful BC, as I feel truly proud to live in a place where adventure possibilities and wilderness landscapes still abound.

# Introduction

In its 950,000 square kilometers, British Columbia packs in more high-impact scenery than almost anywhere else on earth. It has an incredible variety of landscapes and natural environments. BC is a place of superlatives—massive glaciers, whitewater rivers, remote lakes, old-growth rainforests, fierce mountains, dry canyons, gemlike islands, wave-battered coastlines, sinuous fjords—the list goes on and on. It's no wonder that the province is marketed as "Super Natural British Columbia."

BC is the most consistently rugged place in North America. Not only is there very little flat land in the province, but over three quarters of it lie above 3,000 feet in elevation. The province, taller than it is wide, is bordered on the west by the Pacific Ocean and the Alaskan Panhandle, on the north by both the Yukon and the Northwest Territories, on the east by Alberta, and on the south by three US states—Washington, Idaho, and Montana.

BC is far bigger than most people think—it covers 10 percent of Canada, the second largest country on earth, and is nearly two-and-a-half times the size of California and four times larger than Great Britain. Seeing the whole province by highway is a major undertaking. Just to research all of the drives included in this book required over 12,000 kilometers (7,200 miles) of driving. On some of the drives, the scale of the land may surprise you if you are used to smaller places. Particularly up north, the hours and miles melt away and you may not seem any closer to your destination.

On its western edge, BC has over 27,000 kilometers (16,200 miles) of coastline—a place where thousands of islands face the open Pacific and fjords slice deeply into the Coast Mountain chain that forms an almost impassable barrier between ocean and interior. From eastern to western BC, numerous parallel mountain ranges run north-south through the province. Two mountain ranges run the entire length of the province—the Coast Mountains in the west and the Rocky Mountains in the east. Between these two ranges are the Selkirk, Purcell, Skeena, and Cariboo Mountains among others. The vast interior plateau that includes most of the Cariboo, Chilcotin, and Southern Interior regions provides the only real respite from the endless waves of peaks that dominate the province. Here the mountains ease off into the gentle plateau, canyon, and lake country that runs from the international border to north of Prince George.

In addition to the coast and mountains, BC is well known for its lakes, rivers, and forests. Most of the highways in the province follow major river valleys as these are the easiest way to travel through this land of barriers. BC has thousands of rivers and lakes, many of which are still unnamed and virtually unknown. Some of the major rivers include the Fraser, Peace, Columbia, Stikine, and Liard. Perhaps more than anything, it's the endless forests of BC that leave a lasting impression. Almost the entire province is deeply forested, from the huge old-growth trees of the lush valley bottoms to the stunted, windswept trees high in the subalpine zone. Evergreen forests are the predominant type but vary from spindly lodgepole pine in the dry Chilcotin region to massive Sitka spruce on the rain-soaked outer coasts.

Many people come to BC hoping to see wildlife and few are disappointed. BC has the greatest amount and largest variety of wildlife in Canada. For example, BC has 25 percent of the world's remaining grizzlies and 60 percent of the world's mountain goats. With so much of it still untouched, it's no wonder that the province is still home to a significant population of creatures so revered by tourists; bears, eagles, cougars, and moose are but a few examples. Northern BC in particular is considered one of the last bastions of vast wildlife habitat left on earth, a place where the natural cycles continue uninterrupted as they have for thousands of years. In the oceans, the variety of marine life is no less remarkable. Killer whales (orcas), dolphins, sea lions, otters, sharks, and of course the all-important salmon all call BC's waters home.

BC is a distinct place within Canada, partly due to ocean and mountain barriers inherent in the province. British Columbians are shaped by their environment more than anything else. With all the opportunities for outdoor recreation, BC residents are more active than other residents of Canada and have a deep affinity with the land. Indeed, many people in BC feel more of a connection with the US Pacific Northwest than they do with the rest of Canada. Several underground political movements have been pushing the idea of "Cascadia" for years. These movements support increased cooperation between BC and the northwestern US states.

Between greater Vancouver and southern Vancouver Island live three quarters of BC's four million people. In fact, most of the population lives in the southernmost zone of BC along the Canadian/US border, leaving a lot of empty country. In particular, the area north of Prince George is a whole different place and has more in common with Alaska or the Yukon than with southern BC. Huge sections of BC, particularly along the coast and the northernmost areas, hardly have any population at all, a startling fact considering that some of these regions are larger than some US states.

Vancouver, BC's largest city with a population of two million people, is very unlike the rest of the province. You don't really enter the real BC until you leave the cities and venture off into the wilder, less explored areas. Indeed, the view from the North Shore Mountains which rise on Vancouver's northern skyline is a perfect example. To the south, the view is of megacities and urban sprawl. Simply turn around and it's like looking into a different world. The view is now dominated by mountains as far as the eye can see with little human impact visible. If this is the view on Vancouver's doorstep, it boggles the mind to think about just how rugged, lonely, and isolated the rest of the province is.

While much of BC is still in its wilderness state and will likely always be that way, resource industries are slowly chipping away at the wild heart of the province. Environmental issues have been at the forefront in BC for the last 30-or-so years as the rate of resource extraction has accelerated to nearly disastrous levels. As we enter the new millennium, both the commercial fishing and forest industries are struggling to cope with the aftermath of decades of overharvesting. Unlike other places where the environmental damage is more or less hidden, like toxic lakes or poor air quality, in BC most of the impact is readily visible for all to see. As you drive many of the highways in the province you might be disheartened at the amount of logging that has taken place. Forest products are BC's biggest industry, but tourism is rapidly catching up and soon might become the largest industry, hopefully creating a more sustainable economy.

BC as a province is little more than 100 years old. Before the arrival of the first white explorers, what's now BC had been continuously populated since the last ice age by native peoples who lived both along the coasts as well as in the heart of the province. The first white explorers arrived by sea in the late 1700s, namely Captains Cook and Vancouver. By land from eastern Canada, explorers and fur traders, most notably Alexander Mackenzie and Simon Fraser, forged routes through the trackless mountain wilderness in search of routes to the Pacific from the rest of Canada. The fur trade was the primary reason for settlement and development in the province in the first half of the nineteenth century. Even though BC still wasn't an official province, the first governing body was formed in the mid-1800s. Soon thereafter, BC experienced some of the most frenzied gold rushes in history. Starting with the Cariboo Gold Rush in 1858, successive waves of miners came to BC in search of riches and spurred much of the early development of the province. During this time, the first major transportation routes in BC were forged through the wilds in order to move people and supplies to the mining areas. The Cariboo Road and the Dewdney Trail are but two examples of routes that have evolved into major transportation corridors. Salmon fishing and canning were also growing industries in the late 1800s and helped to populate the coastal areas.

Vancouver itself dates back to 1862 when a timber mill was built in order to harvest some of the biggest trees in the world. While Vancouver was to evolve into the largest city in BC, New Westminster, just east, was briefly named as the capital of the colony of BC before it was changed to Victoria where it is located today. With the completion of the Canadian Pacific Railway across Canada in 1885, the Canadian government lived up to the promise it had made to the new province of BC years before, and the railway provided the impetus for the rapid expansion of southern BC and Vancouver in particular.

As part of a conscious decision to diversify the provincial economy and make it less dependent on the fur trade and gold mining, the early government embarked on an ambitious program to develop the forestry and agriculture industries in the hinterlands of the province. These industries remain two of the mainstays of the province today. At the same time, the government realized that the railways were not enough to fuel the growth in the province's economy, and began building roads. From 1900 to 1925, many old wagon roads were converted to pavement for automobile travel. This trend continued in the post–World War II era when car ownership expanded rapidly. Successive BC-government obsessions with "mega" projects have resulted in a 22,000-kilometer (13,200-mile) network of highways. These highways, many cut through trackless wilderness, make BC one of the great driving destinations on earth, especially when combined with the great number of backroads.

### The Regions

BC is broken down into nine geographic and tourism regions. These regions are the creation of the government and are not official boundaries shown on maps. Rather, they divide BC into rough areas that have similar geography, history, environments, and peoples.

**Vancouver Island.** This region includes all of Vancouver Island, the Gulf Islands, and a remote chunk of the mainland coast just northeast of Vancouver Island. Vancouver Island is the largest island off the west coast of North America. The vast majority of its population lives in the southern half of the island. The entire western rim of Vancouver Island is a wild and remote place where the mountains plunge right into the open ocean. Most of the tourism occurs along the gentle east coast and near Victoria, BC's capitol, on the very southern tip of the island. The west coast of Vancouver Island is wet and stormy while the east coast is dry and mild. Drives 1 through 5 are found in this region.

**Southwestern BC.** This region is dominated by BC's fjord-riddled lower coast as well as the rugged bulk of the southern Coast Mountains. Other than the Fraser Valley in which Vancouver, BC's largest city, is located, there is very little flat land in this part of the province. Vancouver's skyline is dominated by the very southern edge of the Coast Mountains that stretch all the way up the west coast and well into Alaska. This part of BC is lush, rain-soaked, and very green, with snow and glaciers on the higher peaks. Over 50 percent of BC's population is found here. Drives 6 through 9 are located in this region.

**Okanagan/Similkameen.** This area in BC's arid Southern Interior is the most unique in the province as it lies in the rainshadow of the Coast and Cascade Mountains and more resembles Southern California than BC. The Okanagan/Similkameen region is the driest part of BC and has Canada's only true desert area in its far southern end. With its good weather, abundance of lakes, sandy beaches, and resort atmosphere, this area is the vacation heartland of BC. Drives 10 and 11 are located in this region.

**Kootenay/Boundary.** Found just east of the Okanagan/Similkameen region, this area lies in the interior "wet belt" of southeastern BC and is dominated by deep forests, snowcapped mountains, and fjord-like lakes. The Selkirk and Purcell Mountains tower above almost everything in this part of the province and are home to nine large mountain parks. The Kootenay/Boundary region has the most picturesque and historic towns in BC, many of which date back to the various mining booms of the 1800s. Drive 12 is located in this region.

**Rocky Mountains.** Although Alberta is better known as the home of the Rocky Mountains, BC has a huge chunk of this magnificent range as well. This long and narrow area lies in the extreme southeastern corner of the province bordered by Alberta to the east and the Kootenay/Boundary region on the west. Both of BC's two Rocky Mountain national parks are found here. Besides the Rockies, the dominant feature is the Columbia River trench which runs right down the center of the area. Drives 13, 14, and 15 are found in this region.

**High Country.** High Country is the most diverse region in the province and stretches from Hope, not far east of Vancouver, all the way northeast to Mount Robson. The region varies from the sun-parched canyons and open grasslands near Lillooet to the lush peak-and-glacier country of the Selkirk and Rocky Mountains. Much of the land here is at high elevations. This region also has some of BC's major highways running through its heart, including a major portion of the Trans Canada Highway. Drives 16, 17, and 18 are located in this region.

**Cariboo/Chilcotin.** This region lies in west-central BC and stretches from the glaciated Cariboo Mountains in the east all the way to BC's remote central coast. The Cariboo area is found to the east of the Fraser River, while the Chilcotin is to the west of it. The main features here are the dozens of large lakes in the Cariboo, the dry gorge of the Fraser River canyon, the immense Chilcotin Plateau, the high and fierce peaks of the central Coast Mountains and finally, a narrow part of fjord and island-riddled coast. The population of this vast area is low, with most people living in the cities of Williams Lake and Quesnel. The two major highways through the region, Highways 97 and 20, provide access to the hundreds of backroads that lead to some truly spectacular places. Much of the land here is dedicated to ranching and forestry. Drives 19, 20, and 21 are located in this region.

**North by Northwest.** This enormous area covers 317,000 square kilometers in the far northwestern corner of the province. Within this area are found the deepest wilderness areas in BC, especially where it borders the Alaskan Panhandle to the west and the Peace River/Alaska Highway region to the east. The two major highways here are the Yellowhead and the Stewart-Cassiar. The area also stretches east to include Prince George, BC's unofficial northern capitol. This region is dominated by the Coast Mountains in the west and the northern Rocky Mountains in the east. The North by Northwest region also includes the Queen Charlotte Islands and the wild north coast of BC. Most of the coastal areas here have a distinctly maritime climate and are wet and mild most of the year. The inland areas have a more continental climate with less precipitation and more distinctive temperature variations between summer and winter. Drives 22 through 25 are found in this region.

**Peace River/Alaska Highway.** This region, covering the whole northeastern corner of the province, is bordered by Alberta to the east, the Yukon and the Northwest Territories to the north, and the North by Northwest region of BC to the west. Peace River/Alaska Highway is a combination of the rugged and desolate beauty of northern Rocky Mountains in the western part and the heavily cultivated flat plateau country near Fort St. John in the east. Much of the area near Dawson Creek more resembles Canada's prairies than mountainous BC. This area is known more than anything for having the entire BC stretch of the world-famous Alaska Highway. In this vast region live only 2 percent of the province's population, not surprising given the remoteness and bitterly cold winters. Drive 26 is found in this region.

## Weather and Seasons
If a single word could be used to describe the weather in BC it would be "unstable." Whatever the weather is doing, don't count on it being the same for long! A basic rule of thumb is that the weather is more changeable in the mountain and coastal regions than anywhere else in the province.

The beginning of the travel season in BC is considered to be mid-March in most of the province—a time when winter begins to ease its icy grip. April is generally rainy and a poor time to travel. May can be a great month to visit BC as it often has sunny, warm weather, but this varies year-to-year. June is generally a mixed-weather month and is often wetter and stormier than May. While statistically July is the hottest month, it is also variable as well. During some Julys it seems to rain every day while in others it's blazing hot and sunny the whole month. Generally the late summer/early fall period—early August to late September—is the most reliable weather window of the year anywhere in BC. This is the best time for almost any drive in this book. The crowds begin to thin, the air is crisp and cool, the bugs are gone, and the fall colors are beginning to occur.

By late October, winter conditions begin to prevail over the whole province with rain at lower elevations and snow higher up. For the most part, winters in BC are a difficult time to travel. Bad weather is the rule and weeks might pass before the sun is seen again. One vigorous storm after another rakes the province, dumping massive amounts of snow almost everywhere and making driving hazardous. The common joke in BC is that people don't grow old, they just rust away.

In a province as big as BC, expect radical climate changes depending upon where you are. For example, Pacific Rim National Park gets on average ten times the rainfall that the Okanagan does and much less sunshine. On some of the longer drives in the book, the highway passes from one climatic zone to another, meaning that weather can change rapidly as you drive. Highway 20 (Drive 21) across the Chilcotin is a perfect example. The highway travels from the hottest, driest zone in the province near the Fraser River to one of the wettest in the lush Bella Coola Valley.

Generally, the farther south you travel in the province, the longer the travel season. Southern Vancouver Island, the Okanagan, and the Columbia River valley generally have the nicest weather in the province and the longest travel season, as they lie in the rainshadow of mountain ranges. On the other hand, coastal BC has the worst, least reliable weather in the province and the shortest travel season. Northern BC has cool, sunny summers and dry, bitterly cold winters on average. The Kootenays and the Rockies have a more continentally-influenced climate. Generally summers are hot and sunny but can be unstable as well, depending upon the marine influence. In winter, temperatures can plunge way below zero as masses of cold air invade from the north or east. The outer coast of Vancouver Island and the entire BC mainland coast are among the wettest places on earth, so expect endless days of rain in the spring, fall, and winter, and only a short respite in summer.

### Parks and Protected Areas
BC is renowned for its system of protected areas and parks. While much of the province has been impacted by industrial use, vast tracts of land are still as pristine as when the first explorers journeyed here over 200 years ago. BC has two main types of parks—national and provincial. There are six national parks in BC, four of which are in the mountains of eastern BC—Glacier and Mount Revelstoke in the Selkirk Mountains, and Kootenay and Yoho in the Rockies. The other two national parks are on the coast—Pacific Rim on Vancouver Island and Gwaii Haanas in the Queen Charlottes.

BC has been on an ambitious mission over the last decade to expand the protected areas to cover 12 percent of the total land base. In the last five years hundreds of new parks have been created, bringing the total to nearly 400 provincial parks alone. In total, almost 6 million hectares (almost 15 million acres) of land are protected parkland. In recent years, BC's provincial parks have attracted over 20 million visitors a year, making them more popular than the entire Canadian national park system.

While many of the parks are small, several are among the largest protected areas on earth. The new editions of provincial maps show the locations of the new parks, particularly the bigger ones. Most of the new parks lie deep in true wilderness and were created to protect wildlife habitat and landscapes rather than for human recreation. The parks near the urban areas tend to be highly geared toward camping and recreation while the parks in the remote areas of the province are more suited to self-propelled backcountry travel and wilderness exploration. The best current sources for information on all of the parks (other than guidebooks) are the various BC Parks Internet sites. For each of the drives, the additional information section lists the BC Parks Internet address for that particular area. The *BC Recreational Atlas* (new edition to be retitled *The BC Road and Recreational Atlas*) also indicates the locations of most parks (except the newest ones) and lists the facilities for each.

**Outdoor Recreation**
To fully appreciate the natural wonders of BC, it's necessary to get away from the highways and into the wilder areas where nature rules supreme. While experienced outdoorspeople will often plan their own outdoor adventures, others will want to travel on a commercially guided trip, leaving the planning and logistics to others. This is the safer option for the inexperienced. With the boom in ecotourism in BC, there is a full range of recreational opportunities from whale-watching to mountaineering. Hiking, skiing, mountain biking, sailing, canoeing, sea kayaking, fishing, rock climbing, rafting, surfing, and backroading are but a few of the possibilities in BC.

Many of the prominent outdoor recreation magazines rate BC among the top places in the world for outdoor adventure. Unlike smaller and more populated places, there is still a spirit of exploration and true adventure in BC. With the majority of the population living in the extreme southern part of the province, the opportunity to really get away from it all is equaled by few other places in North America. The best way to plan an outdoor trip in BC is to read guidebooks. The Adventurous Traveler Bookstore is an excellent source for BC guidebooks (see Appendix). Also, try searching the Internet, or call the government to obtain any of the regional tourist books they publish. These free publications are full of ads from adventure and tour companies and are gold mines of information.

**What to Bring**
Except for Vancouver, Victoria, and a few other large population centers, casual dressing is the norm. You'll be out of place if you are dressed up in most of BC, particularly the rural areas. Dressing for action is the best rule to follow. With the limitless potential for exploration along these drives, you'll want to be able to get out and walk around. If nothing else, bring a

pair of sturdy hiking shoes or boots. Running shoes often result in twisted ankles so avoid them if possible. Be sure to bring a camera and a good supply of film.

With BC's rapidly changing weather, be sure to have enough clothes to keep you comfortable no matter what the weather is. A wind and waterproof jacket is a necessity. Summers are generally warm to hot, even up north, so also be prepared for that. A small backpack or fanny pack to carry snacks, a water bottle, and a jacket are good things to bring along if you'll be walking around a lot. Of course serious outdoorspeople will bring everything they need for their adventures or pick up supplies in Vancouver. A great place to stock up on outdoor clothing and equipment is the nonprofit Mountain Equipment Co-op (see Internet site listed in the Appendix) in Vancouver. This massive store is the best place in the province to get geared up before venturing off into the outdoors.

## Drive Selection

The 26 drives in this book where chosen for a variety of reasons, most important of which was roadside scenery. Many run through the various mountain ranges (an unavoidable fact in rugged BC), while others run along the ocean's edge or deep within dry canyons. The three circle tours combine drives through the heart of BC with unforgettable ferry rides up the wild BC coast and create a driving experience unlike any other in North America. Generally the drives pass through lightly populated wilderness rather than through the heavily built-up regions in the very southern edge of the province. If drivers want to see cities and development, they have many other places to go, but if they want to see the true "Super Natural BC" they need to leave the cities behind and enter the beauty of BC's backcountry. This book will point you in the right direction, and there's a lot of freedom for exploration along the way.

## Safe Driving

Here are some tips to make your BC driving trip a safe and memorable one:

1. Avoid driving at night and in bad weather. Many of the highways are twisty and narrow with all sorts of cliffs and dropoffs nearby. Collisions with wildlife often happen at night as well.

2. Avoid driving BC in midwinter. Snowstorms, cold temperatures, and icy highways are a constant hazard. The exceptions are Vancouver Island, the Sunshine Coast, the Gulf Islands, and the Okanagan. If you do decide to drive in winter, be sure to have extra warm clothes, emergency food, snow tires, and chains.

3. Watch the road, not the scenery. This is hard to do on BC's spectacular highways but your relatives and friends will be thankful you did!

4. Carry emergency equipment. Although emergencies are unlikely to happen, the remoteness of BC's highways means that help is sometimes far away. This is particularly true in the northern half of the province. Having warm clothes, spare food and water, a first-aid kit, a good spare tire, emergency flares, and tire inflator are all wise additions to your travel kit.

5. Let someone know your itinerary and keep in touch as you move around the province.

6. Cell phones are useless in most of the remote parts of BC. Cell phones are useful for emergencies along a few of the major highways in southern BC. North of Prince George coverage is very limited. Ask your provider for a coverage map before you arrive in BC. Short band radios or CB radios are much more useful in emergencies if you know how to use them.

## Backroad Travel

Nowhere else in North America, likely the world, is there such an incredible number of backroads as in BC. For every mile of paved highway there are at least ten miles of backroads ranging from well-groomed access roads to full-on four-wheel-drive country. If you want to give your shiny new sport utility vehicle a workout, BC is the place to do it. Much of the province is the domain of resource industries. The forest industry in particular has created most of the backroads in BC. As the huge old-growth timber is harder and harder to find, logging companies are pushing roads farther into the wilderness in search of valuable wood.

Although the impact of extensive logging in BC is controversial from an environmental standpoint, there is no doubt that these operations have opened up a great deal of the province for intrepid backroaders to see first-hand. The roads through BC's mountainous areas are particularly scenic—many travel alongside rivers, through deep forests, and beneath towering summits. These roads have a short lifespan, though. Once the logging stops, the roads quickly fall apart due to growing bush, washouts, and landslides.

The easiest way to identify where the backroads are is to have a copy of the *BC Recreational Atlas* (new edition to be retitled *The BC Road and Recreational Atlas*) when on any of the drives in the book. With this invaluable mapbook, you'll be able to see the various backroads branching off the paved highway. The atlas differentiates between the good backroads and the lesser maintained ones so you won't get sucked into a road harder than your vehicle or nerves can handle.

The best way to find out more information about a backroad you are interested in (and its present condition) is to contact the BC Forest Service office listed in the back for each drive. A good rule to follow is that if the

Forest Service has never even heard of the road then it's probably washed out or otherwise impassable. They will also be able to tell you if the given road is being used by resource companies when you plan to be there. One encounter on a narrow logging road with a fully loaded logging truck will quickly convince you to stay off these roads during working hours.

**Tips for Backroad Travel in BC**

1. Try to drive backroads used for logging after 5 P.M. on weekdays or, preferably on weekends only.

2. Make sure you don't get in over your head. If the road ahead starts to get too steep or rough then get out and scout it on foot. Remember that help is often far away and getting towed out may be incredibly expensive. Stay well within your comfort zone. Once you start up many roads, it might be difficult to turn around, so make sure you can manage it before you start.

3. Make sure you have the appropriate vehicle for the road and that it's in good mechanical condition. Four-wheel-drive trucks and Jeep-type vehicles are way better when the going gets tough than are fancy SUVs.

4. Try to travel with another vehicle in case someone gets stuck, breaks down, or there is an accident.

5. Have a good spare tire (two preferably), warm clothes, spare food and water to last several days, basic tools, a good map and compass, spare gas (depending on the drive), a shovel, jumper cables, a solid jack and jacking board, first-aid kit, flares, tire inflator, tire repair kit, and small air compressor. Tire chains are useful even in summer in case the road is steep and muddy.

6. As mentioned before, cell phones are useless in most of the remote parts of BC. Short band radios or CB radios are much more useful in emergencies if you know how to use them.

7. Leave word of where you are going and when you plan to return with a friend, relative, or other responsible person and check back in with them when you get back out safely.

8. Try to find out in advance the condition of the road you plan to travel. Either ask locally or call the nearest Forest Service office. This is the easiest way to have a fun and safe trip.

9. Check with your insurance company. You might not be covered if you crash or otherwise damage your vehicle off a paved road. Taking rental cars and trucks off the paved highways often invalidates the insurance.

## Land and Sea Circle Tours

A feature unique to BC is that the extensive ferry system can be used to create loop trips that combine scenic driving with ocean voyages along the remote Pacific coast. BC Ferries runs one of the largest ferry systems in the world and has extensive coverage up and down the coast. These unforgettable trips should be high on the list for anyone planning a driving adventure to BC, especially given the reasonable prices (quoted as of 1999) of the ferry fares. Indeed, the scenery along the ocean-going legs of these tours is the same as seen by people on luxury cruises to Alaska. When combined with the scenic drives, these tours will leave a memorable impression of BC that will make you dream of returning.

All three tours described start and end in Vancouver. The itinerary on the driving legs is entirely up to you. For each of the tours, the quickest way back to Vancouver is listed; however, you are free to customize the trips to include other scenic drives while in the area. The amount of time needed for the tours depends entirely on the number of side trips and the pace of driving. The times quoted are the bare minimum to be able to actually see and experience the sights along the way.

These circle tours will take a little more planning than strictly driving trips. The main source of information for the ocean-going legs of the tours is BC Ferries themselves, as they are actively promoting these land-sea trips. If possible, view their web site at **www.bcferries.com** for schedules, fares, reservations, and other information on the ferry fleet. Call BC Ferries at 250-386-3431 (long distance from outside BC) or 888-BCFERRY (888-223-3779) from within BC. They also can be contacted at:

BC Ferries
1112 Fort Street, Victoria
British Columbia, Canada
V8V 4V2

## The Tours

### 1. Totem Circle

This grand adventure combines a trip up the spectacular Inside Passage of the BC coast with a drive back down the center of the province to Vancouver. It will take most travelers about a week to ten days to complete. It covers about 3,000 kilometers (1,800 miles) in total, with approximately 2,000 kilometers (1,200 miles) of driving and 1,000 kilometers (600 miles) of ferry travel. The trip is named after the wealth of northwest native culture that can be experienced along the way, especially in Alert Bay (near Port Hardy) and in the Prince Rupert and Hazelton areas.

The trip is described clockwise, starting with the ferry ride. There are two options for the start of the trip. From Vancouver, either start the driving by taking the ferry from Horseshoe Bay to Nanaimo, or to see more of Vancouver Island, take the ferry from Tsawwassen to Swartz Bay. Starting at Swartz Bay will add a few hours to the drive up Vancouver Island but you'll be treated to the gorgeous views from the Malahat Highway (Highway 1) on your way to Nanaimo. Either ferry trip takes about an hour to reach Vancouver Island and costs about $50 for two adults and a car.

Once in Nanaimo, head north on the Island Highway (Highway 19) to Port Hardy near the northern tip of Vancouver Island. Just north of Nanaimo, drivers can choose whether to take the "old" Island Highway (Highway 19A, Drive 3) along the oceanfront or save time by staying on the faster "new" Island Highway (19). The trip north from Nanaimo to Port Hardy will take anywhere from 5 to 7 hours and entails about 400 kilometers (240 miles) of driving.

Once in Port Hardy, board the BC Ferry "Queen of the North" and begin the unforgettable cruise up the inside passage on BC's remote west coast. The cost of this one-way ferry ride is $430 for two adults and a car. Reservations are required. The ferry travels northbound every three days (check schedule) in the summer months. June and July are the two ideal months to travel this circle tour as the days are long enough that the entire 15-hour ferry ride will be in daylight.

The ocean leg is one breathtaking scene after another. Once away from the dock, the ferry quickly heads north and encounters the open ocean swells of Queen Charlotte Sound and views of towering coastal peaks in the background. After this often-rough passage, the ferry begins to thread its way through the Inside Passage, a series of narrow protected waterways between islands just off the mainland. Except for a few native settlements along the way, the coast is entirely uninhabited and is as wild today as it was hundreds of years ago. The views combine wave-swept rocky coastlines and extensive old-growth forests with glimpses of high, snowcapped peaks on the western edge of the Coast Mountains.

North of Bella Bella, the ferry runs straight up incredibly narrow Princess Royal and Grenville Channels, both less than a kilometer (0.6 mile) wide and lined by steep, green peaks on both sides. On the ferry ride, watch the magnificent scenery drift by hour after hour and also be on the lookout for whales and dolphins, which are regularly seen.

Once in Prince Rupert, drive the Yellowhead Highway (Drive 22) to Smithers and beyond to Prince George. An excellent two-day side trip is to head north up the Stewart-Cassiar Highway and drive the amazing Glacier Highway (Drive 24). From Prince George, head south on Highway 97 through the Cariboo region to Cache Creek. From Cache Creek, either take Highway 99 to Duffey Lake Road (Drive 8) and the Sea to Sky Highway (Drive 7), or if pressed for time take Highway 1 south down the Fraser Canyon (Drive 16) to Hope and then on to Vancouver. The trip from Prince Rupert to Vancouver will take most drivers anywhere from three to six days depending upon the pace and side trips taken.

**2. Discovery Coast**
This circle tour, much shorter in total distance than the Totem Circle tour, is just as spectacular and takes about a week for most drivers to complete as there is so much to see along the way. This loop trip was made possible by a new BC Ferries route, the Discovery Coast Passage route which began in 1997. This incredibly scenic and varied tour takes in Vancouver Island, the lush island and fjord scenery of BC's midcoast, a trip up one of the longest fjords in the world, and a drive across the Chilcotin Plateau in the shadow of the majestic Coast Mountains. The total driving distance for this loop is approximately 1,400 kilometers—400 kilometers (240 miles) from Nanaimo to Port Hardy and 1,000 kilometers (600 miles) from Bella Coola back to Vancouver. The directions to Port Hardy on the northern tip of Vancouver Island are the same as for the Totem Circle tour previously described.

This tour is only possible in mid-summer when the Discovery Coast Ferry is running—generally early June to early September. The ferry schedule is quite complicated as there are three possible routes for the ocean-going part of the journey. Despite the different trip lengths, the cost for all three options is the same. The ferry sails northbound every few days and reservations are highly recommended. The cost is $440 for two adults and a car for the one-way trip from Port Hardy to Bella Coola.

On some days, the ferry travels directly between Port Hardy and Bella Coola. This trip takes about 14 hours and stops only once in Namu. More commonly, the ferry ride is almost 24 hours long, leaving in the early morning from Port Hardy and arriving the next morning in Bella Coola. On the way it makes stops in Bella Bella, the largest native community on the midcoast. The longest option is the trip from Port Hardy to Bella Coola via Bella Bella, Klemtu, and Ocean Falls. This journey is almost 34 hours long and involves spending two nights on the ferry. There are no overnight accommodations other than reclining seats. Most travelers simply bring a sleeping bag and pad and sleep on the floors or in the seats. A cafeteria on board provides meals.

The longest trip allows for visits to the unique coastal villages of Klemtu and Ocean Falls and passes much more ocean, island, and fjord scenery along the way. Klemtu is a remote native village of the Kitasoo people and is set in a beautiful location between old-growth covered mountainsides on Swindle Island. The ferry generally stops here for four hours, enough time to take a walking tour of this unique spot. Ocean Falls is nearly a ghost town, left abandoned when the local pulp mill closed down in the 1980s. While most of the buildings are empty, a dedicated few hang on in this remote outpost of civilization.

The last leg of the ferry journey is down the Dean Channel, a 70-kilometer (42-mile) long fjord that slices deep into the Coast Mountains. For many this would be the highlight of the trip but unfortunately, the ferry often sails through here in the dark. In the summer, wake up early as the ferry runs through North Bentinck Arm on the last leg of the journey in the morning. The soaring, glacier-clad peaks, waterfalls, old-growth forests, and turquoise waters near Bella Coola are an unforgettable sight.

Once off the ferry in Bella Coola, drive through the towering Coast Mountains, up the infamous "Hill" and across the Chilcotin Plateau on Highway 20 (Drive 21) to Williams Lake. From there, either take the easy way back to Vancouver via Highway 97 to Cache Creek and then Highway 1 for the rest of the drive, or for a more spectacular and exciting trip, take the Chilcotin Backroads (Drive 20) to Lillooet, the Carpenter Lake Road to Gold Bridge (Drive 19), the Hurley River Road to Pemberton, and finally the Sea to Sky Highway (Drive 7) back to Vancouver.

### 3. Sunshine Circle

This scenic loop trip "circles" Georgia Strait, the massive inland sea between Vancouver Island and the BC mainland. The Sunshine Circle covers about 300 kilometers (180 miles) and takes anywhere from three to five days to complete. This is by far the shortest of the three described tours and has the most flexible ferry schedules. The trip can be extended into the "Three Coasts Tour" if the Pacific Rim Highway (Drive 2) is taken to Long Beach from Parksville.

The main components of the tour are two scenic drives in this book—the Sunshine Coast (Drive 6) and the Old Island Highway (Drive 3). The tour can be done in either direction but is described clockwise. Be sure to ask for the "CirclePac" fare at the first ferry terminal. By buying all of the tickets for the trip at once, you save 15 percent over buying them separately. The tickets can be used on any ferry trip, giving you a great deal of flexibility. As of 1999, the coast for the "CirclePac" fare was $105 for two adults and a car.

From Vancouver, either take the ferry from Tsawwassen to Swartz Bay, or for a shorter trip, take the ferry from Horseshoe Bay to Nanaimo and start the tour there. Starting in Swartz Bay is recommended as the ferry on the way there passes through the beautiful Gulf Islands. Before heading south to Victoria, it's possible to include a few scenic dives in the Gulf Islands (Drive 4), a side trip that will take anywhere from a few hours to a few days.

For those who ferried to Swartz Bay, make your way south to Victoria and then north on Highway 1 to Nanaimo on the Malahat Highway, the stretch of Highway 1 between Victoria and Duncan. This section is exceptionally scenic and has panoramic views of the Gulf Islands. Once in Nanaimo, follow the Island Highway (Highway 19) to Parksville and then follow

Highway 19A, the "old" Island Highway (19A, Drive 3) along the shores of Georgia Strait to Courtenay. The side trip to Denman and Hornby Islands from Buckley Bay is highly recommended.

Once in Courtenay, follow the signs through Comox to the Little River ferry terminal just north of town. From there, take the ferry across Georgia Strait to Powell River on the northern end of the Sunshine Coast, passing long Texada Island along the way. Before driving south down the Sunshine Coast (Drive 6), consider the optional side trip north to the very end of Highway 101 at Lund. From there, boat tours can be taken into magnificent Desolation Sound or across to beach-rimmed Savary Island.

Driving south from Powell River, there are two more ferry trips on the way back to Vancouver—the Saltery Bay to Earls Cove ferry across Jervis Inlet and the Langdale to Horseshoe Bay ferry across Howe Sound. See Drive 6 for a full description of the sights along the way. Recommended stops are at Egmont, Pender Harbor, Secret Cove, and Gibsons.

# Vancouver Island

# 1

## West Coast Highway
### Sooke to Port Renfrew

**General description:** The West Coast Highway travels 75 kilometers (45 miles) from the urban areas just to the west of Victoria, BC's capital and second biggest city, out to the wild and stormy Pacific on the southwestern coast of Vancouver Island. This drive is challenging with steep grades, tight corners, and numerous one-lane bridges, but the scenic rewards along the way are well worth the effort. Despite the fact that it runs along the waterfront for almost its entire length, much of the ocean views are blocked by forest. To really see, and more importantly feel, the Pacific you must take any of the access roads that branch off the highway and head down to the ocean.

**Special attractions:** Access to west coast beaches, the waterfront trails in Juan de Fuca Provincial Park, Botanical Beach, and the chance to see whales and other marine life.

**Location:** Southern end of Vancouver Island.

**Drive route numbers:** Highway 14, the West Coast Highway the entire distance.

**Travel season:** Summer is best but the spring and fall are fine except when it's raining, which it often is in this part of the world. Winter brings day after day of pounding rain and vicious winds, making this a time for the dedicated beach-lover only.

**Camping:** The first and easiest place to camp is at French Beach Provincial Park near the start of the drive. More attractive campsites are found in Juan de Fuca Provincial Park but these are not car accessible. Sombrio Beach is the most popular place to camp in the park and is reached by a 15-minute hike.

**Services:** No services between Sooke and Port Renfrew and only the basics there.

**Nearby attractions:** East Sooke Park, just east of Sooke, boating on Juan de Fuca Strait, the world-famous West Coast Trail in Pacific Rim National Park, and backroads to Duncan as a shortcut on the way back to Vancouver.

# Drive 1: West Coast Highway
*Sooke to Port Renfrew*

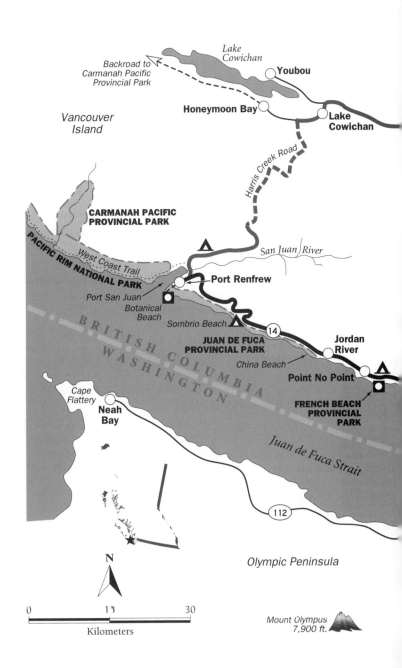

Lake Cowichan

Backroad to Carmanah Pacific Provincial Park

Youbou

Honeymoon Bay

Lake Cowichan

Vancouver Island

Harris Creek Road

CARMANAH PACIFIC PROVINCIAL PARK

PACIFIC RIM NATIONAL PARK

West Coast Trail

San Juan River

Port Renfrew

Port San Juan

Botanical Beach

Sombrio Beach

JUAN DE FUCA PROVINCIAL PARK

China Beach

14

Jordan River

Point No Point

BRITISH COLUMBIA

WASHINGTON

FRENCH BEACH PROVINCIAL PARK

Cape Flattery

Neah Bay

Juan de Fuca Strait

112

Olympic Peninsula

N

0        15        30
Kilometers

Mount Olympus
7,900 ft.

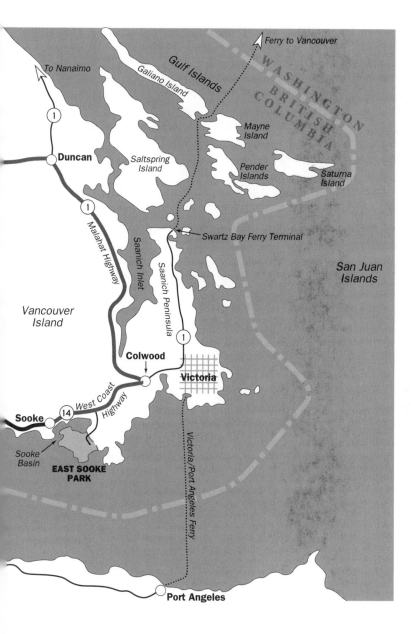

To Nanaimo

Gulf Islands

Galiano Island

Ferry to Vancouver

WASHINGTON

BRITISH COLUMBIA

Duncan

Saltspring Island

Mayne Island

Pender Islands

Saturna Island

Malahat Highway

Saanich Inlet

Saanich Peninsula

Swartz Bay Ferry Terminal

San Juan Islands

Vancouver Island

Colwood

Victoria

Sooke

West Coast Highway

Victoria/Port Angeles Ferry

Sooke Basin

EAST SOOKE PARK

Port Angeles

OLYMPIC NATIONAL PARK

 # The drive

The West Coast Highway begins at the "Welcome to Sooke" sign on the eastern outskirts of Sooke, the last place where you will find full tourist services. Set your odometer here. This is western Canada's southernmost harbor and is known for its seafood and as a gateway to the west coast of the island. Sooke is about an hour's drive west of Victoria on winding and picturesque Highway 14. Along the way, the views across the Juan de Fuca Strait to the Olympic Mountains are spectacular on clear days. The drive winds through dry forest, rare garry oak stands, and past open rock domes, all features unique to the very southern tip of Vancouver Island. The Victoria area enjoys the mildest year-round climate in Canada because it lies in the rainshadow of the stormy Olympic Mountains to the southwest. East Sooke Park, reached by turning off Highway 14 immediately before Sooke Basin (about 15 minutes east of Sooke), is a large waterfront park with numerous trails along the rocky, cove-riddled coastline.

Driving west, Sooke is quickly left behind in a few kilometers. Through this initial section, the highway travels alongside Juan de Fuca Strait, with gravel beaches mere feet from the road. Despite the closeness to the ocean, much of this first stretch is residential and legal beach access is difficult to find.

From here, the entire northern aspect of the Olympic Peninsula in Washington state can be seen. The greatest vertical relief is directly opposite Victoria in the Olympic Mountains. All summer long the snowfields and glaciers in these mountains contrast vividly with the blues and greens of the surrounding landscapes. Looking farther to the west, it's obvious that the peninsula slowly tapers off to low lying hills near its tip. The very northwest point of the continental US, Cape Flattery, is easily seen in the hazy distance. At night the lighthouse on Tatoosh Island, just off the cape, marks the entrance to the Juan de Fuca Strait, a major shipping route to and from the Seattle and Vancouver area.

As the highway moves away from the rainshadow area near Victoria, it enters the temperate rainforest zone with the dry, open arbutus and garry oak forests being replaced by Sitka spruce and western red cedar more typical of the coastal areas. The lush forests here are nourished by one of the highest annual rainfalls on earth which falls mostly between November and May.

The initial portion of the highway does a good imitation of the Oregon coast's famous coastal drive with its frequent ocean views and classic waterfront homes. After this easy first part, the rest of the drive is far more challenging on a road surface that more resembles a paved logging road than a main highway. Highway 14 is best taken at a slow and cautious pace, especially in the tortuous last section. Passing is almost impossible as there are few designated passing lanes and the road surface is often rough and bumpy, despite being paved.

At 23 kilometers (14 miles), French Beach Provincial Park, the first good beach access point, is reached by turning left into the parking area from the highway. This beach is easily the busiest along the entire route as it's a popular day trip for Victoria residents. From the parking area, the ocean and its long gravel beach are a quick stroll away. The park is a popular camping (69 sites), beachcombing, sunset watching, and family picnic area. A scenic walk to the south (left) leads to a rocky headland where numerous tide pools brim with marine life. Although the beach here faces the open Pacific, the waves tend to be small as the Olympic Peninsula in the far distance breaks up the ocean swell. In winter, however, savage storms pound these beaches and have the power to fling driftwood right back into the forest. The nasty weather and heavy rains mean that only hardy storm-watchers venture out here in the depths of the winter months.

Interestingly-named Point No Point, a few kilometers past French Beach, is marked by a prominent teahouse on the waterfront. This spot derives its name from the confusion that early surveyors had over the geography of the area. The point is a popular whale watching location with grey whales passing by in both the spring and fall. In the summer, killer whales (orcas) are sometimes seen swimming close to the rocky, wave-battered shoreline.

Beyond the point, deep forest blocks all views of the ocean until Jordan River is reached at 33 kilometers (20 miles). This small settlement, supported mostly by forestry, is well known as a popular spot with surfers who catch the winter swells that break where Jordan River enters the ocean. By parking anywhere alongside the highway, access to the huge gravel beaches and the water is easier here than in almost any other place along the entire drive. The only service found in this tiny community is a waterfront cafe across from the beach. On clear days, the best time to be here is in the early evening to watch the setting sun paint the sea and the sky in shades of orange.

Much of the land on the rest of the drive has been heavily logged over the last 50 years, leaving little of the original old-growth forests to marvel at. Southern Vancouver Island has already been cut over to the point that the few remaining pristine river valleys have become a battleground between environmentalists and forest companies. The parks that have been created along the west coast tend to protect only a very narrow strip at the ocean's edge, allowing the forests immediately behind to be completely logged off. After seeing the small, spindly second growth forests along the highway, the cathedral-like forests seen later on will be an eye-opening experience and show what the whole area was like less than a hundred years ago.

At 38 kilometers (23 miles) is the access road to China Beach and the southern edge of Juan de Fuca Provincial Park, which stretches from here all the way to Port Renfrew along the coast. This park, created only a few years ago, has a 47-kilometer (28.2-mile) trail, the Juan De Fuca Marine Trail, along the waterfront, which takes about four days for the average backpacker to hike. In its length it passes through old-growth forests, along rocky beaches, and over rugged headlands, all within sight of the vast and mysterious ocean. While often compared to the world-famous West Coast Trail, found just to the north, this trail is both easier to hike and to access. The challenging West Coast Trail runs for 77 kilometers (46 miles) with no access points other than the entry and exit points, while this trail can be accessed in four different places along its length.

The turnoff to Sombrio Beach, the next access point to the park, is reached at 58 kilometers (35 miles). All the park access points are well signed and easy to spot while driving—watch for the blue signs. The gravel road down to the trailhead for Sombrio can be steep and loose but is still suitable for all vehicles. From the parking lot, the beach is about a 15-minute walk down a gravel path that leads though groves of huge Sitka spruce, a tree that grows to massive proportions on the rain-soaked outer coast of Vancouver Island. At the bottom of the trail, stay right, cross the suspension bridge, and walk through the campsite to the ocean. Across the creek you may see the remains of the squatter community that called this once-remote beach home for years. Many of the residents lived in driftwood shacks and spent their carefree days surfing just offshore. With the creation of the park, the residents were ejected for good and most of the rustic structures were dismantled.

Back on the West Coast Highway, the route makes a high traverse through regenerating second-growth forest and has expansive ocean views to the west. Driving this route in the setting sun is beautiful with the ocean shimmering in the distance and nothing between you and Japan. Most of the Olympic Peninsula has faded into the distance and the main views are towards the open Pacific. This stretch is the most challenging of the entire trip with steep grades, exceptionally tight corners, and numerous one-lane wooden bridges. Crossing these bridges can be intimidating as the oncoming traffic isn't easily seen when approaching the bridges. Be sure to fully stop before cautiously proceeding across.

The third and least used access to Juan de Fuca Park is the Parkinson Creek Road at 68 kilometers (41 miles). This 4-kilometer- (2.4-mile-) long access road is rough and best suited to four-wheel-drive vehicles. With the variety of access points, short sections of the Juan de Fuca Marine Trail can be hiked, like Sombrio Beach to Botanical Beach, allowing hikers to break the long trail into shorter segments.

The outskirts of Port Renfrew, home to about 400 residents, is reached at 71 kilometers (42.6 miles) where the highway curves around the south side of Port San Juan, a large bay in front of town. This small community

*View from Botanical Beach looking west at sunset towards the West Coast Trail.*

has the basic tourist services of gas, food, and accommodation but little else. An interesting mix of loggers and outdoor adventurers come to work, fish, surf, and hike in the area. The original trees surrounding the town were among the biggest in the world but few have been spared the logger's axe. Ask locally how to reach the nearby Red Creek Fir, the largest Douglas-fir in Canada, which, before losing its top in a storm, was estimated to be 320 feet high.

Port Renfrew is best known as the southern access point to the world-renowned West Coast Trail. This lengthy backpacking trail through the southern most unit of Pacific Rim National Park was originally built as a lifesaving trail for mariners who found themselves washed up on the beach after their ships ran aground. Many shipwrecks dot the coast here, known as the "Graveyard of the Pacific," and are a testimonial to the power and unforgiving nature of the ocean.

As Canada's most famous trail, quotas have been placed on it to keep it from being mobbed and overused. On any given summer day, people from around the world are experiencing the magic of the west coast along its rugged path. Most hikers start in Port Renfrew and finish in Bamfield, therefore completing the more rugged southern section first. For most backpackers, the trail is a five- to ten-day endurance test as it weaves along the rugged coast through stunted forests, along wide beaches, and over steep headlands. Call the park office at 250-647-5434 for information or do an Internet search, a gold mine of information on the trail. Several detailed guidebooks have been published about the trail and are a great aid in planning this adventure.

Be sure to continue through town and follow the signs to the Botanical Beach trailhead, 3.5 kilometers (2.1 miles) west of Port Renfrew on a good gravel road. There are two access points to the water from here. On the left of the C-shaped parking lot is the trail to Botanical Beach itself, while the trail just to the right accesses Botany Bay. These two rocky beaches are connected by a short waterfront trail that works its way along the ocean's rim and through stately forest. The loop trip down one trail, along the ocean, and up the other will take at least an hour or more if you want to spend time enjoying the classic west coast scenery.

Botanical Beach is named for the myriad of tide pools that cover the rocky shelf at the sea's edge. At low tide, the water in the pools harbors many types of marine life including sea stars, muscles, urchins, anemones, and crabs. At high tide the pools are underwater and inaccessible so be sure to check the tide tables posted on the information boards before heading down. Sunsets here are memorable with the last rays of light reflecting in the tide pools and the constant roar of the surf pounding the rocky shores. As an added bonus, lucky visitors can be rewarded with whale sightings just offshore. In all, this is one of the most beautiful and easily reached seascapes in all of coastal BC.

Although most drivers will opt to retrace the drive back to Sooke (try not to travel back in the dark—the drive is challenging enough during the day) and points beyond, those with the BC Recreational Atlas (new edition to be retitled The BC Road and Recreational Atlas), a good sense of direction, and backroad experience can follow easy roads due east from Port Renfrew to Lake Cowichan near the east coast of Vancouver Island. Despite being gravel, these roads are more relaxing than the West Coast Highway and are a faster way to reach Nanaimo and the ferries back to Vancouver.

If you tackle this route, be sure to gas up in Port Renfrew. The route starts just past the park office trailer for the West Coast Trail on the northern outskirts of Port Renfrew and follows the San Juan River on a paved road for about 20 kilometers (12 miles). From here the road turns to gravel and travels almost due north up Harris Creek, climbs over a low mountain spine and then drops to the south side of Lake Cowichan near the community of Honeymoon Bay. From here, turn right and connect with the paved roads along Lake Cowichan towards Duncan and Highway 1. Be sure to ask in Port Renfrew about the conditions of the road before attempting this shortcut.

# 2

# Pacific Rim Highway
## *Port Alberni to Tofino*

**General description:** The Pacific Rim Highway travels 130 kilometers (78 miles) through Vancouver Island's rugged mountain backbone out to the pounding surf, massive beaches, and old-growth forests of BC's wild west coast in Pacific Rim National Park. The middle section of this drive is among the most challenging in the book as it twists and turns along the contours of the Mackenzie Range before reaching the coast, Tofino, and island-dotted Clayoquot Sound.

**Special attractions:** Exciting driving, mountain views, interesting forests, the best beaches in Canada, the coastal communities of Ucuelet and Tofino, excellent fishing, whale watching, and sea kayaking in Clayoquot Sound.

**Location:** The west coast of Vancouver Island due west of Nanaimo.

**Drive route numbers:** Highway 4 the entire way.

**Travel season:** Any time of year. Summer is by far the most popular time to come and is therefore busy. The heavy rains and powerful winds in winter are popular with storm-watchers.

**Camping:** Early in the drive, Sproatt Lake Provincial Park is a popular campsite. More scenic campsites are located in Pacific Rim National Park or in commercial campgrounds in and around Tofino.

**Services:** None between Port Alberni and Ucuelet.

**Nearby attractions:** The Broken Islands south of Ucuelet and Clayoquot Sound to the north of Tofino are the main nearby attractions. In both places fishing and whale watching are very popular. Hot Springs Cove on the north end of Clayoquot Sound is a popular boat trip.

 # The drive

Port Alberni, the start of the drive, is reached from Parksville on Vancouver Island's east coast in about an hour's drive via Highway 4. The highlight of that section of highway is Macmillan Provincial Park, at about the halfway point between the two towns. The park, also known as Cathedral Grove, is a refuge of old-growth forests surrounded by a sea of clearcuts and second-growth forests. Through here, the highway is surrounded by majestic trees on both sides and does a good impersonation of the driving through the redwood forests of California. Nowhere else in BC (on a paved road) does a highway travel through a nicer stretch of forest. From the parking lots on both sides of Highway 4, short loop trails wander through the forests and

# Drive 2: Pacific Rim Highway

*Port Alberni to Tofino*

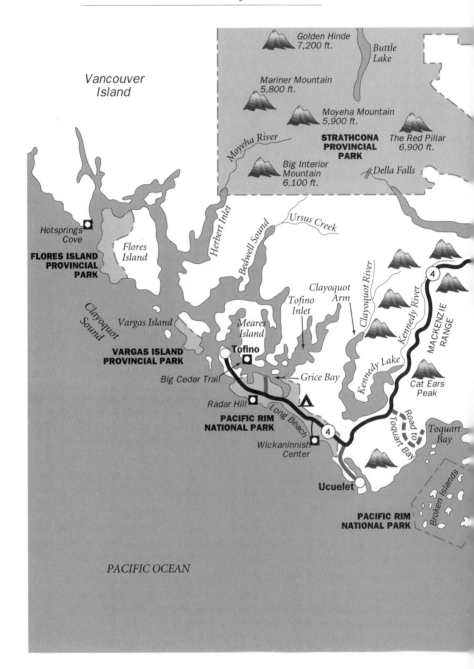

Vancouver
Island

Golden Hinde
7,200 ft.

Buttle
Lake

Mariner Mountain
5,800 ft.

Moyeha Mountain
5,900 ft.

*Moyeha River*

**STRATHCONA
PROVINCIAL
PARK**

The Red Pillar
6,900 ft.

Big Interior
Mountain
6,100 ft.

*Della Falls*

*Herbert Inlet*

*Bedwell Sound*

*Ursus Creek*

Hotsprings
Cove

**FLORES ISLAND
PROVINCIAL
PARK**

Flores
Island

*Clayoquot River*

*Clayoquot
Sound*

Vargas Island

Clayoquot
Arm

Tofino
Inlet

*Kennedy River*

**MACKENZIE
RANGE**

Meares
Island

**4**

Tofino

**VARGAS ISLAND
PROVINCIAL PARK**

*Kennedy Lake*

Big Cedar Trail

Grice Bay

Cat Ears
Peak

Radar Hill

*Long Beach*

**PACIFIC RIM
NATIONAL PARK**

*Road to
Toquart Bay*

Toquart
Bay

**4**

Wickaninnish
Center

Ucuelet

*Broken Islands*

**PACIFIC RIM
NATIONAL PARK**

*PACIFIC OCEAN*

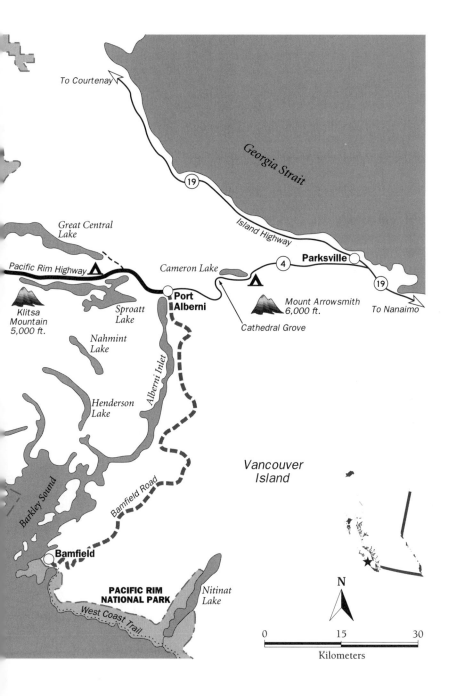

To Courtenay

Georgia Strait

19

Island Highway

Great Central
Lake

Pacific Rim Highway

Cameron Lake

4

Parksville

19

To Nanaimo

Port
Alberni

Klitsa
Mountain
5,000 ft.

Sproatt
Lake

Mount Arrowsmith
6,000 ft.

Cathedral Grove

Nahmint
Lake

Alberni Inlet

Henderson
Lake

Barkley Sound

Bamfield Road

Vancouver
Island

Bamfield

PACIFIC RIM
NATIONAL PARK

Nitinat
Lake

West Coast Trail

N

0        15        30
Kilometers

11

beneath these giants. Some of the largest Douglas fir trees in BC grow here, many being over 800 years old. A major natural disaster struck the park in the winter of 1997 when severe winds blew over dozens of old trees, most of which still lie where they fell.

Port Alberni, whose fortunes are closely linked to commercial fishing and logging, has fallen upon hard times as these industries face an uncertain future. Affordable housing and sport fishing are helping to keep the town vibrant despite the problems in the traditional industries which are suffering due to resource depletion. With the increasing interest in the west coast of the island, Port Alberni is also in a good position to capitalize on the tourist boom by offering tours and services for the growing ecotravel market. The town is situated at the head of Alberni Inlet, the longest indentation of Vancouver Island's rugged and inlet-riddled west coast. In the late 1960s, an earthquake-induced tidal wave traveled all the way up the inlet and hit the town hard, causing considerable damage along the waterfront.

Be sure to fill up with gas here as there are no services until Ucuelet near the end of the drive. Set your trip odometer at the "Welcome to Port Alberni" sign. Port Alberni is also the turnoff (well signed) for the gravel-road drive to Bamfield on the south side of Barkley Sound. Expect to take two hours to reach this classic coastal village with its quaint boardwalks and high percentage of marine biologists who work at the Bamfield Marine Station.

Beyond Port Alberni, the highway travels through scattered residential development for several kilometers before heading into the deep forests of the core of Vancouver Island. Just northwest of the town is Great Central Lake, one of the biggest lakes on the island and located partially within Strathcona Provincial Park. Adventurers canoe up the lake and hike a long, poorly maintained trail to the base of 1,400-foot Della Falls, the highest waterfall in North America and the sixth highest in the world.

At 15.5 kilometers (9.3 miles), the main access point to Sproatt Lake Provincial Park is reached. Sproatt Lake is a popular boating, camping, and day use area for Port Alberni residents. The highway runs along the northern shore of the lake for many kilometers although it's not often visible through the deep forest. Though scenic, the mountainsides around the lake have been heavily logged so stop here for a break and then press on to the more pristine areas later in the drive. At the head of the lake, the dark bulk of Klitsa Mountain dominates the scene and stands out boldly on the horizon, being covered with snowfields most of the year.

Despite their relatively low elevations which range from 4,000 to 5,000 feet, these peaks on the island's mountainous backbone are steep, rugged, and often more challenging to climb than far higher summits on the mainland. Much of the land here is intricately folded, cliffy, and surrounded by jungle-like V-shaped valleys. Furthermore, the abundant rainfall of the area ensures that these peaks are storm-lashed and buried in deep snow for much of the year.

Henderson Lake, just to the south of Sproatt Lake, is deluged by an annual rainfall of 6,500 millimeters (almost six times Vancouver's annual rainfall), and is said to be the wettest place in North America, although Hawaii and southeast Alaska also claim that dubious title. Whatever the case, the area is pounded by storm after storm from October to April as vigorous low pressure systems sweep in off the Pacific and collide with the uplift on the leading edge of the island's mountain ranges. As witnessed by the grotesquely twisted forests along the outer coast, the winds here can be near hurricane force and never allow the trees to grow straight and tall.

Much of the area to the west of Port Alberni is in a Tree Farm License, a permit system whereby forest companies are able to log on Crown (government) land in exchange for creating employment and paying stumpage fees for the trees cut. Although environmental pressures are decreasing the total allowable cut, this area is still heavily utilized by the logging industry to meet their timber needs. It's easy to spot the new clearcuts, but differentiating between the old-growth and maturing second-growth is challenging for most people.

Past the head of Sproatt Lake, the Pacific Rim Highway climbs to Sutton Pass and then starts to descend into the Kennedy River valley on its way to the ocean. By now the highway is much more demanding than before as it twists and turns to match the contours of the mountains. The deep forests encountered before slowly start to give way to stunted, twisted caricatures of trees as the outer coast is approached. These trees, part of "bog forests," are endlessly fascinating as no two are alike, with many resembling large bonsai trees.

Although the peaks of the Mackenzie Range are barely 5,000 feet high, the vertical relief is great and their ruggedness impressive from below. Most are of volcanic origin and are made of exceptionally dark rock that contrasts vividly with the permanent snow on their flanks. More often than not, the mountains through here will be hidden in a deep blanket of clouds and drizzle. It takes an exceptionally strong high pressure system on the outer coast to tear away the clouds and reveal the exceptional views. Although the scenery is beautiful here, the narrow, twisty highway makes it difficult to take a good look around. The highway shoulders are too narrow to park on so be sure to look for the designated pullout areas if you want to stop.

At about 45 kilometers (27 miles) is the turnoff for the Clayoquot Witness Trail, accessed from the signed Upper Kennedy Logging Road which leaves Highway 4 to the right. To locate this key logging artery, continue about 400 meters past the Sutton Pass sign on the highway. The trailhead is 7.5 kilometers (4.5 miles) away on a well-graded gravel road. The trail was built by environmentalists through the extensive old-growth forests of southern Clayoquot Sound in order to help preserve the area. The sometimes rugged trail is nearly 60 kilometers (36 miles) long (one-way) but short there-and-back day hikes can be done from this, the northern trailhead. On the way, the trail passes through majestic old-growth forests and enters the newly created

*Old-growth forest, Cathedral Grove, MacMillan Provincial Park, Highway 4 near Port Alberni.*

Clayoquot Plateau Provincial Park. Call BC Parks for details on the trail at 250-954-4600.

Once into the Kennedy River valley, the landscape becomes more pristine looking, partly due to the rugged terrain which makes logging difficult and also to the fact that much of the forest is stunted and commercially worthless. At 81 kilometers (49 miles), the northern end of Kennedy Lake is reached at the start of the most challenging portion of the entire drive.

All along the shores of deep blue Kennedy Lake, the highway is blasted out of the cliffs which fall into the lake, making for several kilometers of narrow and intimidating driving. Try to avoid driving this section in the pouring rain or in the dark.

Along here, the highway travels past the southern edge of Clayoquot Sound, one of the five large indentations (sounds) in Vancouver Island's convoluted west coast. For the past decade, Clayoquot Sound has been the site of the most bitter environmental debate in Canada. Although most of Vancouver Island's commercially viable old-growth forests have already been logged, the Clayoquot area has the highest concentration of intact river valleys on the whole island.

In 1993, the debate came to a boiling point when protesters blocked a logging road leading into virgin forest. The blockade grew quickly, bolstered by environmental activists from around the world. In the largest mass arrest in Canadian history, over 800 protesters were jailed for holding up logging during that controversial summer. As a result of the protests, Clayoquot has been largely spared the loggers axe as strict new rules have been imposed as to the amount of cutting and the methods to be used.

As a result of the controversy, several new parks were created in the area including Kennedy Lake, situated alongside the highway on the lake's western end and Clayoquot Arm, an offshoot of the lake's northern shores. The latter park is only reached by the boat launch at Kennedy Lake Park.

About halfway down the lake's southern coast, an important side road cuts to the left and leads to Toquart Bay on the shores of Barkley Sound. The turnoff should be signed. The boat launch at Toquart is a popular starting point for boaters and sea kayakers to reach the myriad of islands and waterways in the Broken Islands.

Where the highway leaves the mountains behind and meets the ocean on a narrow isthmus of land, the major T-junction on Highway 4 is reached at 96 kilometers (58 miles). From here Ucuelet is to the left while Pacific Rim National Park and Tofino are to the right.

Ucuelet, 7 kilometers (4 miles) from the junction, is something of Tofino's twin sister, although it is much more dependent on resource industries than Tofino. Ucuelet has always been a center for both sport and commercial fishing and features a busy series of docks strung out along the town's waterfront. When in Ucuelet, compare the ugly clear-cuts behind the town with the pristine views backing Tofino and see the visual difference that logging makes. Ucuelet is the bigger of the two communities and is where more services are found. The town is also known as the gateway to the Broken Islands in Barkley Sound to the south.

This picturesque archipelago of over a hundred islands situated out in the open Pacific is the one of the three parts of Pacific Rim National Park (Broken Islands, Long Beach, and West Coast Trail). Boats can be chartered in town for fishing or sightseeing trips into these small, storm-lashed islands. By continuing past the town center, the highway ends at the Amphitrite Point Lighthouse, one of the many lighthouses on the west coast of Vancouver Island. The distinctive red and white lighthouse may be open for tours when you arrive. Another attraction here is the *M.V. Lady Rose,* a cargo and passenger ship that plies the waters of Barkley Sound between Port Alberni, Ucuelet, and Bamfield. Call for a brochure or schedule (see Appendix for phone number).

Back at the T-junction, stay straight and reset your trip odometer to zero to accommodate those who skipped Ucuelet. The western boundary of Pacific Rim National Park is reached only a kilometer (0.6 mile) from the junction. For those stopping in the park, day-use passes must be purchased at either one of the manned or self-pay park facilities. At 2.6 kilometers (1.6 miles), a small visitor information center on the right is a great place to pick up a free park map, to ask questions of the rangers, and to see the interpretive displays.

At 5 kilometers (3 miles) is the turnoff to the Wickaninnish Center, a must see place for visitors and the first real opportunity to get out on the beaches. The center was named after a leading native chief in the Clayoquot Sound area in the 1800s and is just a few minutes off the highway on Long Beach Road. Along the way, the turnoff to Florencia Bay is passed as is the short and easy Bog Trail which leads through a magical forest of strange and twisted trees. At the end of the road, turn left into the Wickaninnish Center parking area with massive sandy beaches and the pounding surf mere feet away.

For much of the late summer, a thick blanket of fog sits along the coast and creates cool temperatures and relief from the heat of summer. August is typically the foggiest month, often referred to as "Fogust" by locals. Summer brings the nicest weather but even then, it's rare to go more than a week at a time without a pounding rain storm. Winters are often brutal on the exposed coast, making this a time of few visitors.

The Wickaninnish Center is a multistory building housing all sorts of interpretive displays detailing both the human and natural history of the park. Of particular interest are the massive whale jaw bones as well as the simulated underwater submersible. Also housed in the building is a cafe with panoramic views of the beach and several decks with telescopes for whale watching.

In the spring months, approximately 20,000 grey whales pass by here on their way to the Bering Sea from Baja, Mexico. The whales are most easily identified by looking for the distinctive mist as they surface and breathe.

An even better way of seeing the whales is to take one of the many whale watching tours offered out of Tofino or Ucuelet. In the summer months, the focus shifts to spotting the killer whales (orcas) who both reside in and transit throughout Clayoquot Sound.

From the Wickaninnish Center, the beach is easily accessed and can be walked northwards for a long distance. The expanse of beach known collectively as "Long Beach" stretches for 30 kilometers (18 miles) along the coast, with 19 kilometers (11.4 miles) of that distance being beach and the rest being pocket coves and rocky headlands that separate one named beach from the next. The rewarding South Beach Trail heads behind the center to a beautiful beach flanked by rocky headlands in about a half hour of easy hiking on a broad trail. Although not far away, this area is much quieter and more secluded than the ever-busy Long Beach area. The park map available from any of the manned visitors centers shows all the trails and facilities in the park.

Back on Highway 4, the next stretch brings the signed turnoffs for the Rainforest Trail and the access to Combers Beach. Soon after, the highway travels along within feet of the beach and has one of the few ocean views from the main highway itself. At 15.5 kilometers (9 miles) is the turnoff for Long Beach and the main access point for most people to reach the sweeping beaches of the park. The uninterrupted 10 kilometer (6 mile) long golden sand beach here allows for easy wandering in any direction. Watching a sunset from here is a long-remembered experience.

This spot is considered to have the best surfing in Canada. When the swell picks up, surfers are commonly seen riding the waves just offshore, often surprising visitors who think of it as a warm-water activity. Although the summer surf might look tame, the hard-core surfers that tackle the stormy winter surf here will vouch for the power of these waves. In winter, heavily clad in thick wetsuits, surfers brace themselves against the frigid waters and cold, wet weather at a time when other visitors are few and far between.

The turnoff to Grice Bay is found at 20 kilometers (12 miles) and leads in about 15 minutes to a good view into Clayoquot Sound and Meares Island, part of Tofino's backdrop. Although this is a popular spot for boating, be aware of the strong currents that run along these shores. The Radar Hill access road is reached on the left at 22.5 kilometers (13.5 miles) and leads in just over a kilometer (0.6 mile) to a high viewpoint over the stunted forests and the open Pacific in the distance. This narrow and bumpy road is unsuitable for trailers and RVs. The hill was once the site of a radar facility that watched for Japanese ships during World War II.

Just past the turnoff, the highway leaves Pacific Rim National Park and reaches the start of the luxury resorts that dominate Cox Bay and Chesterman Beach, both just south of Tofino. These resorts always rate high on any list of romantic destinations in the entire Pacific Northwest, with many of them being four-star quality. Trails from the resorts allow access to these beaches to those who aren't paying customers.

Tofino is reached at 32 kilometers (19 miles) where the superlative views of Clayoquot Sound and its many islands, mountains, and old-growth forests are seen for the first time. It is spectacularly situated on the tip of a narrow peninsula with the open Pacific on one side and Clayoquot Sound on the other. The area, a unique combination of California-like beaches and the fjord and mountain seascapes of the BC coast, is an unforgettable place.

To the north is pristine Meares Island while to the west is flat Vargas Island. Although the snowcapped peaks of Vancouver Island's mountains are not readily visible from the village, a short boat ride out into the sound reveals a truly "ocean to alpine" panorama.

Tofino has flourished in recent years and has become a leading recreational, environmental, and artistic community of about 1,000 people. Numerous galleries sell original art, much of which has a west coast and native Indian theme. In the summer months, the village is as busy and touristy as Whistler or Lake Louise and rivals any resort community for the number of nearby attractions. Although there are many places to stay in town, expect high prices as you would in any tourist-oriented spot.

Fishing and tourism dominate the Tofino economy like almost no other place in BC. Clayoquot, with its combination of stately forests, protected waterways, and surf-pounded islands, has become a very popular sea

*View looking north into Clayoquot Sound at sunrise from Grice Bay,*
*Pacific Rim National Park.*

*Old building in Tofino used as a whale-watching base.*
*Meares Island in Clayoquot Sound rising in background.*

kayaking destination. At the government dock at the foot of First Street, kayakers are often seen launching for trips to either the inner or outer coasts, depending upon experience. Several kayaking companies located in Tofino take people on lessons and tours in the sound, allowing those without the experience or equipment to have an intimate look at the unique seascapes and marine life found here.

In the battle over the fate of Clayoquot Sound, Tofino, mostly in favor of preservation, was pitted against Ucuelet, whose residents, many of whom are loggers, were for logging the sound. Overall, the laid-back, west coast ambiance in Tofino is a far cry from the more industrial, working feel of Ucuelet.

Other than the beaches, many visitors are drawn to Tofino to go whale watching. Numerous companies offer tours ranging from a few hours to all day. Many of the tours are combined with a stop at the Big Cedar Trail on Meares Island or, with more time, a trip to Hot Springs Cove on the north end of Clayoquot Sound where visitors walk on a short boardwalk through the rainforest to natural hot springs. The searing water pours off a small cliff and down into a series of pools right on the edge of the ocean making this a highly recommended trip for those with the time and money.

Once done in Tofino, the only way to reach the rest of BC is by retracing the drive all the way back to Parksville.

# 3

# Old Island Highway

## Parksville to Campbell River

**General description:** This civilized seaside drive follows the "old" Island Highway (19A) along the eastern shores of Vancouver Island for 130 kilometers (78 miles) and links together numerous picturesque coastal towns. Much of the drive is within sight of Georgia Strait, the long inland sea between Vancouver Island and mainland BC. Like the Okanagan, this area is well suited to leisurely and relaxing travel. The opportunities to go on side trips off the highway to islands and into the mountains is a major part of the drive's attraction.

**Special attractions:** Frequent ocean views, some of the best beaches in BC, well-developed tourist facilities and resorts, boating and fishing opportunities galore.

**Location:** On the east coast of central Vancouver Island between Parksville and Campbell River.

**Drive route numbers:** Highway 19A. Any map over a few years old will show this route as Highway 19. On newer maps, Highway 19 is the new Island Highway, well away from the waterfront.

**Travel season:** Any time of year. This is the mildest place in Canada and hardly ever sees snow or severe conditions. In winter, some of the tourist facilities may close but that's more than compensated for by the solitude on the beaches and the winter recreation opportunities like skiing.

**Camping:** Miracle and Rathtrevor Beach Provincial Parks are the most desirable places to camp. The bigger towns along the drive have commercial campgrounds as well.

**Services:** Services are found regularly along this drive.

**Nearby attractions:** Lesquiti Island, Denman and Hornby Islands, the BC Ferry across to Powell River (Land and Sea Circle Tour 3), alpine hiking in Strathcona Provincial Park, two ski areas near Courtenay, Quadra Island, and the drive to Buttle Lake (Drive 3).

 The drive

Now that the "new" Island Highway (19) has diverted most of the commercial traffic away from the waterfront on a well-inland and more efficient route, this scenic drive is left to sightseers and locals to enjoy. For much of its distance, Highway 19A, the "old" Island Highway, runs along Georgia Strait with frequent ocean views and access to wide, sandy beaches. Unlike many of the drives in the book, this one is distinctly civilized with little wilderness and few remote areas. Much of the drive is reminiscent of the Oregon Coast due to its resort feel and oceanfront setting. While Vancouver Island on the whole is a rugged and unforgiving place, the very eastern edge of the island is gently sloping and without great vertical relief so the driving here is nothing like the tortuous routes to the west coast of the island (Drives 1 and 2).

The drive begins on the southern outskirts of Parksville where Highway 19A crosses the Englishman River on a prominent bridge. Set your trip odometer here. Parksville is 35 kilometers (21 miles) north of Nanaimo and is easily reached from both Vancouver and Victoria, both about three hours away.

The Island Highway is a nearly 400-kilometer (240-mile) route from Nanaimo to Port Hardy near the northern tip of Vancouver Island. When combined with the Malahat Highway (Highway 1 from Victoria to Nanaimo), this route is a long and memorable introduction to Vancouver Island and its principal communities. In an effort to speed up the drive from one end of the island to the other, the BC Government initiated an ambitious multi-billion dollar project to move the Island Highway (19) well inland from the ocean to make it a faster and easier drive. At present, the highway is complete from Nanaimo to near Campbell River, the northern extremity of the majority of the population base on the island. While the new route is faster, the old highway (19A) along the waterfront is less congested and far more scenic.

Parksville, with a population of just over 10,000, is a well-known resort community famous for its beaches. Nowhere else on the east coast of Vancouver Island are the beaches as big and plentiful as the ones facing the town. At low tide, the gently sloping waterfront here exposes miles of wide sandy beaches perfect for sunbathing and beachcombing. Looking across the water, the view is dominated by the mountains backing the Sunshine Coast (Drive 6). Numerous islands can be seen out in Georgia Strait, most notable of which is long Texada Island on the northern horizon. At night the lights of Vancouver twinkle in the distance less than 20 kilometers (12 miles) away directly across the strait.

Parksville offers all services and has a holiday atmosphere, especially in the summer months. Numerous seaside resorts, restaurants and waterfront parks lie alongside the water, many of which cater to families. With its mild climate, Parksville is a popular retirement spot, possibly second only to the Kelowna area as a choice for Canadians fleeing the bitterly cold winters of the majority of Canada. As it sits in the rainshadow of Vancouver Island's mountainous backbone, the climate is positively mild and dry in comparison to the storm-pounded west coast of the island.

Rathtrevor Beach Provincial Park, one of Vancouver Island's busiest parks, lies along Georgia Strait on the eastern outskirts of Parksville. The full-facility campground there has 174 campsites.

# Drive 3: Old Island Highway
*Parksville to Campbell River*

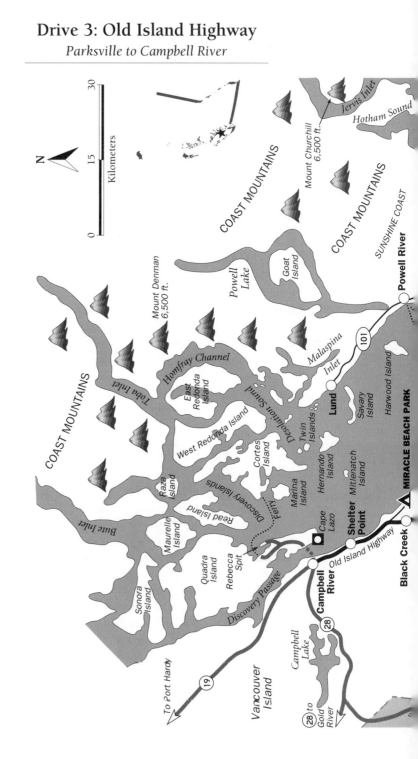

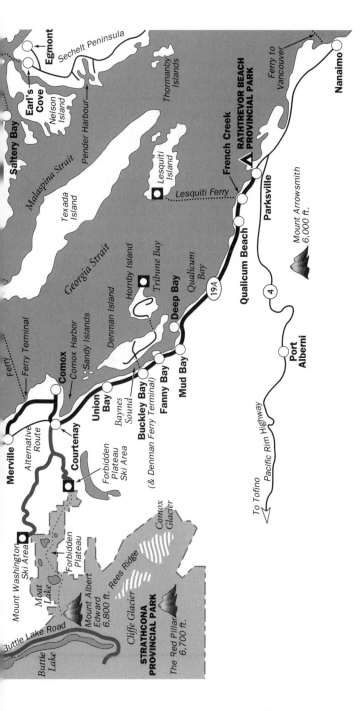

Egmont

Sechelt Peninsula

Earl's Cove

Nelson Island

Pender Harbour

Saltery Bay

Malaspina Strait

Texada Island

Georgia Strait

Sandy Islands

Comox Harbour

Comox

Ferry Terminal

Ferry

Merville

Alternative Route

Courtenay

Forbidden Plateau Ski Area

Mount Washington Ski Area

Moat Lake

Forbidden Plateau

Buttle Lake Road

Buttle Lake

Mount Albert Edward 6,800 ft.

Rees Ridge

Cliffe Glacier

Comox Glacier

STRATHCONA PROVINCIAL PARK

The Red Pillar 6,700 ft.

Denman Island

Baynes Sound

Union Bay

Buckley Bay
(& Denman Ferry Terminal)

Fanny Bay

Mud Bay

Hornby Island

Tribune Bay

Deep Bay

Qualicum Bay

19A

Qualicum Beach

Lesquiti Ferry

Lesquiti Island

Thormanby Islands

French Creek

RATHTREVOR BEACH PROVINCIAL PARK

Parksville

Mount Arrowsmith 6,000 ft.

4

Port Alberni

Pacific Rim Highway

To Tofino

Ferry to Vancouver

Nanaimo

23

Many of the towns along this route developed with the fishing industry and although tourism has become one of the largest parts of the island economy, many of these seaside communities still have substantial harbor facilities for commercial and recreational boats alike. An important component of the economy is the sport fishery based in Georgia Strait, a major migratory route for salmon heading towards the Fraser River.

Georgia Strait is the massive inland sea that separates Vancouver Island (the largest island on the west coast of North America) from mainland BC. From its southern reaches where it merges with Puget Sound in Washington state's San Juan Islands, Georgia Strait runs all the way to Campbell River where the Discovery Islands mark its northernmost point. For most of its distance, the strait is 10 to 20 kilometers (6 to 12 miles) wide and forms the southern part of the famed Inside Passage, the protected sea route to Alaska. Although the waters here are usually calm, wind storms occasionally pound the coast, creating large waves when the winds howl across the open waters of the strait. Boaters in Georgia Strait have a great deal of respect for the "Qualicum Winds" that whistle eastwards across Vancouver Island through a gap in the mountains west of Parksville and whip up dangerous seas in a heartbeat.

Traveling north on 19A from Parksville, French Creek and the turnoff for the Lesquiti Island ferry is reached in 6.7 kilometers (4 miles). The marina here is one of the biggest and busiest on the island and caters to both commercial and sport fishery. The foot-passenger-only ferry that runs several times a day from here to Lesquiti Island is an interesting side trip to a large, storm-lashed island lying at the mid-point of the strait. Lesquiti Island has a reputation as being one of the last refuges of hippies in BC and as a place to escape the hustle and bustle of the modern world. Not only have the 300-or-so islanders refused BC Ferries access that would bring more visitors and development, they have also resisted efforts to bring electricity to the island. Lesquiti is a model of self-sufficiency as all islanders rely on various forms of alternative power generation. As is commonly found on remote islands, the residents drive Lesquiti's few gravel roads in a motley collection of old cars that would hardly be allowed off the island and onto BC's highways.

Qualicum Beach, Parksville's sister city and home to equally beautiful beaches, is reached only 10 kilometers (6 miles) north of Parksville. This resort and retirement community is well-groomed, exceptionally pleasant, and is known for its fishing, golfing, and beachcombing. All along the ocean here, waterfront parks allow for easy access to the wide sandy beaches and panoramic views up and down the strait. Boasting some of the warmest waters in Canada, the beaches here offer the best ocean swimming opportunities in BC. Photographers will want to be on the beaches early in the day as this side of Vancouver Island faces east and is known for sunrises rather than sunsets. Although scenic, don't expect the kind of raw energy and powerful scenery here as on the west coast of Vancouver Island. Except in storms, the ocean here is placid and very unlike the surf and crashing waves found on the island's outer edge.

North of Qualicum Beach, the large towns are left behind as the highway travels through a lightly populated stretch of coastline. After running just inland and away from the ocean views, the highway regains the ocean's edge at 25 kilometers (15 miles), just south of wide Qualicum Bay. At 27 kilometers (16 miles) is the turnoff to the left to the Horne Lake Caves, 15 kilometers (9 miles) up a side road to the west. This cave system is accessible to anyone on a self-guided basis. Bring a flashlight and a lot of common sense if you want to explore the caves. Call BC Parks for park information (see Appendix).

After passing through the small waterfront communities of Bowser, Deep Bay (just off the highway), Mud Bay, and Fanny Bay, the highway reaches Buckley Bay at 53 kilometers (32 miles) and the BC Ferry terminal for Denman Island which lies just across Baynes Sound. Much of the area's waterfront consists of mud flats commonly used by both migratory birds and shellfish harvesters. The optional ferry ride across to Denman is just a few minutes long. Once on Denman, another ferry can be used for another short crossing to Hornby Island, Denman's sister island. Both of these pastoral islands have long stretches of beautiful shorelines as well as several hills from which panoramic views of Georgia Strait can be gained.

Hornby Island, the more popular of the two islands, can see its population swell from 1,000 (full-time residents) to over 10,000 in the summer months as visitors flock here from all over BC. The area on the south end of Hornby near Helliwell Bluffs and Tribune Bay is particularly beautiful for its combination of sandstone cliffs, turquoise waters, and vast stretches of white sand beaches that create an almost tropical setting. For details of the BC Ferries fares and schedules to these islands, call BC Ferries or visit their website (see Appendix).

Back on the highway, at 56 kilometers (34 miles) is a rest area with beach access and washrooms. A few minutes further is the settlement of Union Bay, situated across from Sandy Islands Marine Park, which can be seen on the eastern horizon. Now that the highway is past Denman Island, the views of Georgia Strait once again open up to include the long spine of Texada Island lying far out in the strait.

Courtenay is reached 73 kilometers (42 miles) from Parksville at the prominent intersection that marks the southern outskirts of town. Although the drive description includes a right turn here and into Comox, just to the east, you can opt to continue north on 19A and rejoin the route description at Merville if pressed for time.

The turnoff to Forbidden Plateau and Mount Washington ski areas is also found here. These ski areas, about 14 kilometers (8.4 miles) and 20 kilometers (12 miles) west of Courtenay (on Mount Washington Road) respectively, are the main downhill skiing centers on Vancouver Island. This alpine area regularly gets one of the deepest winter snowfalls in the whole province. In summer, head for Forbidden Plateau on the very eastern edge of Strathcona Provincial Park if you would like to go hiking through subalpine meadows complete with numerous lakes, snowfields, and views across Georgia Strait to the snowy Coast Mountains. Mount Washington, a little further from Courtenay, uses its lift system in summer to transport visitors to the top of Mount Washington for a 360-degree view of mountains, ocean, and islands.

To follow the route description, turn right at the intersection and follow the signs for Comox and the Powell River ferry. The road curves around the head of wide Comox Harbor before reaching another key intersection at 79 kilometers (47.4 miles). Comox is the home of Canadian Forces Base Comox, the main air force base in BC and a major search and rescue center for southwestern BC. Military aircraft are frequently seen overhead in the area. Comox is a seafaring community and an important military base. Comox dates back to 1849 when the Royal Navy established a base of operations here. The town has one of the busiest ports on Vancouver Island and is a popular recreational base where it's possible to go skiing in the morning and boating in the afternoon.

Looking across Georgia Strait from here, the spire of Mount Churchill dominates the eastern horizon above hidden Jervis Inlet, a long fjord branching off Georgia Strait. On clear days, the nearly level Comox Glacier in Strathcona Park glistens on the western horizon. Several beaches on Georgia Strait, including Kye Bay, Seal Bay, and Goose Spit are all accessible from Comox—ask locally for directions.

After sightseeing in Comox, backtrack to the intersection described before and turn right, following the signs for the Powell River ferry. Go 5.6 kilometers (3.4 miles) beyond the intersection, turn left at the Y-junction, and follow this pastoral route (be sure to stay left at the two intersections) back to Highway 19A at Merville to rejoin those who skipped the drive into Comox. This point is reached 97 kilometers (58 miles) from the beginning of the drive in Parksville for those following the route as described.

At the aforementioned Y-junction, the Powell River ferry is reached by staying right and driving 1.7 kilometers (1 mile) farther. This ferry connects the mid-Vancouver Island communities with the Sunshine Coast and is an important link in the Sunshine Circle tour (Land and Sea Circle Tour 3).

The next section of highway runs well inland from the waterfront through alternating forests and commercial developments before rejoining the ocean at 108 kilometers (64.8 miles). At 114 kilometers (68.4 miles) is the turnoff to the right for Miracle Beach Provincial Park, a large and popular camping park with 193 sites on the waterfront.

In the next stretch, the highway closely follows the shores of Georgia Strait and has excellent beach access all the way to Campbell River. By now, the highway is nearing the northernmost reaches of Georgia Strait where it fades into the intricate Discovery Island archipelago. Across the strait, the mountains towering above the famous boating destination of Desolation Sound are now seen, as is the southern tip of Quadra Island, marked by high sand cliffs and the Cape Lazo Lighthouse. Halfway across the strait is the barren rock of Mitlenatch Island, an ecological reserve and the most important sea bird nesting site in Georgia Strait. From these beaches, bald eagles, harbor seals, and less frequently, killer whales (orcas) can often be seen out (and above) on the water.

Campbell River, situated at the entrance to the Discovery Passage, is reached at 125 kilometers (75 miles). Just south of the city is Oyster Bay Shoreline Park, a pleasant rest area with good views. Campbell River is strung out along the waterfront with condominiums and resorts being met well before the town center itself. Downtown Campbell River and the end of the drive is reached at 130 kilometers (78 miles) where the must-see Discovery Pier is located. This large waterfront park serves as both the main harbor for Campbell River and as a popular tourist destination.

Much of Campbell River is newly developed as the population (and popularity) has been growing for years, making for a clean and very livable community. Although the city is only slightly more than halfway up the island, it marks a definite boundary between the populous southern Vancouver Island and the nearly empty northern half. Only about 3 percent of the island's 700,000 people live north of here.

Campbell River is famous for its sportfishing and promotes itself as the "salmon fishing capitol of the world." With new restrictions on salmon fishing designed to protect the stocks from extinction, the sport fishery has hit hard times but you would never know it as the harbor seems as busy as ever. With surveys indicating that well over half of the visitors to Campbell River come here to fish, it's not surprising that the city is home of the Tyee Club, a group of dedicated fishermen who live to catch trophy-sized salmon. The current record fish is a 70-pound salmon caught in the late 1960s. Discovery Passage, known for its narrowness and tricky currents, is a virtual salmon highway where the fish transit through on their way to their spawning grounds. In addition to fishing, Campbell River is also known as the gateway to Strathcona Provincial Park (Drive 5) and as a popular saltwater diving spot.

From Campbell River, the scenic driving options are numerous. A short and easy side trip is to take a ferry across Discovery Passage from downtown Campbell River to Quadra Island. Although there are few roads on Quadra

*Discovery Pier and docks, Campbell River waterfront
with Discovery Passage and Quadra Island in background.*

other than on the very southern tip, the road leading to Rebecca Spit Marine
Park and its sandy beaches makes for a very rewarding half-day trip from
Campbell River. With an extra day to spare, another ferry can be taken to
Cortes Island where a pastoral road system leads to quiet bays, isolated coastal
villages, and views into famed Desolation Sound to the east.

Other options include Drive 5 to Strathcona Provincial Park or the
trip up the northern stretch of the Island Highway (19) to Port Hardy and
from there continuing on backroads leading northwest towards Cape Scott
on the very northern tip of the island. This is the outback part of Vancouver
Island, home to classic west coast fishing villages, surf-pounded beaches,
and a hardy breed of residents who live far from urban BC. North and west
of Campbell River, the weather often deteriorates into the stormy weather
so common in the remote areas of Vancouver Island.

# 4

# Gulf Islands

*Drives on Saltspring, Saturna, Pender,*
*and Galiano Islands*

**General description:** The Gulf Islands, lying between BC's two biggest cities, allow visitors to combine seaside driving with ocean cruising on the extensive BC Ferries fleet. Four of the most popular islands are described— Saltspring, Saturna, Pender, and Galiano. On the islands, quiet roads run along the picturesque coastlines, past quaint seaside communities, and to the summits of miniature peaks with stunning ocean and mountain views. The Gulf Islands are readily accessible from both Vancouver and Victoria and make for a perfect weekend getaway.

**Special attractions:** Seaside driving, the mildest climate in BC, unique shorelines, small artistic communities, opportunities for marine life sightings including killer whales and sea lions, and west coast ambiance.

**Location:** In southern Georgia Strait between Vancouver and Victoria, immediately north of the San Juan Islands in Washington state.

**Drive route numbers:** Various local roads, no highways.

**Travel season:** All year. Some of the tourist facilities and services close in the winter months. Long weekends in summer bring overcrowding and long waits at the ferry terminals. If you want to get out on the ocean, come spring, summer, or fall.

**Camping:** As most land on the Gulf Islands is private, camp only in designated sites. The best places to camp are in the provincial parks found on Saltspring (Ruckle and Mouat Parks), Galiano (Montague Park), and North Pender (Prior Park) Islands. There is no camping at all on Saturna.

**Services:** Saltspring has the most services by far; Saturna has the fewest. Besides their tourist services, each of the islands has at least one gas station and grocery store—expect high prices.

**Nearby attractions:** Dozens of uninhabited islands where the delicate ecosystem of the Gulf Islands is still intact, unlimited boating, sailing and kayaking possibilities, and the San Juan Islands just to the south.

 The drives

The exquisite Gulf Islands, a collection of hundreds of islands with a mild, Mediterranean climate, interesting coastlines, and a quiet, pastoral beauty, lie in the very southernmost reaches of Georgia Strait, BC's great inland sea.

*Sea kayaker at Montague Harbor Provincial Park
enjoying idyllic paddling below an old arbutus tree.*

Although there is a lot to see by road on the islands, it's necessary to get out on the water or hike up one of the small mountains on the islands to really experience the true nature of this spectacular part of BC.

More than anything, it's the island's edges that make the Gulf Islands so special. The coastlines of the islands are a beautiful combination of sculpted sandstone cliffs, distinctive red-barked arbutus trees, and South Seas-like lagoons with white sand beaches and turquoise waters. In addition, marine life like sea lions and porpoises is surprisingly common here despite the proximity of two big cities. A pod of resident killer whales (orcas) resides in the Georgia Strait area and whale watching tours in the islands often spot these icons of the Northwest. For kayakers and sailors, these islands are paradise; for drivers nearly so, given the wealth of scenic driving found on all the car-accessible islands. For those without boats, there are numerous places in the islands to either rent or charter powerboats, canoes, and kayaks to explore the scenic coastlines and waterways.

Nowhere else in Canada is the climate as mild as in the Gulf Islands where, more often than not, the weather is never too hot or cold for comfort. On the rain-soaked coast of BC, the aridity of the Gulf Islands comes as a bit of a novelty. While good weather on the majority of the coast cannot be expected to hold for long, in the Gulf Islands weeks of blue skies are the norm from May to October. Long a popular escape, the Gulf Islands are a busy place in midsummer and accommodations might be hard to book on the spot so some advance planning is usually in order.

Besides the large, well-known islands, there are over 200 others ranging from mere rocks to substantial but unpopulated ones. Since 1974, the Gulf Islands have been administered by the Islands Trust, a unique governing body with the mandate to protect the islands from overdevelopment. In order to recognize these unique islands, a new national park is in the process of being created that will encompass several islands.

The larger, populated islands are served by the BC Ferries system, which has frequent connections between the islands and to and from both Vancouver Island and the Vancouver area. Overall, the Gulf Islands are far more accessible from Victoria than Vancouver. Sailing between the islands is easy but be sure to check the schedule carefully as there are usually only two interisland ferries per day from each island. The main BC Ferries terminals are at Tsawwassen, just south of Vancouver, and Swartz Bay, just north of Victoria. For fare and schedule information, call BC Ferries or go to their website (see Appendix). From Vancouver, it is often necessary (if you miss the direct connection) to sail to Swartz Bay and then transfer to a Gulf Island ferry. If doing this, ask for a through-fare and pay the same as if you were traveling to the Gulf Islands directly.

A Washington state ferry from Anacortes (the main terminal for the San Juan Islands) has a run to Sydney on Vancouver Island. From there a quick drive north leads to Swartz Bay and connecting ferries to the Gulf Islands. By starting the trip in Anacortes, American visitors can combine both the San Juans and Gulf Islands in a trip from a single starting point.

Because the islands are small and the drives short, each of the four islands is listed separately. For each of the islands, there are no fixed driving itineraries, rather a general description of the various scenic driving opportunities on each. In a weekend trip, it's possible to see at least two islands. With a week available, it would be possible to sail from one to another and enjoy each island's unique character. Before traveling to the Gulf Islands, it helps to have a detailed map as the road systems can be confusing. A good source for maps and a description of the main island's services and attractions is the annual publication *The Gulf Islander.* See Appendix for contact information.

### Saltspring Island

The largest and most populous of all the Gulf Islands, Saltspring is also the easiest to reach, especially from Vancouver Island. With around 10,000 full-time residents, Saltspring has more people than the rest of the islands combined. Artists flock to Saltspring as do home businesses and cottage industries, all seeking a peaceful existence virtually within sight of BC's urban heart.

There are several ways to reach Saltspring by car. The main ferry terminal for the island is at Long Harbor on its east coast which serves as the

*Sunrise from Mount Tuam, Saltspring Island looking west to the Pender Islands and the North Cascades on the far horizon.*

# Drive 4: Gulf Islands

*Saltspring Island*

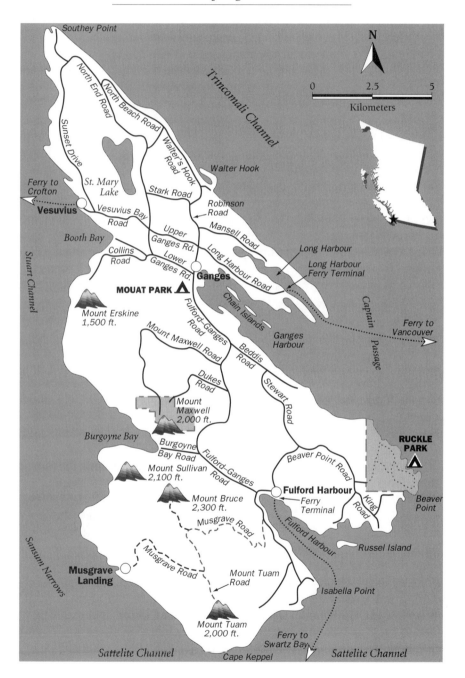

Southey Point

North End Road

North Beach Road

Walter's Hook Road

*Trincomali Channel*

Sunset Drive

Ferry to Crofton

St. Mary Lake

Walter Hook

Stark Road

Robinson Road

**Vesuvius**

Vesuvius Bay Road

Mansell Road

Upper Ganges Rd.

Booth Bay

Long Harbour

Long Harbour Ferry Terminal

Collins Road

Lower Ganges Rd.

Long Harbour Road

*Stuart Channel*

**Ganges**

**MOUAT PARK** ▲

Fulford-Ganges Road

Chain Islands

*Captain Passage*

Mount Erskine 1,500 ft.

Beddis Road

Ganges Harbour

Ferry to Vancouver

Mount Maxwell Road

Dukes Road

Stewart Road

Mount Maxwell 2,000 ft.

**RUCKLE PARK** ▲

Burgoyne Bay

Burgoyne Bay Road

Fulford-Ganges Road

Beaver Point Road

Mount Sullivan 2,100 ft.

Mount Bruce 2,300 ft.

**Fulford Harbour**

Ferry Terminal

King Road

Beaver Point

Musgrave Road

Fulford Harbour

*Sansum Narrows*

Russel Island

**Musgrave Landing**

Musgrave Road

Mount Tuam Road

Isabella Point

Mount Tuam 2,000 ft.

*Sattelite Channel*

Ferry to Swartz Bay

Cape Keppel

*Sattelite Channel*

N

0    2.5    5

Kilometers

gateway to the island from the mainland. To reach Saltspring from Vancouver Island, take either the Fulford Harbor ferry which leaves from Swartz Bay or the Vesuvius ferry which leaves from Crofton, a little farther north up Vancouver Island.

In the middle of the Saltspring's east coast is Ganges, reached by a 10- to 15-minute drive from any of the ferry terminals. Ganges serves as the commercial hub of the Gulf Islands and nearly all drivers eventually stop here for a tour. Ganges is a colorful place with many art dealers, a busy marina, and a relaxing coastal atmosphere. In a way, it's like Whistler on the water.

For scenic driving, several areas on the island stand out. The Walter's Hook Road near the north end features excellent views of Trincomali Channel as well as access to several sandy beaches. Vesuvius, on the northwest coast and only a few minutes from Ganges, is a picturesque village with a busy dock, ferry terminal, and views across to nearby Vancouver Island. Just south of Ganges on the main Fulford-Ganges Road is the well-signed turnoff for Mount Maxwell. Initially paved, the Mount Maxwell Road turns to gravel and climbs to a spectacular viewpoint on one of Saltspring's highest mountains. From the parking area, the 2,000-foot summit is a quick walk away. The viewpoint, perched dramatically on the edge of a high cliff, has excellent views of the Gulf Islands to the south and of Vancouver Island to the east. Try and be here at sunset for a memorable experience.

Fulford Harbor on the south end of the island is the gateway to two beautiful spots—Ruckle Provincial Park and Mount Tuam. Fulford Harbor is small village with a BC Ferry dock, marina, and a small cluster of services. Ruckle Park, a five minute drive from Fulford, is reached by turning right onto Beaver Point Road from just up the hill from the ferry terminal. From the end of the road, the waterfront is a short walk away. This park is popular with campers who enjoy the sunny, dry weather as well as the spectacle of ferries passing by all day long. For the more adventurous, longer trails head to the park's more remote eastern shorelines.

For those who don't mind a little more challenging driving, the Mount Tuam Road on the very southern tip of the island adds a little adventure to a Saltspring trip. From Fulford Harbor, turn left and follow the Fulford-Ganges Road for about a kilometer (0.6 mile) and then stay left and along the water on the Isabella Point Road. In a few hundred meters and just beyond a local park on the water, the road divides. Take Musgrave Road to the right and begin to climb steeply. Although gravel, this road is fine for almost any car. The road quickly flattens out and traverses high above Fulford Harbor with views to Mount Baker, the prominent 10,800-foot volcano in northwestern Washington state. Just past several homes, the road turns a corner, passes a turnoff (stay right), enters deep forest, and begins to gain elevation in several tight switchbacks.

After about 10 kilometers (6 miles) from the turnoff onto Musgrave, the road crests out on a plateau and then works its way back south. The turnoff to Mount Tuam is marked with a sign nailed to a tree stating "Mount Tuam Retreat." Turn left here and take the Mount Tuam Road for about 2 kilometers (1.2 miles) where it dead-ends at a gate. Park here and walk up the road. In about 500 meters (0.3 mile), an aircraft communications tower is reached at the beginning of the extensive views. Walk past the towers towards the ocean on a faint trail and soak in the incredible vista of islands, ocean, and mountains from the 2,000-foot summit of Mount Tuam. The panorama includes much of the North Cascades and Olympic Mountain ranges in Washington state as well as the San Juan and southern Gulf Islands.

## Saturna Island

Other than Saltspring, Saturna has the finest scenic driving of any of the Gulf Islands. In contrast to Saltspring's high population, less than 500 people call Saturna home. Much of the island is semiwilderness and peaceful. There are few services, no camping, and little accommodation on the island other than a few bed and breakfasts so if you're staying overnight on this island, be sure to consult the *BC Accommodatio ns Guide* and book as far ahead as possible. The main reason for the low population is that Saturna doesn't have a direct ferry connection to Vancouver. Reaching Saturna entails a transfer at either Galiano or Mayne Islands, a fact that greatly complicates travel arrangements. There are direct sailings between Swartz Bay and the Lyall Harbour ferry terminal on Saturna, making this the ideal way to reach the island.

Two outstanding trips on Saturna are recommended for visitors. The drive up Mount Warburton Pike is the most easily attained and spectacular vantage point in all the Gulf Islands. From the ferry terminal, head inland on East Point Road. In less than a minute, pass the island's main grocery store and turn right on Harris Road. This road is gravel but well-maintained and fine for any vehicle with the exception of those pulling trailers and motorhomes. At the next junction, take Staples Road on the left for the rest of the trip to the summit. The drive from the ferry terminal to the summit takes about one half-hour.

Mount Warburton Pike is marked by a microwave repeater tower and open, grassy slopes that yield panoramic views of the San Juan Islands to the south, the Gulf Islands and much of southern Vancouver Island to the west, and the snowy Olympic Mountains in the far distance. Sunsets from the mountain are often spectacular as it faces almost due west.

Back down on East Point Road, turn right and follow it around the end of Lyall Harbor and up a steep hill. Where it bends sharply right, the signed Winter Cove Road to the left leads quickly to Winter Cove Marine Park. Although BC's marine parks are usually only accessible by water, this one

# Drive 4: Gulf Islands
## *Saturna Island*

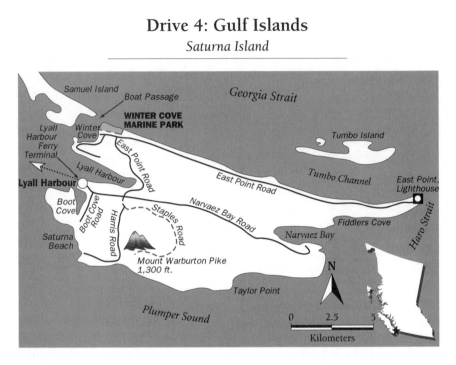

can be reached by road. From the parking lot on the waterfront, take the short path east (right) to Boat Passage between Saturna and Samuel Islands. This narrow gorge is known for its rapids as strong currents rip through the passage with the changing tides. The intricately sculpted rocks of the waterfront here also make for interesting exploration.

Once back on East Point Road, stay straight at the intersection and follow it along the shores of Georgia Strait all the way to East Point on the prettiest stretch of road in the Gulf Islands. Where the road ends, park and walk past the lighthouse and onto the open, grassy point and be treated to a sublime view of Mount Baker, the Coast Mountains, and much of Georgia Strait.

### Pender Islands
The Pender Islands are comprised of two islands—North and South Pender. Earlier in the century the two islands were one but the dredging out and bridging of Pender Canal created two separate islands. The Penders are the second most populous of the Gulf Islands after Saltspring, with most of the population living on the west side of North Pender. The highlight of the Penders is the driving, hiking, and boating possibilities on South Pender. Before heading to South Pender from the ferry terminal at Otter Bay on the north island, take the scenic side trip left onto Otter Bay Road (well signed) to Port Washington on the island's northern tip. The buildings here are among the oldest in the Gulf Islands with one dating back to the 1800s.

# Drive 4: Gulf Islands
*Pender Islands*

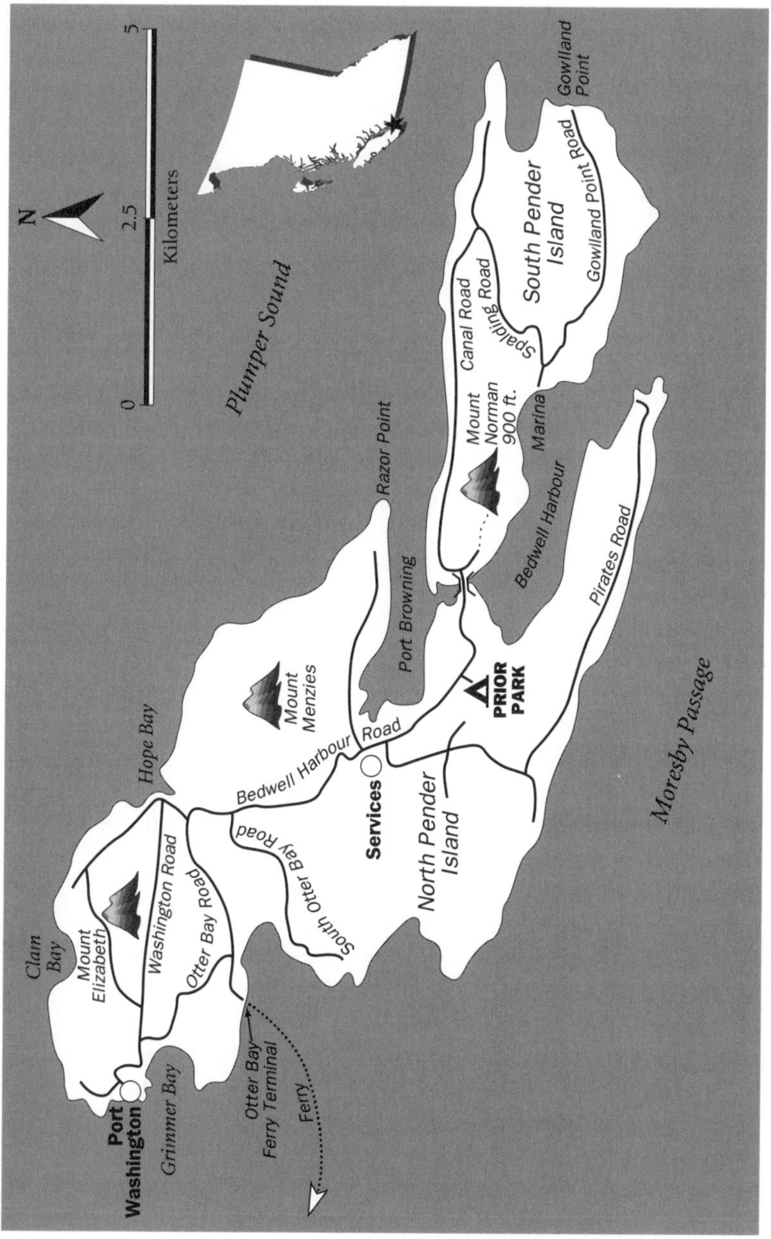

South Pender Island

Gowlland Point

Gowlland Point Road

Spalding Road

Canal Road

Mount Norman 900 ft.

Marina

Bedwell Harbour

Plumper Sound

Razor Point

Port Browning

Pirates Road

Mount Menzies

PRIOR PARK

Hope Bay

Bedwell Harbour Road

Services

North Pender Island

Moresby Passage

Clam Bay

Mount Elizabeth

Washington Road

Otter Bay Road

South Otter Bay Road

Grimmer Bay

Port Washington

Otter Bay Ferry Terminal

Ferry

N

Kilometers

0    2.5    5

From Port Washington, head back to the ferry terminal and then follow the signs to South Pender Island. On the way, you pass the commercial center of North Pender, which includes a well-stocked grocery store, gas station, and several other shops. Just beyond is small Prior Centennial Provincial Park, the only place to legally camp on the island.

The Pender Canal Bridge connecting the two islands was built in the 1950s and has great views into Bedwell Harbor to the right and Port Browning to the left. Immediately past the bridge is a fork to the right for Ainslie Point Road. If you have the time and energy for a short but steep hike, stay right here and drive a short distance to the trailhead for Mount Norman. The hike up to the summit of the Penders is about a kilometer (0.6 mile) up a steep gravel road that gains over 700 feet in several tight switchbacks. From the viewing platform atop the summit, the views to the west, south, and north are a breathtaking sweep of islands, ocean, and mountains. This is one of the premier viewpoints in the Gulf Islands.

Once back on Canal Road, the main road on South Pender, curve around to the east side of the island and gain excellent views across Plumper Sound to Saturna Island. Canal Road curves around Mount Norman (becoming Spalding Road) and passes the short side road to Bedwell Bay Marina before ending at Gowlland Point on the very southern tip of the island. From the delightful beach there, the views to the San Juan Islands and Mount Baker are superb, especially at sunrise.

### Galiano Island

Long and narrow, Galiano is the second largest and driest of the Gulf Islands and has a population of about 1,000 people. Most people's impression of the island comes from taking the ferry through Active Pass, the gorge-like waterway between Galiano and Mayne Islands. From the ferry terminal at Sturdies Bay, the commercial center of the island, take the main road inland for a few hundred meters, pass by the end of Whaler Bay, and then turn left and proceed along Burrill Road. In a short distance, Jack Drive branches off to the left at the end of which is tiny Bellhouse Park. From this waterfront park, ferries pass by seemingly within arm's reach as they enter Active Pass. Just across the pass is the Georgina Point Lighthouse on Mayne Island.

Back on Burrill Drive, follow it to where it curves around a sharp corner and becomes Bluff Drive. Shortly this road turns to gravel as it climbs gently to a ridge crest. From the high point, a side road to the left enters Bluffs Park and leads to an excellent viewpoint down into Active Pass. Sit here and watch the ferries glide through the narrow waterway and bald eagles soar with the thermals high above.

Continuing on Bluffs Road, drop steeply down the other side of the ridge and connect with the paved Georgeson Bay Road at the bottom. Turn right here and follow this pastoral road north to the intersection with the

# Drive 4: Gulf Islands
## Galiano Island

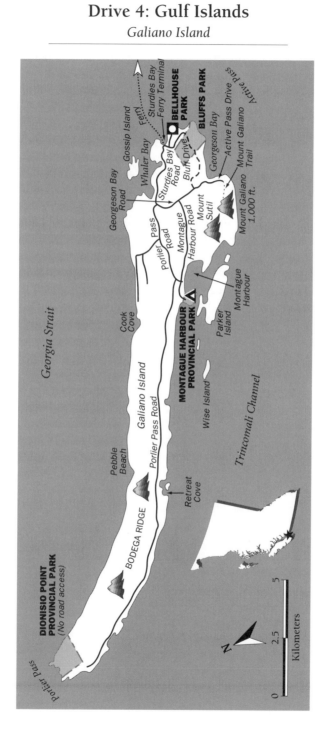

DIONISIO POINT
PROVINCIAL PARK
(No road access)

BODEGA RIDGE

Porlier Pass Road

Porlier Pass

Pebble
Beach

Galiano Island

Retreat
Cove

Cook
Cove

Georgia Strait

Georgeson Bay
Road

Whaler Bay

Gossip Island

Sturdies Bay
Road

BELLHOUSE
PARK

BLUFFS PARK

Sturdies Bay
Ferry Terminal

Ferry

Bluff Drive

Georgeson Bay

Active Pass Drive

Mount Galiano
Trail

Active Pass

Mount Galiano
1,000 ft.

Montague
Road

Mount
Sutil

Harbour Road

MONTAGUE HARBOUR
PROVINCIAL PARK

Montague
Harbour

Parker
Island

Wise Island

Trincomali Channel

N

2.5

5

0

Kilometers

Montague Harbor Road in a few minutes. Turn left on Montague and follow the signs to Montague Harbor Provincial Park. Encompassing a small peninsula, Montague is one of the most popular spots in the Gulf Islands with sailors, kayakers, and campers. The bays here are usually packed with sailboats and yachts in the summer months. The beaches in the park are some of the best in the Gulf Islands and the water is often warm enough for swimming. A scenic loop trail around the edge of the peninsula accesses several more secluded beaches.

One of the premier short hikes in the Gulf Islands is the 6-kilometer (3.6-mile) round trip up 1,000-foot Mount Galiano which has an amazing view of Active Pass and much of the Gulf Islands chain. The mountain lies on the very southern tip of Galiano and is easily seen from Bluffs Park. Find the marked trailhead by turning left onto Active Pass Drive from the intersection of Georgeson Bay Road and Bluffs Drive mentioned above.

Another scenic drive on Galiano is along its long west coast, reached by backtracking on the Montague Harbor Road a short distance and then turning left onto the Porlier Pass Road. This road runs along Trincomali Channel and often has ocean views across to Saltspring Island and several smaller, more remote islands to the west.

# 5

# Strathcona Provincial Park

## *Campbell River to Buttle Lake*

**General description:** This short but challenging 90-kilometer (54-mile) drive travels from the gentle east coast of Vancouver Island to Strathcona Provincial Park, BC's oldest, situated deep within the island's rugged core. Although most of the park is the domain of the wilderness hiker and mountaineer, the road along the eastern shores of Buttle Lake allows drivers to see one of the island's greatest concentrations of scenic wonders. This is a there-and-back drive with the option of making the side trip to Gold River near the Pacific coast.

**Special attractions:** The largest protected area on Vancouver Island, exciting driving along Buttle Lake, excellent mountain and lake views, and access to hiking trails into the high alpine.

**Location:** Central Vancouver Island between Highways 4 and 28.

**Drive route numbers:** Highway 28 to the Gold River turnoff and then the Buttle Lake Road for the remainder of the drive.

**Travel season:** Highway 28 is well maintained and driveable anytime. Spring, summer, and fall are best for the Buttle Lake Road. The road is open in winter but might be treacherous.

**Camping:** The best camping is at either Elk Falls Provincial Park (122 sites), just west of Campbell River, or at either of the two campgrounds along Buttle Lake in Strathcona Park.

**Services:** None between Campbell River and Buttle Lake other than accommodation at Strathcona Park Lodge. Gold River has all the basic tourist services.

**Nearby attractions:** Quadra and Cortes Islands, accessed by BC Ferry from Campbell River; Gold River and access to the ocean; all types of outdoor recreation.

 The drive

The drive begins in Campbell River where Highway 19, the Island Highway, and Highway 28 meet. Set your trip odometer here. The turnoff to Highway 28, Strathcona Provincial Park, and Gold River is well signed and hard to miss. The fastest way to get to this point from either Vancouver or Victoria is the new Island Highway (19) from Nanaimo, but if you have a little more time, be sure to take the old Island Highway (19A, Drive 3) along the shores of Georgia Strait to Campbell River.

41

# Drive 5: Strathcona Provincial Park
*Campbell River to Buttle Lake*

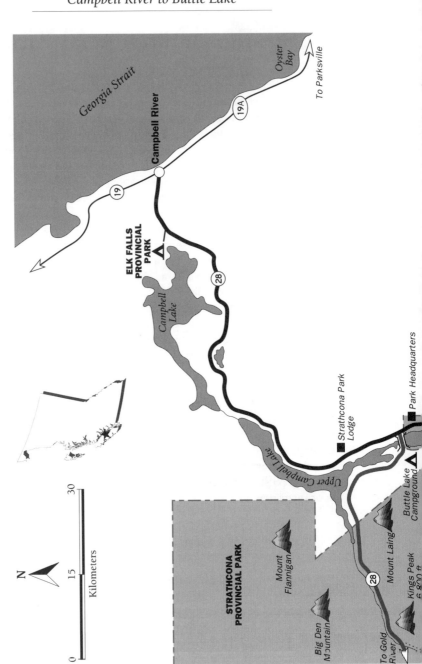

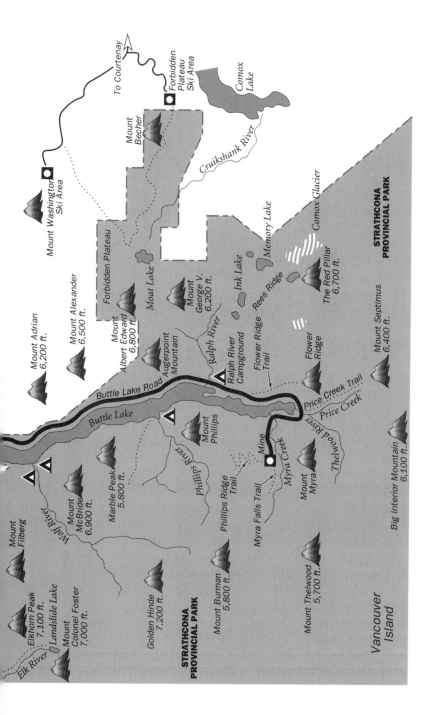

To Courtenay

Forbidden Plateau Ski Area

Comox Lake

Mount Becher

Cruikshank River

Mount Washington Ski Area

Comox Glacier

Memory Lake

Rees Ridge

The Red Pillar 6,700 ft.

STRATHCONA PROVINCIAL PARK

Mount Adrian 6,200 ft.

Mount Alexander 6,500 ft.

Forbidden Plateau

Moat Lake

Mount Albert Edward 6,800 ft.

Mount George V. 6,200 ft.

Ink Lake

Flower Ridge Trail

Flower Ridge

Mount Septimus 6,400 ft.

Augerpoint Mountain

Buttle Lake Road

Ralph River

Ralph River Campground

Buttle Lake

Price Creek Trail

Price Creek

Phillips River

Mount Phillips

Marble Peak 5,800 ft.

Thelwood River

Big Interior Mountain 6,100 ft.

Mount Filberg

Wolf River

Mount McBride 6,900 ft.

Phillips Ridge Trail

Mine

Myra Creek

Mount Myra

Elkhorn Peak 7,100 ft.

Landslide Lake

Mount Colonel Foster 7,000 ft.

Golden Hinde 7,200 ft.

STRATHCONA PROVINCIAL PARK

Mount Burman 5,800 ft.

Myra Falls Trail

Mount Thelwood 5,700 ft.

Vancouver Island

Elk River

43

Once on Highway 28, the route begins to climb up the long and gently sloping eastern scarp of Vancouver Island and into the foothills of the island's mountains. The access to Elk Falls Provincial Park is reached just a few minutes into the drive. This large camping-oriented park on the confluence of the Elk and Quinsam Rivers is a great place for families, with short hikes to waterfalls, fishing, and swimming opportunities. The park has two components, a day-use area and camping area. The campsites are 6.5 kilometers (3.9 miles) past the day-use area.

After passing through deep second-growth forests and traveling past several small lakes, the highway reaches the eastern tip of Upper Campbell Lake at 30 kilometers (18 miles), the second of the three large lakes on or near the drive. The lake is nearly connected to Buttle Lake and has the highway running along its southern shores for a few memorable kilometers. The lake is notable for its deep blue color, cliff-lined shorelines, and mountainous backdrop. Although large and scenic, this lake is marred by logging on the surrounding mountainsides. Campbell Lake, the closest of the lakes to Campbell River, is not readily visible from the highway.

Along the lake the drive becomes more demanding as the eastern edge of Vancouver Island's mountainous spine is reached. With every corner a little more of the peaks that tower above Buttle Lake are revealed. Although not high, these mountains are rugged by any standard and feature huge vertical relief out of their low valley footings.

At 41 kilometers (24.6 miles) is the rustic Strathcona Park Lodge, known for its outdoor education programs. The COLT (Canadian Outdoor Leadership Training) program is an intensive 105-day course that trains outdoor enthusiasts to take on leadership roles in outdoor recreation through a combination of leadership training, environmental awareness, and land and water based skills. Strathcona Park is the setting for much of the field experience which includes canoeing the lakes, kayaking the rivers, and mountaineering in the alpine regions. For less ambitious travelers, the lodge is open for overnight stays and canoe rentals. If you want to stay there it's best to call ahead to book a reservation (see Appendix).

Although much of Strathcona Provincial Park lies unseen, nestled deeply in true wilderness, the remainder of the drive skirts along the eastern shore of Buttle Lake and allows drivers to see at least the edges of the apex of Vancouver Island. The island has lost much of its remoteness in the past few decades as logging and mining have chipped away at its wild heart bit by bit. Luckily, Strathcona was created in 1911, long before large-scale logging took hold in the province. The park protects 250,000 hectares of forests, glaciers, alpine meadows, and high elevation lakes of the rugged central portion of the island in perpetuity. The park stretches almost all the way across the central part of Vancouver Island from the Pacific coast on the west all the way to Forbidden Plateau, just above Georgia Strait on the island's east coast. In all, Strathcona is the premier wilderness and outdoor adventure playground on Vancouver Island.

At 46 kilometers (27.6 miles), the highway enters Strathcona Provincial Park where a small information and rest area are found. Just over a kilometer (0.6 mile) past the park entrance is the junction to Gold River on the right. To continue with the drive stay straight and begin to travel along narrow Buttle Lake, deep within the heart of the park. By turning right here, Highway 28 continues through the northern section of Strathcona Park and ends at the small and isolated community of Gold River, just inland from the ocean. From there, a paved road continues to saltwater at the head of Muchalat Inlet on the eastern edge of remote Nootka Sound.

Buttle Lake was named for Commander John Buttle who explored the area and discovered his namesake lake in the 1860s. With the separation of Vancouver Island from mainland BC, several species found here, including Roosevelt elk and Vancouver Island marmots, are genetically distinct from those on the mainland. This separation also means that several species of mammals on the mainland such as grizzly bears, coyotes, and porcupines are not found here.

Just beyond the turnoff to Gold River is the park headquarters, the best place for inquiries about the park. One kilometer later (0.6 mile) is the Buttle Lake boat launch and picnic area. There are two main campsites in the park. The Buttle Lake campground (85 sites) is situated on the north end of the lake and is reached by turning right as for Gold River and then turning immediately left into the campground just on the other side of the lake. The other main campground is the Ralph River campground towards the lake's

*A carving of a Roosevelt elk at the entrance to Strathcona Provincial Park. Roosevelt elk in British Columbia are found only on Vancouver Island.*

southern end. For those with boats or canoes, several water-access-only campsites are located along the western shore of Buttle Lake opposite the road. The free park map available at the entrance or park headquarters shows the location of all of the features and facilities in the park. Call the park office to inquire about these campsites (see Appendix for phone number).

The 37-kilometers (22.2-miles) of road along the eastern shore of Buttle Lake twists and turns, following the contours of the land and usually staying within sight of the narrow, steep-sided lake. Driving along the lake on a clear winter day is splendid with views to snowcapped peaks contrasting boldly with the sky.

Except for the few large parks on Vancouver Island, all of the valuable old-growth stands of forest have been logged or are scheduled to be logged. In truth, a lot of Vancouver Island is still wilderness but most of it is high elevation forest or alpine terrain with little economic value. BC is often criticized for creating "rock and ice" parks that protect breathtaking mountain landscapes but few trees. Most park boundaries are conveniently drawn to exclude valuable forests coveted by the logging companies. Nowhere else is it more obvious than in Strathcona Park where a recent controversy has erupted over clearcutting on the eastern shores of Buttle Lake in an area most park visitors think of as pro-tected. In fact, the boundaries of the eastern edge of the park were drawn to leave out much of the forest on the mountainsides above the Buttle Lake Road.

In several places along here, fresh clear-cuts scar the mountainsides right down to the road. The Wesmin Mine, another source of controversy, is located in the park and its massive ore trucks regularly travel the road, intimidating drivers with their size. With the many tight corners, use caution along here and watch for these trucks where possible.

At 53 kilometers (32 miles) is the parking area for the short walk to Lupin Falls, the first of a series of waterfalls that are encountered along the lakeshore. The trail to the waterfall takes about 20 minutes one way. The Auger Point picnic area is reached at 69 kilometers (41.4 miles) while the Karst Creek Day Area is reached just a kilometer (0.6 mile) past it. A short and easy trail from Karst Creek passes limestone features such as sinkholes, disappearing streams, and waterfalls.

Across from the lake, but unseen, is the highest point of Vancouver Is-land, the Golden Hinde at 7,200 feet. A majestic pyramid of rock, this peak is a fitting climax to the ruggedness of Vancouver Island and a popular challenge for wilderness mountaineers who endure a long approach just to get to the base of the mountain. Across the lake from here, 6,900-foot Mount McBride and 5,800-foot Marble Peak soar skyward and merely hint at the sea of peaks stretch-ing away to the west. The western shore of Buttle Lake is fully protected and is pristine looking from the water's edge all the way to the summits. Many of the peaks above the lake are snowcapped well into the summer, an indication of the severity of the winter storms that rake this range in the winter months.

At 74 kilometers (44.4 miles), the road meets the second major campground on Buttle Lake, the Ralph River campground (76 sites). Past here, the lake narrows as its southern end is approached. At 78 kilometers (47 miles) is the parking area for the Flower Ridge Trail, a strenuous trail that climbs to a high, meadow-covered ridge with good views of the park. This is only one of the many wilderness trails that start near the southern end of the lake. The Marble Meadows Trail (boat access only) climbs steeply on the opposite side of the lake to a high limestone ridge to close-up views of the Golden Hinde. For the easiest access to the alpine regions of the park, head to the Forbidden Plateau on the park's very eastern edge, accessed from Courtenay on Drive 3. There the roads climb much higher and closer to the treeline, making the hikes much easier than from along Buttle Lake which lies at a low elevation. For a good description of all the hikes in the park, see *Hiking Trails III—Central and Northern Vancouver Island.*

In the last portion of the road, the views are dominated by the peaks south of Buttle Lake on the gateway to the truest wilderness on all of Vancouver Island. Several of the peaks seen here are high enough to also be seen from the open ocean far to the west. From the end of the drive at 83 kilometers (50 miles), several more challenging trails lead south to some exceptionally remote and spectacular mountain areas brimming with glaciers, meadows, and high alpine lakes. These hikes are very strenuous and best suited to experienced mountain hikers.

The road dead-ends at about 89 kilometers (53.4 miles) at the Westmin Mine site, which is the starting point for several more trails into the alpine on the west side of southern Buttle Lake. The trails that start from here are the Phillips Ridge and the Myra Falls Trails. Of the two, the Myra Falls Trail is easier and much shorter. The Phillips Ridge Trail climbs steeply to above treeline and gives good views in all directions, especially to the scores of peaks west and south.

After soaking up the views here, retrace the route back to Campbell River or, if time permits, drive out to Gold River to see more of the park. From Gold River, a short drive west reaches the ocean at narrow Muchalat Inlet in about one half-hour of driving. Located west of Muchalat Inlet in Nootka Sound is Bligh Island, named after the infamous British navy captain who accompanied Captain Cook here while exploring Canada's Pacific coast in 1788.

The *Uchuck III*, a former WWII minesweeper converted into a ferry and transport ship (see Appendix for phone number), heads out into Nootka Sound from the dock west of Gold River and sails to the wave-swept outer coast of Vancouver Island to supply small, isolated coastal villages. Although a working ship, it takes passengers on a memorable and highly recommended trip into some of the wildest places on the island.

# Southwestern British Columbia

# 6

# Sunshine Coast Highway
### Langdale to Lund

**General description:** The Sunshine Coast Highway (101) is a 130-kilometer (78-mile) seaside drive along the narrow strip of land between the massive barrier of the Coast Mountains and the inland sea of Georgia Strait. Most of the attraction of the drive is based on the ocean views, the unique coastal communities, and the novelty of two ferry rides across two of BC's coastal fjords. The opportunities to get out on the ocean along this drive are unmatched in the entire book with numerous rental, charter, and tour companies allowing access to rocky coastlines, islands, and narrow fjords that surround the Sunshine Coast.

**Special attractions:** Frequent ocean views, two ferry trips, rugged coastlines, offshore islands, lighthouses, marine life viewing, excellent boating and kayaking opportunities, and picturesque coastal towns.

**Location:** The Sunshine Coast, immediately northwest of Vancouver on the east side of Georgia Strait.

**Drive route numbers:** Highway 101 the entire way.

**Travel season:** Any time of year. Summer brings the best weather but also long ferry waits. If you plan on getting out on the water, be sure to come in summer. Much of the tourist infrastructure closes in the winter months.

**Camping:** The best camping is at Roberts Creek, Porpoise Bay, or Saltery Bay Provincial Parks. Each of the major towns have commercial camping as well.

**Services:** Found at regular intervals along the drive.

**Nearby attractions:** The waters of Georgia Strait, Sechelt Inlet, Princess Louisa Inlet, Powell Lake, and Desolation Sound.

 The drive

This scenic drive travels up the Sunshine Coast from Langdale to Lund on the very northern extremity of Highway 101, the series of coastal roads (Pan American Highway) that run down the west coast of the Americas all the way to the southern tip of South America. Nowhere else along the Pacific coast of mainland BC does the highway actually run alongside the ocean. So convoluted and rugged is the 27,000-kilometer-long BC coast (16,200 miles) that north of Lund, the ocean is reached in only two other places—Bella Coola and Prince Rupert.

The Sunshine Coast is very much defined by its location, sandwiched between ocean and mountains. Though Georgia Strait is visible along the drive, the Coast Mountains lie for the most part unseen, blocked from view by lower peaks. To really appreciate the mountain scenery, it's necessary to boat into one of the steep-sided fjords that radiate off the Sunshine Coast. The Sunshine Coast is nearly an island, being connected to the mainland only by a narrow isthmus of land at Sechelt. The peninsula is called the Sunshine Coast because it is both sunnier and drier than Vancouver. Although it has one of the mildest climates in Canada, it still gets its share of bad weather, proving that everything is relative when weather is concerned.

As scenic as the driving is here, the boating is even better, not surprising given the sheer amount and variety of the water-accessed destinations. The coast is beautiful to explore by boat but the cliff-lined shores make landings difficult in most places. Beaches are few and far between anywhere along the BC coast and this area is no exception.

For much of its distance, the Sunshine Coast Highway travels close to the ocean but has infrequent views of it. To see the sheltered bays, quaint fishing harbors, and island views, it's necessary to exit off the main road and go exploring. In order to complete the drive, it's necessary to take two scenic ferry trips. While adding to the attraction of the drive, they must be factored into the driving time and planning.

The drive begins in Langdale on the shores of western Howe Sound. Langdale is reached via BC Ferries from Horseshoe Bay, located in West Vancouver. From downtown Vancouver, the drive to the ferry terminal takes about 20 minutes and is accessed via Highway 1 westbound. For fare and schedule information, call BC Ferries or view their Internet site (see Appendix). Even though the driving distances are not long, the ferry rides must be added in, so expect to take a minimum of five hours to reach Lund at the end of the drive.

The 45-minute cruise across Howe Sound is a great introduction to the seascapes of coastal BC. As the ferry pulls away from the dock, the sheer mountain walls on all sides of triangular Howe Sound seem to grow higher as the ferry moves out and into the sound. The ferry sails between massive Bowen Island to the south and equally large and multipeaked Gambier Island to the north. Both have summits over 3,000 feet high. At the mid-point of the trip, look way north towards the head of the sound to see the volcanic peak of Mount Garibaldi, nearly 9,000 feet high and covered in glaciers. Looking back towards the serrated Howe Sound Crest to the east reveals

# Drive 6: Sunshine Coast Highway
*Langdale to Lund*

Mount Denman
6,500 ft.

COAST MOUNTAINS

*Toba Inlet*

*Homfray Channel*

*West Redonda Island*

East
Redonda
Island

Beartooth
Mountain
5,800 ft.

*Powell
Lake*

Cortes
Island

**DESOLATION SOUND
MARINE PARK**

Goat
Island

*Dodd
Lake*

*Desolation Sound*

Marina
Island

Twin
Islands

*Malaspina Peninsula*

*Logging roads*

*Hasam Lake*

Hernando
Island

**Lund**

Mitlenatch
Island

Savary
Island

**Sliammon**

**Homesite**

*Louis
Lake*

**MADIERA
PARK**

Harwood Island

**Powell
River**

101

**Saltery Bay**

*Ferry*

*Malaspina Strait*

**Merville**

Ferry Terminal

Ferry
Terminal

Nelson
Island

**Courtenay**

**Comox**

*Georgia Strait*

Texada
Island

*Garden Bay*

**MADIERA
PARK**

Sandy Islands

19A

Denman Island

Hornby Island

Lesquiti
Island

**Buckley Bay**

*Tribune Bay*

*Vancouver
Island*

*Qualicum
Bay*

*Old Island Highway*

**Qualicum Beach**

To Nanaimo

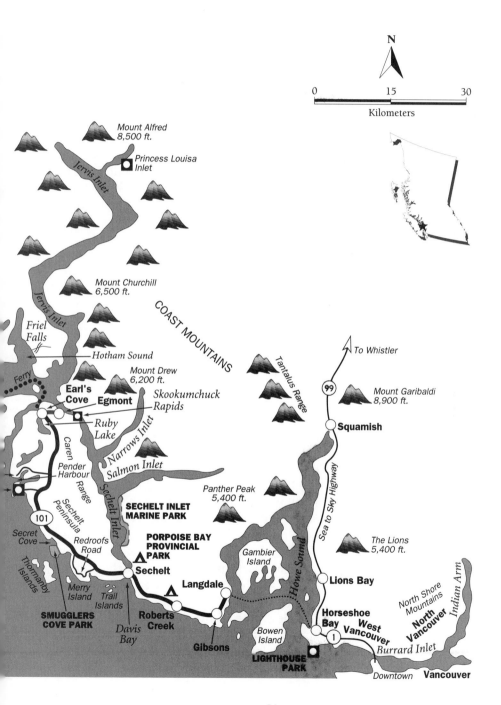

N

0        15        30
Kilometers

Mount Alfred
8,500 ft.

Princess Louisa
Inlet

Jervis Inlet

Mount Churchill
6,500 ft.

COAST MOUNTAINS

Friel
Falls

Jervis Inlet

Hotham Sound

Mount Drew
6,200 ft.

Ferry

Earl's
Cove   Egmont

Skookumchuck
Rapids

Ruby
Lake

Caren

Narrows Inlet

Pender
Harbour

Range

Salmon Inlet

Tantalus Range

To Whistler

99

Mount Garibaldi
8,900 ft.

Squamish

Sechelt Inlet

Panther Peak
5,400 ft.

101

SECHELT INLET
MARINE PARK

Sechelt
Peninsula

Sea to Sky Highway

Secret
Cove

Redroofs
Road

PORPOISE BAY
PROVINCIAL
PARK

The Lions
5,400 ft.

Thormanby
Islands

Sechelt

Gambier
Island

Merry
Island

Trail
Islands

Langdale

Lions Bay

North Shore
Mountains

Indian Arm

SMUGGLERS
COVE PARK

Davis
Bay

Roberts
Creek

Horseshoe
Bay   West
Vancouver

North
Vancouver

Gibsons

Bowen
Island

Howe Sound

1

Burrard Inlet

LIGHTHOUSE
PARK

Downtown   Vancouver

**51**

views of the famed Lions, Vancouver's signature peaks. As the ferry approaches Langdale, it passes between Gambier and Keats Islands and provides views out into the open waters of Georgia Strait to the south.

Once off the ferry, set your trip odometer and stay sharply left at the Y-junction signed for Gibsons and drive along the waterfront. Staying right here is a shortcut to Highway 101 that bypasses most of Gibsons. In the 4-kilometer (2.4-mile) drive to the quaint seaside community of Gibsons, the narrow highway passes numerous typical west coast homes lining the shores of Howe Sound, and has excellent views of the sound and its mountain fringe.

Gibsons, despite being very close to Vancouver, is one of BC's most beautifully situated coastal communities. The ocean gap between here and Vancouver means that Gibsons is an escape from the urban sprawl of the Lower Mainland. Gibsons is famed as the home of the long-running CBC Television series "The Beachcombers" which was set both in town and out in Howe Sound. The series ran for many years and had a worldwide audience. Mollies Reach, the cafe often featured in the series, is in the center of town above the main harbor.

Downtown Gibsons is a rewarding place for a stroll with a long stretch of tourist and marine-oriented shops. As is the case all along the drive, there are plenty of seafood restaurants as well. Be sure to wander around the main harbor to see an interesting mix of old commercial fishing boats and new, sleek pleasure craft. Just southwest of Gibsons on the corner where Howe Sound merges with Georgia Strait is Gower Point. Here a cairn marks the point where Captain George Vancouver first met BC's Pacific coast while mapping the west coast of North America in the late 1700s.

Just above the harbor, Highway 101 curves up and around a steep hill to gain the upper and newer section of Gibsons where many of its services are found. Traveling northwest, the highway runs inland for a stretch before passing Roberts Creek at 9 kilometers (5.4 miles). This seaside community is reached by exiting off the highway and driving through its quiet roads that run past the ocean. Roberts Creek Provincial Park, a little further north on Highway 101 is a popular and well-groomed camping park set in deep forest. This is the best place to camp along the beginning of the drive.

Just before Sechelt, the highway skims along the water's edge at Davis Bay where a new waterfront park offers the easiest access to the ocean on the entire Sunshine Coast. Beautifully situated, this beach looks far across Georgia Strait to Vancouver Island and is a fantastic sunset watching location. Several motels located across from the beach tempt a stay here.

After curving around and bending back to the west, the highway reaches Sechelt at 27 kilometers (16.2 miles). This is the point where the ocean waters of Sechelt Inlet, just to the north, almost pinch off the Sunshine Coast into an island separate from mainland BC. Sechelt has a large native Indian presence with the Sechelt Nation being the first of BC's many native bands to sign a modern day treaty with the provincial government. As you enter Sechelt, the Sechelt Cultural Center is seen on the left and has been built in the traditional long house style. Sechelt itself has a long waterfront park with excellent views toward Vancouver Island and closer in, the Trail Islands, which lie just offshore. On clear days Mount Baker, the soaring 10,800-foot volcano in northwestern Washington, can be seen on the far southern horizon.

A very worthwhile side trip from Sechelt is to follow the signs north through town to Porpoise Bay Provincial Park, a large and busy camping park located on the waters of Sechelt Inlet. From here, Sechelt Inlet runs north to Jervis Inlet near the well-known Skookumchuck Rapids. Canoes and kayaks can be rented in Sechelt to explore the placid waters of the inlet. The Sechelt Inlet Marine Park, located farther up the fjord, is a series of tropical-looking sandy beaches set below towering mountainsides. This is a very popular sea kayaking destination.

After leaving the bustle of Sechelt behind, the highway quickly enters deep forest and tranquility once again. Although close to the ocean in the next section, a screen of trees and waterfront homes often block views to the water. Just a few minutes past Sechelt is the turnoff to Redroofs Road on the left. Turn here and follow the waterfront, or if pressed for time, stay on Highway 101. Redroofs Road resembles a quiet country lane as it passes little cottages and quaint shops. Most of coastal BC has a laid back, relaxing atmosphere and this area is the closest place to Vancouver to really feel it. The coast here seems a world apart from the Lower Mainland despite being only a couple of hours away.

Sergeant Bay Park, found at the tip of the peninsula, is only a few minutes off Highway 101. This waterfront park features several beaches perfect for sunbathing and swimming, or for the more ambitious, the launching of canoes or kayaks. Continuing on Redroofs Road, Coopers Green regional park is quickly reached, located directly across Halfmoon Bay from Smugglers Cove Marine Park. From the picnic and boat launch here, the views include the craggy Thormanby Islands offshore in the distance, the Merry Island lighthouse farther to the south, as well as the calm waters of Halfmoon Bay in the foreground. This is a popular launch point for boating and kayaking trips to the surrounding coastlines. In the winter months, sea lions are often seen and heard from here.

Following Halfmoon Bay, Redroofs Road quickly links back up with Highway 101. Turn left and continue north. Fourteen kilometers (8.4 miles) past Sechelt is the well signed turnoff to Smugglers Cove Marine Park. This small but scenic marine park is popular with sailboats plying the Inside Passage to Alaska and is known for its challenging anchorages. The park is laced with small rocky coves, turquoise lagoons, and numerous tiny islands— a boater's paradise. The park is a about a 6-kilometer (3.6-mile) drive off

*The rocky coastline of Smugglers Cove Marine Park,*
*typical of the rugged waterfront on the entire British Columbia coast.*

Highway 101 on Brooks Road. Although best explored from the water, Smugglers Cove is accessible by a short trail that leads to the water's edge at the head of a small bay. From here, rough trails traverse along the coast to rocky overlooks into Welcome Passage which lies between the mainland and South Thormanby Island.

Back on the highway, the signed turnoff to Secret Cove is reached within minutes. The short road down into the marina here is a delightful little side trip to see a picture-perfect west coast scene complete with dozens of sailboats tied to the docks. The cove is "secret" because it is well hidden by an island and is tucked into a small inlet not visible from Malaspina Strait, the main body of water just offshore.

Traveling north on Highway 101, the next point of interest is the Pender Harbor area, well known as a series of vibrant coastal communities nestled around the convoluted waterways at the mouth of Jervis Inlet. This is one of the main boating centers for the entire coast and most of the traffic here is marine related. Throughout Pender Harbor there are numerous marinas and other facilities built to serve the massive influx of summer boaters who pass through on their way up the Inside Passage, or more commonly, on their way to Desolation Sound or Princess Louisa Inlet.

While widely known for its fishing, Pender Harbor is even better known as the gateway to the world-famous Princess Louisa Inlet, a magical fjord at the head of Jervis Inlet, a few hours away by boat. The inlet, widely known as one of the most beautiful places in the world to drop an anchor, is 6 kilometers (3.6 miles) long and exceptionally narrow. It is ringed by glacier-clad peaks that rise to 8,500 feet straight out of the water. Up to 60 water-falls have been counted on the fjord's cliffs, with the most famous being Chatterbox Falls at its head. Tours to the inlet can be arranged in Pender Harbor or in Egmont, a little farther up the highway. Contact either BC Parks or the Sechelt Infocenter for a list of tour operators (see Appendix).

The main commercial center of Pender Harbor, Madiera Park, is reached nearly 59 kilometers (35.4 miles) from Langdale and is located on the south-ern half of the harbor. Continuing a little farther north, the highway passes the turnoff to Garden Bay and Irvines Landing. Garden Bay in particular is highly recommended but the whole area is well worth a side trip. Along the way to Garden Bay, the road passes a small lake before reaching a classic coastal scene of intricate shorelines, historic buildings, and dozens of moored boats. Pender Harbor is heavily geared to tourism so expect a full range of services, accommodations, and restaurants.

For excellent views of this jigsaw puzzle of lakes, ocean inlets, and mountains, take the easy trail up 750-foot Pender Hill which is located on the north side of Pender Harbor. The trailhead is reached via Garden Bay Road to Irvines Landing Road and then to Lee Road. The 1.5-kilometer (0.9-mile) trail starts at a turquoise-colored pole and takes about 30 min-utes to reach the top. A map will help to identify all of the land and water features of the surrounding area.

Beyond the delightful environs of Pender Harbor, Highway 101 travels high above Ruby and Sakinaw Lakes, both set below forested mountain-sides that rise sheer from the ocean's edge along here. The whole area is fascinating geographically due to its juxtaposition of mountain and ocean scenery. The Caren range, rising to the east of the highway, has some of Canada's oldest trees, many well over 1,000 years old.

The second ferry terminal of the trip is reached at Earl's Cove where the highway dead-ends at Jervis Inlet. Just before the terminal is the signed turnoff to Egmont. This small coastal village is about 6 kilometers (3.6 miles) east on this side road. The main reason for going there is the 4-kilometer (2.4-mile) trail to Skookumchuck Rapids. Located where Sechelt Inlet emp-ties into Jervis Inlet, the Skookumchuck Rapids which mean "turbulent wa-ters" in the local native language, are caused when huge volumes of water traveling with the tides are forced to flow through a narrow gap. Be sure to make the walk to the rapids at peak ebb or flood to see them at their thrill-ing best. Adventuresome kayakers are sometimes seen playing in the rapids that at times resemble a large-volume white-water river.

On a clear day, this second ferry ride across Jervis Inlet is a breathtak-ing panorama of BC's typical mountain, island, and fjord seascape that is found few other places on earth. Once away from the dock, the view up

*Sea kayaker near Chatterbox Falls at the head of Princess Louisa Inlet, an offshoot of long Jervis Inlet. The cliffs in the background soar to glaciated summits over 8,000 feet high.*

Jervis Inlet is astonishing, with the 6,500-foot spire of Mount Churchill rising sheer out of the water to the north. Closer in, the ferry passes cliff-lined Captain Island and travels across from the mouth of Hotham Sound, the next major body of water to the west (left) of Jervis Inlet. By looking closely you will see threadlike Friel Falls dropping over 1,000 feet into the sound.

The ferry dock at Saltery Bay is the beginning of the upper Sunshine Coast. From here, the highway runs slightly inland from the ocean for much of its distance to Powell River. The turnoff to Saltery Bay Provincial Park is reached only a kilometer (0.6 mile) past the ferry terminal. On the waterfront across from Nelson Island, this park has 45 sites for both tents and RVs and is popular with campers, boaters, and divers.

On the way north, the occasional ocean views are dominated by the long spine of Texada Island, which lies just across Malaspina Strait. Powell River, reached about 30 kilometers (18 miles) past Saltery Bay, runs for many kilometers along the waterfront in a series of loosely connected communities. The city is situated on a very thin strip of land between the remote wilderness of the Coast Mountains to the east and the waters of Georgia Strait to the west.

With its combination of ocean and mountain scenery, Powell River, the largest community on the Sunshine Coast, is a popular outdoor recreation location. The city calls itself the "dive capital of Canada" for its numerous excellent saltwater diving locations. Powell River is a major center for both pleasure and commercial boating and has several marinas strung out along its waterfront. Of course, the seafood dining in town is excellent, as is the opportunity to head out on a charter boat to catch your own dinner. Those interested in backroading will find numerous logging roads that lead into the Coast Mountains behind the city. Use the *BC Recreational Atlas* (new edition to be retitled *The BC Road and Recreational Atlas*) to locate their starting points.

The main part of the city is Westview, where most of the shops and services are located. This is also the location of the BC Ferry terminal which gives access to Comox on Vancouver Island (see Land and Sea Circle Tours) as well as to Texada Island. The 850-foot Valentine Mountain (reached by stairs to the top) at the end of Crown Avenue (ask locally) has a panoramic view of the ocean, mountains, and lakes that envelop the area.

A few kilometers beyond Westview is the historic community of Homesite, the old area that sprang up with the major pulp mill seen below the highway. The collection of old homes and businesses here, over 440 of them, have been declared a National Historic Region by the Canadian government as a well-preserved example of a single company town.

Just past Homesite, Highway 101 curves around and drops to cross the mouth of fjord-like Powell Lake before climbing back up to above the ocean and quickly passing through the native settlement of Sliammon. Powell Lake is the setting for the multi-day Powell Lake Canoe Circuit, a series of twelve lakes that connect together via portage trails to make a popular loop trip through this lake-dotted mountain country. Consult *Adventuring in British Columbia* for details (see Appendix).

Lund, and the end of Highway 101, are reached 23 kilometers (13.8 miles) north of Powell River where the highway curves and abruptly drops into this tiny seaside community. Lund is yet another picturesque and laid-back coastal harbor town serving boaters who tie up here for supplies or to spend the night before moving on. The town is the gateway to famous Desolation Sound Marine Park, just to the north, the most popular boating destination on the whole coast.

Desolation Sound, named by captain George Vancouver who explored here in 1792, is a boaters haven of inlets, bays, and tiny island groups all set below the high western edge of the Coast Mountains. Pyramidal Mount Denman, which lords above the sound, is easily the most distinctive peak seen from the ocean on BC's west coast. Lund has several charter companies that take people on tours into the sound. Ask locally or call the Powell River Infocenter for details (see Appendix).

Savary Island, just offshore from Lund, is also a worthwhile trip and is closer and cheaper (about $14) to reach than Desolation Sound. From the main dock area, the Savary water taxi crosses over to the island several times a day during summer (call for details, see Appendix). Savary Island is called the "Hawaii of BC" for its sand-fringed coastlines and South Seas atmosphere. Although there are a few residents here, the narrow dirt roads are quiet and more resemble trails than roads. Be sure to pick up an island map from the water taxi operator. About a 15 minute walk from the ferry dock leads to the south side of the island where the massive yellow sand beaches beckon. The waters here are reported to be amongst the warmest in BC, tempting a quick dip in the ocean. The views in all directions are superb with both the Sunshine Coast and Vancouver Island in full view to the south.

After sampling the delights of the Sunshine Coast, either head back to Vancouver the way you came or cross over to Vancouver Island at Powell River and continue down the old Island Highway (19A) and back to Vancouver via Nanaimo to complete an excellent coastal loop trip (see the Land and Sea Circle Tours section for more information).

# 7

# Sea to Sky Highway

## *Horseshoe Bay to Pemberton*

**General description:** Beginning on Vancouver's doorstep, the Sea to Sky Highway (Highway 99) is a spectacular introduction to the landscapes that are the hallmarks of British Columbia—snowcapped peaks, cathedral-like forests, a myriad of islands, thundering waterfalls, and the shimmering beauty of the ocean. In few other places on earth can you be transported from a major urban area to such magnificence as quickly as on this famous highway. The 135-kilometer (81-mile) drive is a study of contrasts—ocean views in the first half and mountain views in the second.

**Special attractions:** The islands of Howe Sound, Shannon Falls, the glaciated Tantalus Range, the Squamish Chief, Mount Garibaldi, volcanic features and hiking trails in Garibaldi Provincial Park, Brandywine Falls, Whistler Village, Nairn Falls, the Pemberton Valley.

**Location:** Southwestern BC, due north of Vancouver in the lower Coast Mountains.

**Drive route numbers:** Highway 99, the Sea to Sky Highway the entire drive.

**Travel season:** All year. The highway is just as busy in winter as summer. From December to March, snow is often encountered on the highway north of Squamish.

**Camping:** Best campgrounds are, south to north along the drive: Porteau Cove, Brandywine Falls, Alice Lake, and Nairn Falls Provincial Parks.

**Services:** Services are found only in Squamish, Whistler, and Pemberton with nothing in between.

**Nearby attractions:** A wealth of hiking and climbing opportunities, especially in Garibaldi Provincial Park, four-wheel driving and backroading on the side roads, the Duffey Lake Road (Drive 8), and the Pemberton River valley.

 **The drive**

The beginning of the Sea to Sky Highway is a mere 15 minutes away from downtown Vancouver. Along this route there is so much to see that the first-time driver will need hours to sample its many viewpoints and attractions. The drive can be divided easily into two segments, the first being West Vancouver to Squamish, where the primary attraction is island-dotted Howe

# Drive 7: Sea to Sky Highway
## Horseshoe Bay to Pemberton

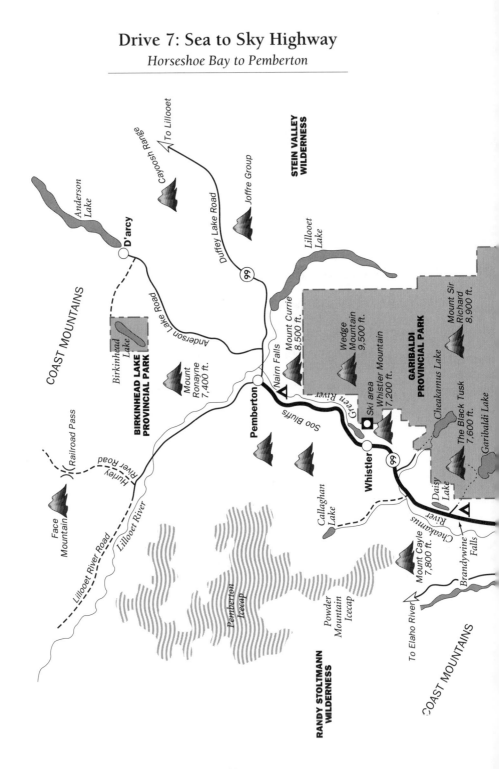

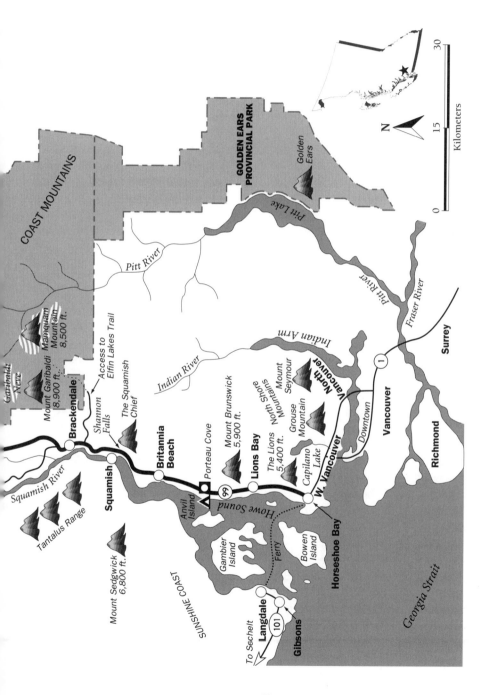

Sound; and the second being Squamish to Pemberton, which is dominated by mountains, glaciers, and alpine scenery.

The drive begins at Horseshoe Bay, located on the Trans Canada Highway (Highway 1) just west of Vancouver. Where the highway curves around and above Horseshoe Bay, stay right for Highway 99, following the signs for Whistler. Turning left here leads to quaint Horseshoe Bay and the BC Ferry terminal for both Vancouver Island and the Sunshine Coast. Set your trip odometer to zero where the highway begins just past the turnoff to Horseshoe Bay. Right from the beginning of the drive an ocean-to-alpine panorama is revealed to the north, a startling contrast to the views of Vancouver seen a just a few minutes before.

For many Vancouverites, this highway is *the* gateway to adventure, with almost any kind of outdoor activity possible along this route including world-class rock climbing, skiing, windsurfing, and mountain biking. This area is a true recreational paradise and is gaining international attention, primarily due to the incredibly popular ski resort at Whistler. Although this route was pioneered by rail in the early part of the century it wasn't until the 1970s that the drive along the first section of highway to Squamish was commonly traveled by car. In those days, most of the travel beyond Squamish was on rough backroads leading to logging operations where Whistler now lies. Before the roads, the only way into the area was to boat up Howe Sound and then take the Pacific Great Eastern Railway from Squamish north to the Cariboo. Pemberton wasn't even accessible by car until 1975 when Highway 99 was completed north from Whistler.

Highway 99 is winding and narrow in many places and takes a lot of concentration to drive. Locals call this the "killer highway" for good reason—it has more than its share of fatal accidents every year. Although there have been calls by many to improve and straighten the highway, most of the accidents are due to aggressive driving, inattention, or bad weather. Be sure to drive here during good weather to not only see the scenery but to also ensure a safe trip. The highway was blasted out of sheer cliffs that fall into Howe Sound and in the rainy season, waterfalls often pour directly onto the side of the road. The debris chutes along the first few kilometers are insurance against potentially disastrous landslides that have in the past swept away homes and blocked the highway for days at a time.

Several pullouts along the start of the highway allow for a picture-perfect image of Horseshoe Bay and the ferries slipping in and out of the terminal. The first stretch of the drive is the most demanding of the entire highway as it weaves around the cliffs of Black Mountain, the very southernmost peak in the Coast Mountain chain that runs from Vancouver all the way north up the west coast to Alaska. Through here, the westernmost summits of the North Shore Mountains soar above the ocean's edge to heights nearing 6,000 feet. The strenuous Howe Sound Crest Trail climbs and traverses these peaks for 30 kilometers (18 miles) from the Cypress Bowl ski area in West Vancouver all the way to Porteau Cove. Along the way, hikers are granted airplane like views of the highway below as well as the mountains and islands that define Howe Sound. For details on this strenuous hike, consult *103 Hikes in Southwestern BC* (see Appendix).

At 4 kilometers (2.4 miles) is the turnoff to Sunset Marina which is situated across from Bowyer Island, the first prominent island near the highway. It's a short but steep drive down to the marina where a boat launch, docks, and restaurant all feature water-level views of the sound. At 7 kilometers (4 miles), the first major concrete debris chute is seen beside the highway. Although only a small trickle of water may be flowing down the chute when you pass, be assured that these imposing structures protect the highway from the ravages of torrential rains and landslides during powerful winter storms.

Between here and Lions Bay, the panorama of ocean views to the west calls for frequent pullouts, especially in the warm light late in the day when the islands are silhouetted against the setting sun. The prominent islands directly across from the highway are Bowen to the south and Gambier to the north. Both of these mountainous islands appear to merge with the rugged backdrop of the Sunshine Coast but are of course separate. The bare Christie Islets, not far out into the sound, are an important sea bird nesting site. Closer to the highway, distinctive red-barked arbutus trees are seen clinging wildly to the cliffs while bald eagles are commonly seen circling high above in the thermals.

Looking up Howe Sound toward its head reveals small but massively bulky Anvil Island, noted for its steep sides and pyramidal summit. At 10 kilometers (6 miles), the picturesque village of Lions Bay is reached, steeply arrayed up the mountainside. Nearly every home here has a panoramic mountain and ocean view. The 5,400-foot Lions, the twin-summited Vancouver landmark, towers above Lions Bay and can be seen from the major concrete bridge across Harvey Creek. Every summer, hikers pass through Lions Bay on their way to climb the West Lion, a strenuous hike involving huge elevation gains.

Howe Sound is one of the two most southerly fjords that deeply indent BC's Pacific coast. The views here are typical of the marvelous seascapes found all up and down the coast with the exception that human impacts are more visible here than elsewhere. There are few beaches on the BC coast as most of it is cliffy and rugged. Howe Sound is no exception, being framed on both sides by peaks that clearly define its edges. Nearer to Squamish, the cliffs that shoot hundreds of feet out of the sound are easily seen to the west.

At 24 kilometers (14.4 miles) is Porteau Cove Provincial Park, the only easy place to reach the ocean along the whole drive. The 59 campsites here are almost always full so arrive early if you want to spend the night. Be sure to stop here and walk out onto the ferry dock to take in the sweeping view both up and down the sound. To the south, Leading Peak, the jagged

*Looking south down Howe Sound from near Britannia Beach
with Anvil Island prominent in the distance.*

summit of Anvil Island, is a prominent landmark, while to the north the glaciers in the Tantalus Range draw the eye upwards. The summits of the Tantalus Range are an astonishing 8,500 feet above the sea-level viewpoint at Porteau Cove. The park is also popular with divers who are treated to clear, deep waters and a proliferation of marine life. A ferry dock is located here in case the highway between Squamish and Vancouver is severed by slides. In that case, vehicles can be loaded here and transported back to Horseshoe Bay by ferry.

The new development at Furry Creek, marked by its golf course set on Howe Sound, is reached at 26 kilometers (15.6 miles). Britannia Beach, just beyond, was home to the biggest copper mine in the British Empire in the early 1930s. Today, the Britannia Mine and the BC Museum of Mining are open to tours (summer only). The mine has been making news for several years as one of the most polluted sites in Canada. A cleanup is now underway to lessen its toxic runoff into the sound. The town of Britannia Beach, situated beside the mine, hosts an eclectic collection of businesses including a diner, a grocery store, and several native Indian craft stores all hoping to snare some of the tourist traffic along the highway. Across the narrowing waters of the Sound, the smokestacks of the Woodfibre Pulp Mill compete for attention with the snowy peak of 6,800-foot Mount Sedgwick which rises just behind.

Past Brittania Beach, the highway turns away from Howe Sound for good but the lack of ocean views is quickly compensated for by striking views of high summits in the next few kilometers. Murrin Lake, a popular picnic and rock climbing area, is reached at 35 kilometers (21 miles) on the way to the first views of Mount Garibaldi, The Squamish Chief, and Shannon Falls. The combination of the three Squamish landmarks in one view is remarkable. Mount Garibaldi, namesake of Garibaldi Provincial Park, is on the volcanic "Ring of Fire" that runs along the west coast of the Americas and is the next volcano north of Mount Baker in Washington state. This ancient volcano, 8,800 feet high, dominates the town of Squamish and is a popular climbing objective. Mount Garibaldi is a collection of three summits with the most dramatic being the spire-like Atwell Peak. Although dormant now, the alpine area around Garibaldi is strewn with ancient lava flows and other reminders of the peak's fiery history.

From along here, also notice how the color of Howe Sound has changed in its northern reaches. Fed by runoff from the numerous glaciers north of Squamish, the turquoise color of the inlet more resembles a lake in the Rocky Mountains than the ocean. At 40 kilometers (24 miles) is Shannon Falls Provincial Park on the right. Be sure to stop here and take the 10-minute walk to the base of this 1,100-foot-high waterfall that thunders down over massive granite slabs. In some winters, a sudden cold snap often freezes the waterfall and it becomes a popular challenge for ice climbers to scale.

Within a kilometer (0.6 mile) of Shannon Falls comes The Squamish Chief viewing area at the base of this soaring granite monolith. Regarded as the second largest hunk of granite on earth, The Chief is known worldwide for its extraordinary and difficult rock climbing routes. Some 2,200 feet high and as sheer as a skyscraper, the Grand Wall, in full view, is a multi-day climb for expert climbers and is one of the finest rock climbs in the world. On summer days be sure to scan the face for climbers slowly working their way toward the top. Mere hikers can achieve the summit of The Chief by a rough hiking trail that climbs the backside of the rock.

Squamish is reached at 44 kilometers (26.4 miles) and is accessed by turning left at the second intersection on Highway 99 and proceeding west into downtown. A rapidly growing town of 18,000, Squamish is an interesting blend of outdoor recreation destination and industrial town. Although Squamish has its roots firmly planted in the forest industry, the growth of Whistler to the immediate north combined with its outdoor recreation potential is slowly transforming the place. Besides rock climbing, Squamish is known for its windsurfing, bald eagle viewing, and for Garibaldi Provincial Park, which rises on the eastern skyline. A proposed ski resort on the flanks of Mount Garibaldi will only add to Squamish's reputation as an outdoor adventure center.

Past Squamish, the rest of the highway is much easier, except for a canyon section halfway to Whistler which is tight and curvy. Seven kilometers (4.2 miles) north of Squamish is Brackendale, set beside the Squamish River and the gateway to one of the largest winter concentrations of bald eagles in the world. Between the months of November and February, between 2,000 and 3,000 eagles gather here, attracted by salmon in the Squamish River, which unlike more northerly rivers, never completely freezes over. Brackendale competes with the Chilkat Eagle Preserve in Haines, Alaska, for the title of the bald eagle capital of the world. It's a breathtaking sight to see a cottonwood tree with 20 eagles perched haphazardly on it with the multitude of glaciers and serrated peaks of the Tantalus Range as a backdrop. Ask locally in winter about the best places to see the eagles.

The major set of lights on Highway 99 at 48.5 kilometers (29 miles) is a local service center as well as the turnoff to southern Garibaldi Provincial Park. The popular trail to Elfin Lakes, accessed from here, leads to numerous volcanic features and towards the Garibaldi Neve, the sprawling sheet of ice below Mount Garibaldi itself. By driving up the 16-kilometer (9.6-mile) access road, a high viewpoint is reached which takes in Howe Sound, The Chief, Squamish, and the Tantalus Range.

At 53.5 kilometers (32 miles) is the turnoff to Alice Lake Provincial Park on the right, a popular camping park, and the Squamish River Road to the left. The Squamish River Road leads through a rugged canyon deep in

*A view of the Tantalus Range from the road to the Elfin Lakes Trail in southern Garibaldi Provincial Park.*

the mountains and would be a popular backroad drive if it wasn't filled with heavily loaded logging trucks. The views of glaciers along this route are unparalleled anywhere near Vancouver. The road eventually leads into the Elaho River area where environmental activists are fighting to preserve groves of rare old-growth forest in the truest wilderness in the southwestern corner of the province. Some of the Douglas fir trees there are over 1,500 years old and are among the oldest trees in Canada.

At 61 kilometers (36.6 miles), be sure to turn right at the viewpoint marker and take the short side road to gain a panoramic view of the Tantalus Range, Squamish, The Chief, and Howe Sound. The Tantalus Range, buried in snow by one winter storm after another, is one of the most dramatic set of peaks visible from a BC highway. Even in midsummer, this mountain massif remains dazzling white and is arrayed in a row of serrated peaks on a north-south orientation. Mount Tantalus, the highest summit, has a remarkable 3,000-foot icefall on its northeast face that plunges daggerlike into a small lake. These mountains, despite their proximity to Vancouver, are difficult to reach as the Squamish River must be crossed by boat and then over 5,000 feet of mountain must be overcome before gaining the base of the glaciers.

At 66 kilometers (40 miles) is the start of a canyon where the highway weaves in and out of a series of granite cliffs. Needless to say there are no pullouts in this section and caution is required as the rocks are mere feet away. Beyond here, Highway 99 begins to run alongside the Cheakamus River canyon, popular with whitewater kayakers and rock climbers. At 71 kilometers (42.6 miles) is a pullout on the left with a good view back to the Tantalus Range as well as into the brooding, granite-walled canyon far below.

The Black Tusk, one of the most impressive areas in Garibaldi Provincial Park, is accessed at the turnoff to the Garibaldi Lake trailhead at 77 kilometers (46 miles). This alpine wonderland is one of the most beautiful in the province and also one of the busiest. The Garibaldi Lake Trail climbs through cool forest before reaching turquoise Garibaldi Lake and its glacial backdrop. A side trail from here climbs steeply to above treeline to where hikers attempt to climb the volcanic spire of 7,600-foot Black Tusk, the core of an ancient and well-eroded volcano. The Black Tusk can easily be seen from the highway just to the north where it runs alongside Daisy Lake—it appears as a finger of black rock stabbing the sky over 5,000 feet above.

The Barrier, a volcanic dam, holds back the waters of Garibaldi Provincial Lake and is the reason for the "Barrier Civil Defense Area"—a no-stopping area along the highway surrounding the Black Tusk. The fear is that the Barrier might give way due to an earthquake (or natural causes) and unleash the waters of the massive lake into the valley below with predictably catastrophic results.

Popular Brandywine Falls Provincial Park, 85 kilometers (51 miles) from the start of the drive, is an almost mandatory stop. Park here and follow

*A hiker below The Black Tusk looking out to Garibaldi Lake, with Mount Garibaldi, a volcano, on the far horizon.*

the gentle, 10-minute-long trail to the viewing platform above the falls and witness the dramatic sight of Brandywine Creek free-falling 200 feet into a deep black gorge cut by centuries of erosion.

Since Brackendale, the Sea to Sky Highway has been traveling between Garibaldi Park on the right and the mountainous spine of the Squamish/Cheakamus divide to the left. This icy divide is home to numerous jagged peaks and volcanic features but is much less known than Garibaldi Park. At 89.5 kilometers (54 miles) is the turnoff to the popular Mad River cross-country ski area and high-elevation Callaghan Lake, found at the end of the valley (summer access only).

Just before Whistler is the signed turnoff for Cheakamus Lake. This large turquoise lake nestled beneath glaciated summits is easily reached by a mellow trail in about an hour's hike. For an easy but scenic hike in the Whistler area, this one is hard to beat.

Soon after the turnoff, the ski runs on Whistler Mountain come into view as the Sea to Sky Highway nears the southern outskirts of Whistler Village. This, the premier resort community in BC, has its humble roots back in the 1960s when Whistler Mountain opened for skiing in this once almost unknown area. Until the 1970s the present-day village was the site of a garbage dump more popular with hungry bears than people. Now home to 7,500 people and two world-class ski areas, Whistler is a hit internationally and draws visitors from all over the world in both summer and winter.

For the past few years, the twin ski areas here have been rated number one in North America by several ski magazines. The main attractions of the mountains are the biggest vertical drop of any ski area in North America, over 5,000 feet, and plentiful snow. The pedestrian-only village is full of interesting architecture influenced by European ski resorts and is a very worthwhile stop for drivers. Development and architecture are strictly controlled here to stop runaway growth and conflicting design. As an international resort, Whistler has prices to match so if you're on a tight budget, you won't want to stay long.

For a look at Whistler's multimillion-dollar chalets, turn off at the sign for Blueberry Hill at 101 kilometers (60.6 miles). Some of these massive homes are worth nearly ten million dollars and show off some beautiful west coast architecture.

The southern part of Whistler, called Creekside, is reached about 5 kilometers (3 miles) before Whistler Village proper and is the home of the World Cup ski races held in Whistler every winter. The turnoff to the main part of the village is hard to miss at 102 kilometers (61 miles). Turn here and follow the signs to the main parking area. More than any other place in BC, Whistler caters to the wealthy jet-set crowd. The village center has numerous places to eat, shop, and book adventure trips into the surrounding areas. The accommodations are plentiful but expensive except in the off-season. A recommended trip is to take either the Whistler or Blackcomb chairlifts to the high alpine (summer only) and walk on the groomed trails to viewpoints overlooking the sea of mountains in all directions. A unique attraction here is the summer skiing on the glaciers of Blackcomb Mountain.

North of Whistler, the highway quickly passes back into the wilds and leaves the hustle and bustle of the village behind. Through this stretch, turquoise Green Lake straddles the highway for several kilometers, backed by the aptly named Wedge Mountain, the highest peak in Garibaldi Provincial Park. This cluster of mountains, some rising to nearly 10,000 feet, are clad in glaciers easily seen from the highway.

Nine kilometers (5.4 miles) north of Whistler is the signed turnoff to the left for the Cougar Mountain Ancient Forest, a grove of large cedars reached after a drive up a gravel road and a short hike. As much of the valley was logged before the resort was even a dream, this grove is among the few bits of old-growth forest that are easy to reach from the resort.

Just beyond this turnoff is the Whistler airport where air tours can be arranged for sightseeing flights to the many glaciers that surround this area. Many of the flights include landing on a glacier, surely a unique experience for many. At 114 kilometers (68.4 miles) is the turnoff for the strenuous Wedgemount Lake Trail which leads to a turquoise high mountain lake with a glacier flowing into it from the north face of Wedge Mountain. Although the destination is breathtaking, the trail is steep and challenging and best suited to those with the experience and equipment for serious mountain hiking.

During the last portion of the drive, the mountain walls close in and loom higher above the highway. Much of the land here is more pristine than any area to the south. Nairn Falls Provincial Park, reached at 131.4 kilometers (79 miles), is a popular campground and the access point for the short hike to Nairn Falls itself. Jet boats can sometimes be seen traveling up the Green River from Pemberton to have a close-up look at the falls.

The end of the Sea to Sky Highway is reached at the T-junction in Pemberton at 134.5 kilometers (81 miles) under the soaring north face of 8,500-foot Mount Currie, the valley icon. Turn left here to enter Pemberton within a kilometer (0.6 mile) or fill up with gas at the junction and turn right to travel east on the mountainous Duffey Lake Road (Drive 8).

# 8

# Duffey Lake Road
## *Pemberton to Lillooet*

**General description:** The Duffey Lake Road is a 100-kilometer (60-mile) drive from the mountain-lined Pemberton Valley, through a high traverse of the Coast Mountains to Lillooet on the edge of BC's arid Southern Interior. The road is difficult in places with steep grades, tight corners, and numerous one-lane bridges, but rewards drivers with some of the best roadside scenery in southwestern BC.

**Special attractions:** Challenging driving, close-up views of glaciers and mountain peaks, the opportunity to see a cross-section of the Coast Mountains from the wet western side to the dry eastern side, and wildlife sightings.

**Location:** Southwestern BC between Pemberton and Lillooet.

**Drive route numbers:** The Duffey Lake Road (Highway 99) the entire distance.

**Travel season:** Spring, summer, and fall are best. In winter, the road is open but four wheel drive and chains are recommended.

**Camping:** Numerous places, the best being the Forest Service campsites near Duffey Lake at the mid-point of the drive. Near the end of the drive at Lillooet there is a large BC Hydro campsite near Seton Lake.

**Services:** None between Mount Currie and Lillooet. Be sure to pick up anything you need in either Pemberton or Whistler.

**Nearby attractions:** Mountain wilderness in all directions, opportunities for exploration and adventure, challenging backroading up the side valleys, boating on Lillooet, Duffey, and Seton Lakes, access to the Stein Valley wilderness, and excellent hiking trails in the alpine.

 The drive

The paving of the Duffey Lake Road in the late 1980s opened up the most scenic mountain drive in southwestern BC, a place dominated by ice-clad peaks, cool forests, and high mountain lakes. Nowhere else in this corner of the province is it so easy to access the alpine world of the Coast Mountains. Although the scenery along the road itself is breathtaking enough, it's the side trips on roads and trails that make this area unique.

About a three-hour drive from downtown Vancouver, the core area of the road at over 4,000 feet has become one of the province's main hiking and mountaineering centers. For those not having the time or ability to

# Drive 8: Duffey Lake Road
## *Pemberton to Lillooet*

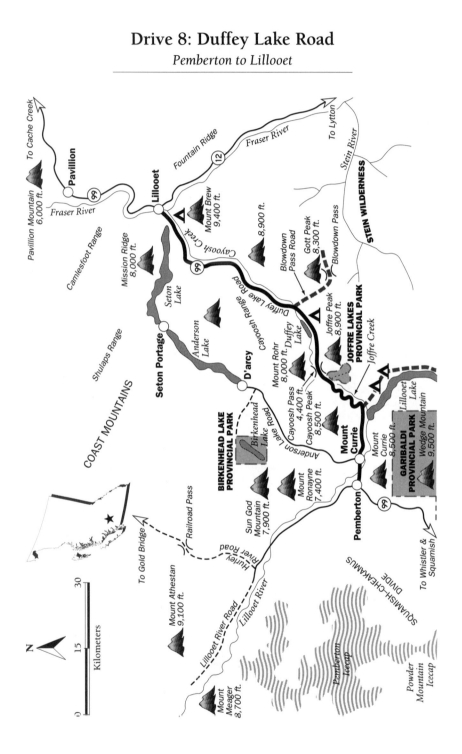

explore off the main road, the spectacle of the glaciers of the Joffre Group, the turquoise beauty of Duffey Lake, and the dramatic descent into Lillooet are reason enough for driving here. Not only did the paving of the road open up a new recreational area, it also created the missing link in what's now called the Coast Mountain Circle, a 600-kilometer (360-mile) loop trip starting in Vancouver that links the Sea to Sky Highway (Drive 7), Duffey Lake Road, and the Fraser Canyon (Drive 16) with Highway 1 from Hope to Vancouver to create a memorable two-day tour through a cross-section of quintessential BC scenery.

This drive begins where the Sea to Sky Highway ends at the T-junction just east of downtown Pemberton. Turn right here following the signs for Lillooet and set your trip odometer to zero. Be sure to fill up here and get any last minute supplies as there are no services on the way to Lillooet, almost 100 kilometers (60 miles) away.

The Duffey Lake Road travels through rugged mountain country, making it a slow and tortuous drive with the most challenging parts being the steep climb near the beginning and the steep descent at the end. Before being paved, the road was rough and the domain of serious backroaders who reveled in the scenery without the crowds. The road is open all year long but in winter it can be a hazardous drive due to the steep grades at the ends and the potential for avalanches in the high altitude middle section. If the route were more traveled, snow sheds to protect the road from avalanches would have to be built similar to those on the Coquihalla Highway or at Rogers Pass on Highway 1.

The flat Pemberton Valley was formed over time by the rich alluvial sediment from the silty Lillooet River changing its course within the confines of the surrounding mountains. Although the Pemberton Valley is becoming an outdoor recreation hotspot and a bedroom community to Whistler (20 minutes to the south), its main claim to fame is its Swiss-like scenery and potato farming. Few peaks in southwestern BC are as awe-inspiring as Mount Currie, which soars right out of the flat valley bottom to its 8,500-foot summit in great walls of rock and ice. Like Mount Cheam in Chilliwack, Mount Currie is *the* landmark of the valley and the focal point for residents.

With the quiet and pastoral scenery along the road in this first gentle stretch it's easy to forget the valley is surrounded by massive peaks. One only has to glance up to realize the true nature of the area. The Lil'wat native community of Mount Currie is quickly reached and has several new businesses catering to the increasing traffic on this route. The road curves around a sharp corner in the village, and at 6.9 kilometers (4.1 miles) an important junction is reached. Turn right to continue on the Duffey Lake Road (Highway 99).

By continuing straight ahead, the residential portion of Mount Currie is passed through on the way to Anderson Lake, D'arcy, and Birkenhead Lake Provincial Park. These destinations are all rewarding and scenic and can be seen on a 74-kilometer (44.4-mile) round trip that will take at least two hours, if not longer, for those awed by the mountain and lake scenery along the way.

Once past the junction, the road is flat but winds around as it makes its way through the Mount Currie Indian reservation. For several years, the natives did not allow the road to be paved through here and this stretch was miserably rough, slow, and dusty. In the early 1990s, the Mount Currie band blockaded the road for a full summer one year to help to press for their land rights. The reservation lies below the northern reaches of Garibaldi Provincial Park and its peaks and glaciers can be seen high above, close at hand, but very hard to reach.

For much of the drive so far the road has been following the placid Lillooet River which gently meanders toward Lillooet Lake. At 16 kilometers (9.6 miles) is a long one-lane bailey bridge over the mouth of the lake. Be sure to stop and yield to oncoming traffic. Once across the bridge, the milky blue lake stretches as far as the eye can see to the south and is surrounded by snowy peaks that line it on both sides in an unbroken mountain chain. The waters of the lake drain south via the Lillooet River into Harrison Lake and finally into the Fraser near Chilliwack.

At 17 kilometers (10.3 miles)—the start of the climb to Cayoosh Pass— is the turnoff to the Lillooet Lake Road which runs down the east side of the lake and accesses a key hiking area (Lizzie Lake in the Stein) as well as numerous Forest Service campsites and lodges. The road is gravel and is heavily traveled by logging trucks so caution is required if taking this side trip.

Just past the turnoff, the Duffey Lake Road begins its 3,000-foot climb toward Cayoosh Pass. The corners are steep and tight and on the ascent you'll almost certainly smell the brakes of those heading downhill. On each corner, runaway-truck lanes attest to the steepness of the road as does the roar of your hardworking engine. Prior to being paved, this section was a white-knuckle affair, especially on the descent into the Pemberton Valley. Although the road still climbs steadily uphill, a small amount of relief comes at 20 kilometers (12 miles) with the end of the tight switchbacks. Along this section, exciting mountain views are gained periodically through the trees. A large gravel viewpoint on the left at the top of the climb has panoramic views back into the Pemberton Valley as well as of the heavily glaciated peaks in northern Garibaldi Park.

Resuming the climb, the road flattens out as it approaches Joffre Lakes Provincial Park, reached at 30 kilometers (18 miles). Be sure to stop here and take the easy 10-minute walk to Lower Joffre Lake to see the ice-clad summits of 9,100-foot Mount Matier, 8,900-foot Joffre Peak, and 8,700-foot

Slalok Mountain. These mountains tower over this turquoise gem. This popular trail continues to the highest of the three Joffre Lakes, situated directly below the Matier Glacier. The glacier occasionally launches car-sized chunks of ice crashing into the lake. The Joffre Lakes hike has gained a great deal of popularity as a good day trip from Whistler and crowds are to be expected along its short but rugged path. The summits of the Joffre Group have become one of the most popular set of peaks for wilderness mountaineering and alpine rock climbing in all of southwestern BC due to their rugged bulk, extensive glaciation, and relative ease of access.

Beyond the park, the road continues to climb for a short distance before cresting out at Cayoosh Pass at 4,400 feet and beginning its long descent to Lillooet. Throughout this section, wildlife is frequently spotted, with deer being most common but bears sometimes seen as well. The Stein Valley, just south, is thought by biologists to be the most southerly extent of significant grizzly bear habitat in BC.

Some clear-cutting has occurred along the Duffey Lake Road through here, dating back from when the present route was a mere logging track through the wilderness. With today's stricter forestry rules, "visual quality objectives" would have most likely nixed any plans to log alongside the road in full view of all drivers.

At Cayoosh Pass and the next few kilometers beyond, several large avalanche slopes cross the highway, easily identified by their light green and

*The northeast face of 8,900-foot Joffre Peak*
*as seen from the Duffey Lake Road just east of Cayoosh Pass.*

bushy appearance. These slopes are crushed by massive avalanches every winter that kill any new tree growth. So well defined are these slopes that the transition from ancient and protected forest to avalanche path happens over only several feet. In winter be sure not to stop under these paths.

Anywhere along the flat stretch after the pass, be sure to pull off the road and look back toward the Joffre Group. The savage north face of Joffre Peak is plastered with steep icefields that cling in extreme angles to its jagged spine. Joffre's southern neighbor, Mount Matier, is a graceful pyramid of ice and is the highest peak in this corner of the Coast Mountains. Contrast this view with the one to the east and it becomes evident that the road is traveling through a transition in the mountains from wet to dry. The glaciers clinging to the flanks of the Joffre Group are the last significant glaciers in this section of the Coast Range. The peaks to the east, although still high, fall within the rainshadow of the icy peaks to the west, leaving little precipitation to spare. By the time the maximum rainshadow in Lillooet is reached the peaks have a barren, desert-like appearance.

A cabin in Cerise Creek, situated beneath Joffre Peak, is a popular hangout for mountaineers and backcountry ski tourers. The trail to the cabin is reached via the Cerise Creek logging road which branches off the main road 12.5 kilometers (7.5 miles) past Joffre Lakes Park (just before reaching Duffey Lake itself). The logging road doubles back and traverses above the highway for 6 kilometers (3.6 miles) to the marked trailhead. The 4-kilometer (2.4-mile) trail to the cabin usually takes most hikers about 2 hours to complete and rewards the effort with close-up views of the Anniversary Glacier.

The western edge of Duffey Lake is reached at 44 kilometers (26 miles) with the best viewpoint for the lake coming 2 kilometers (1.2 miles) farther. The lake is named for explorer James Duffey who discovered it in 1860 while scouting out a route between the Pemberton area and Cayoosh (now called Lillooet). On sunny days, Duffey Lake glows a gorgeous turquoise color and contrasts sharply with the white glaciers and dark green forests of the area. Several primitive Forest Service campsites (marked by brown poles) are strewn along this part of the road with the most scenic one being situated beside the lake at 50 kilometers (30 miles). Several more are passed on the left in the next stretch of road just east of the lake.

Beyond Duffey Lake, the road begins to descend into an ever-narrowing mountain valley following raging Cayoosh Creek on its sharp descent toward Lillooet. At 53.5 kilometers (32.1 miles), a tight turn to the right (marked by a "NO THROUGH ROAD" sign) is the start of the slowly deteriorating Blowdown Pass Road, the gateway to a spectacular alpine region on the northern edge of the Stein Valley. Most rugged vehicles can drive to the 11-kilometer (6.6-mile) mark in the valley where the road noticeably roughens. Although most hikers park here and walk up the last 4 kilometers (2.4 miles)

*Backroading up the last few feet of the Blowdown Pass Road*
*to 7,300-foot Blowdown Pass on the Stein Divide, Coast Mountains.*

of road to 7,300-foot Blowdown Pass, those with four-wheel-drive vehicles and off-road experience can drive the old mining road the rest of the way. Although the mountain views from the road itself are incredible, the moderate hour-long hike up 8,300-foot Gott Peak from the pass reveals a breathtaking 360-degree mountain panorama not seen from below. Consult the book *103 Hikes in Southwestern BC* for details of this memorable side trip and "high" point of the drive.

Not far east of Duffey Lake is the proposed ski area in Melvin Creek that would capitalize on the dry powder snow and often sunny weather of the area. The environmental impacts of the ski area are being studied by the government, with particular concern about the large herd of mountain goats that roam the peaks there. If built, the ski resort would compete with Whistler, about an hour drive away, and boost Lillooet's resource-based economy.

The next section feels claustrophobic as the road drops into a confined gorge and the mountains close in and loom higher and higher above. Several one-lane bridges and Forest Service campsites are encountered in the next few kilometers. The grades ahead are some of the steepest on any BC highway, so slow down and use caution this next section as the road loses 3,000 feet in its decent to Lillooet. As the road drops and curves around towering mountainsides, Cayoosh Creek is entrenched in a deep canyon, hundreds of feet below the road.

In several places in this stretch, the valley is so narrow that high cliffs across from the road are seemingly within arm's reach. Around 84 kilometers (50.4 miles), the road traverses the mountain wall on the north side of the creek and several pullouts along here are good viewpoints for Phair Peak and Mount Brew, both well over 9,000 feet high. At 90 kilometers (54 miles) several tight corners are dominated by Cayoosh Wall, the local name for a 4,500-foot-high cliff of loose grey and orange rock that towers above Lillooet. These peaks are the very easternmost summits in the Coast Mountains and are located where the range quickly dissolves into the Interior Plateau.

Relief comes a few kilometers later at the bottom of the steep grades where a well deserved break can be taken at the Seton Lake viewpoint. Seton Lake was dammed in 1956 to help generate hydroelectric power in conjunction with the dams in the Bridge River valley encountered along Carpenter Lake (Drive 19). This beautiful green lake was named after Alexander Seton, a friend of the pioneer who blazed the route from Fort Langley in the Fraser Valley to present day Lillooet.

Just east of Seton Lake, the road crosses a bridge and enters the hot and dry landscapes of Lillooet at 100 kilometers (60 miles). The sagebrush and sun-baked hills here are a fitting contrast to the blue glaciers, moist forests, and cold lakes encountered along the drive and highlight the diversity that BC packs into such short distances. Lillooet is the hub of several

*Looking west up Seton Lake at sunset from the Duffey Lake Road near Lillooet.*

scenic driving options described in this book. To complete the Coast Mountain Circle, head south along the Fraser River on Highway 12 (Drive 16) to Lytton and then on to Vancouver on Highway 1. Two exciting drives that explore BC's arid rainshadow landscapes also start in Lillooet—Chilcotin Backroads (Drive 20) and Carpenter Lake Road (Drive 19).

# 9

# Chilliwack River Valley
## *Cultus Lake Turnoff to Chilliwack Lake*

**General description:** The Chilliwack River valley is a 50-kilometer (30-mile) drive through some of the finest mountain scenery anywhere near Vancouver. The drive starts near the eastern end of the Fraser Valley and ends at Chilliwack Lake, situated right on the Canadian/US border deep in the North Cascades. The opportunity for all kinds of outdoor adventure as well as the chance to drive backroads up side valleys below towering peaks makes the area a perfect escape from the cities of the Lower Mainland.

**Special attractions:** Close to Vancouver, beautiful scenery, some of the finest peaks in southwestern BC, and Chilliwack Lake itself.

**Location:** At the eastern end of the Fraser Valley, southeast of Chilliwack. The road parallels the Canadian/US border the whole way.

**Drive route numbers:** The Chilliwack River Road is not a designated highway and starts off Highway 1 at Chilliwack.

**Travel season:** Any time of year. Summer is the busy season but the valley is popular year round, especially with fishermen. In winter, the main road is regularly plowed but may be temporarily blocked during snow storms.

**Camping:** There are many places to camp. In addition to informal camping off the logging roads, Chilliwack Lake Provincial Park at the end of the drive is the main campsite. Along the way, the road also passes several Forest Service campsites with lesser facilities than in the park.

**Services:** Be sure to pick up everything you need in Chilliwack or Sardis as there are no services beyond the 8-kilometer (4.8-mile) mark in the valley.

**Nearby attractions:** Cultus Lake, a popular boating and camping park; numerous bold peaks that challenge hikers and climbers; fishing on the Chilliwack River; canoeing or boating on Chilliwack Lake; four-wheel driving up the side roads; mountain biking—the list goes on and on. Almost any outdoor recreational pursuit is available here.

 The drive

The Chilliwack River, flowing from the deepest wilderness in the continental US into the Fraser Valley just east of Vancouver, is the setting for this spectacular drive beneath the high peaks of the North Cascades. This valley is a recreational hotspot and is a favorite of fishermen, hikers, kayakers, rafters, backroaders, and mountaineers. Despite being close to the two million people of the greater Vancouver area, the valley is large enough to never seem overly crowded. Cultus Lake, at the beginning of the drive, is far busier then the Chilliwack Valley itself. With so many rewarding side trips off the main road, it's easy to escape the crowds by venturing off the beaten track. In all, this dramatic area is a perfect showcase for the beauty of southwestern BC.

To access the start of the drive, travel eastbound on the Trans Canada Highway (Highway 1) east from Vancouver or west from Hope. Take the main Chilliwack turnoff (Exit 104) which is signposted with a Chilliwack Lake Provincial Park sign. Once off the highway, travel south through Sardis for approximately 7 kilometers (4.2 miles), passing numerous places along the way to stock up on supplies. When you reach the Vedder Canal Bridge across the Chilliwack River, set your trip odometer, turn left, and proceed east up the valley. By continuing straight and across the bridge, Cultus Lake is quickly reached. Situated just north of the border, Cultus is one of BC's most visited parks and is popular with both family campers and thrill-seeking water skiers.

At first, the road travels right alongside the Chilliwack River through low, forested mountains. Along here, the river is heavily braided and fishermen are often spotted trying their luck in the early morning hours. For the first few kilometers, houses dot the river banks and the setting is distinctly pastoral. As you travel east however, the high peaks of the North Cascades are soon glimpsed through the trees and give a taste of the dramatic scenery just ahead. At 9.4 kilometers (5.6 miles), pass the turnoff to the Slesse Memorial, a cairn honoring the 56 people who died when their airplane crashed into the east face of Mount Slesse in 1956.

Long before the first white people explored the Chilliwack Valley in search of gold, it was used by the Salish Indians for hundreds, perhaps thousands, of years as both a source of food and a transportation route through this rugged and unforgiving area. Today the Sto:lo people are direct descendants of the first inhabitants of the river. Chilliwack means "valley of many streams" in their native language.

Continuing east on the main road, a bailey bridge across the Chilliwack River is reached at 10.5 kilometers (6.3 miles). The Tamihi Rapids below the bridge are popular with both fishermen and kayakers who gather here almost every weekend. Several commercial rafting companies who use the Chilliwack River consider these rapids to be the best on the entire river. In the winter months, the Canadian National Whitewater Kayaking team practices in the slalom course to the left of the bridge. A local kayaker who trained in these rapids for years was crowned world champion in 1999.

Beyond the rapids, civilization is left behind and the sense of deep wilderness grows as you enter the mountains. Along this stretch, the river is

# Drive 9: Chilliwack River Valley
## *Cultus Lake Turnoff to Chilliwack Lake*

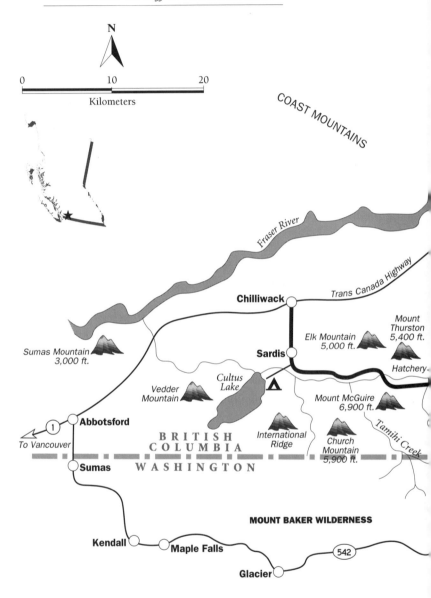

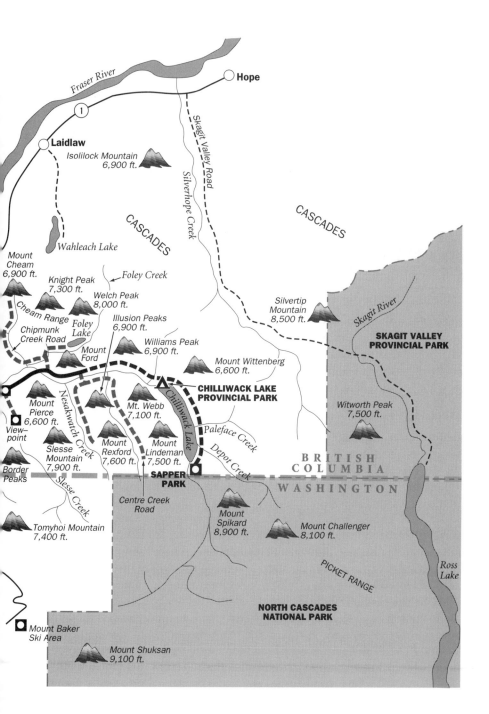

Fraser River

Hope

1

Laidlaw

Isolilock Mountain
6,900 ft.

Skagit Valley Road

Silverhope Creek

CASCADES

CASCADES

Wahleach Lake

Mount
Cheam
6,900 ft.

Foley Creek

Knight Peak
7,300 ft.

Welch Peak
8,000 ft.

Silvertip
Mountain
8,500 ft.

Skagit River

SKAGIT VALLEY
PROVINCIAL PARK

Cheam Range

Foley
Lake

Illusion Peaks
6,900 ft.

Chipmunk
Creek Road

Mount
Ford

Williams Peak
6,900 ft.

Nesakwatch Creek

Mount
Pierce
6,600 ft.

Mt. Webb
7,100 ft.

Mount Wittenberg
6,600 ft.

CHILLIWACK LAKE
PROVINCIAL PARK

Witworth Peak
7,500 ft.

Chilliwack Lake

Paleface Creek

View–
point

Slesse
Mountain
7,900 ft.

Mount
Rexford
7,600 ft.

Mount
Lindeman
7,500 ft.

Depot Creek

BRITISH
COLUMBIA

Border
Peaks

Slesse Creek

SAPPER
PARK

WASHINGTON

Centre Creek
Road

Tomyhoi Mountain
7,400 ft.

Mount
Spikard
8,900 ft.

Mount Challenger
8,100 ft.

PICKET RANGE

Ross
Lake

Mount Baker
Ski Area

NORTH CASCADES
NATIONAL PARK

Mount Shuksan
9,100 ft.

*White-water kayakers in the Tamihi Rapids, a challenging section of the Chilliwack River.*

to the left and there are frequent pullouts, usually packed with fishermen's vehicles. High on the northern skyline are the meadowlands of Mount Thurston, a popular launch point for paragliders who soar over the valley in the summer months. At 16.7 kilometers (10 miles), a Forest Service campsite on the left features ample space for pitching a tent.

There are several marked and maintained hiking trails in the Chilliwack Valley. Most are strenuous but do lead to high vistas of the "sea of peaks" that envelop the Chilliwack. The best source for detailed information on the hikes here is the book *103 Hikes in Southwestern BC*. Of the trails, the Pierce, Radium, and Greendrop Lake Trails are the most popular. Although the trailheads are minimally signed, it's best to have a hiking guide to precisely locate the trails.

At 19.8 kilometers (11.9 miles), the bridge across Slesse Creek is reached at the beginning of the spectacular second half of the drive. To the left of the bridge is the Chilliwack River Hatchery where salmon are raised to be released into the river in an attempt to keep the fishery thriving. Tours are available—call for details (see Appendix for number). Immediately after the bridge, the road climbs steeply for a short distance to gain elevation.

At the top of this short hill, the Slesse Creek logging road is reached. Turn right here for a short, optional side trip to an excellent viewpoint. By following this flat and gentle gravel road for about 1 kilometer (0.6 mile), a fork is reached. Turn right and drive for less than 100 feet to a high lookout up the Slesse Valley and towards the Border Peaks rising dramatically along the Canadian/US border. American Border Peak, at 8,000 feet the highest of the two summits, rises in a great wedge skyward while Canadian Border Peak, just inside Canada, is a little lower but no less rugged. Just below the summits are a series of hanging glaciers that thrive in the deep shade of the mountains' north faces. With vertical relief of nearly 6,000 feet, these twin peaks are an unforgettable sight, especially in winter when coated in snow and standing out proudly against a deep blue sky.

Once back on the main road and heading east, the high summits of the Cheam Range tower on the northeastern horizon. Welch Peak, the jagged pyramid, is the highest point in this compact range of peaks that rise right out of their footings at sea level along the Fraser River to a long row of summits between 7,000 and 8,000 feet high. These mountains are easy to access and have become a popular winter mountaineering area. At 25.7 kilometers (15.4 miles) is a short side road to the left which is a good place to park and see these peaks since the range soon disappears from view behind a forested ridge.

At 26.6 kilometers (16 miles), cross the Chilliwack River on another wooden bridge. A Forest Service campsite is located on the river here and is accessed by turning hard left just past the bridge. A few meters further the turnoff to the Foley Creek logging road appears on the left. This road system is the main access for hikers and climbers venturing into the peaks of the Cheam Range. For those driving four-wheel-drive vehicles, the Chipmunk Creek Road (stay left at all junctions—the start of the road is signed) climbs right to treeline below 6,900-foot Cheam Peak. From the end of the rough road, a short trail reaches the summit in less than two hours of hiking and rewards the effort with an incredible view of the North Cascades as well as the Fraser Valley stretching away to Vancouver.

As with all logging roads in the valley, a large Forest Service sign indicates the name of the road system as well as its status. If the signs indicate active logging, avoid the road, especially during working hours. Logging traffic is a mixed blessing. Although you risk a frightening encounter with a fully loaded logging truck if traveling up an actively used road, the road will be in peak condition. Once logging stops, so does road maintenance, meaning that within a couple of years access is lost due to washouts, landslides, or bush growing in. In BC, logging roads are built only to extract timber. Unfortunately, recreational usage of logging roads means very little to the Forest Service, meaning that popular hiking areas are often rendered inaccessible when the access road is deactivated or is otherwise destroyed.

Continuing east on the Chilliwack Valley Road, the views now are mainly to the south into the heart of the fierce peaks arrayed along the border. While the Chilliwack Valley runs east to west, the side valleys between the peaks run north to south, many of which end in Washington state. At highway speeds, the views up the gorge-like valleys are fleeting at best so slow down if you want to look into them.

At 29.5 kilometers (17.7 miles) there is a large clearing alongside the road to the right with a glimpse of the spire of 7,900-foot Slesse Mountain towering above the surrounding peaks. The first sight of this incredible fang of rock is breathtaking—both a climbers dream and nightmare. From this vantage point you can see only the upper third of its legendary Northeast Buttress, one of the great climbing challenges in North America.

Just beyond this point at 30 kilometers (18 miles) is a major side road to the right. By turning here and onto the Chilliwack South Forest Road, owners of four-wheel-drive vehicles, SUVs, and rugged cars can take side trips up the two most spectacular side valleys along this trip— Centre and Nesakwatch Creeks. For this memorable side trip, continue straight ahead about 400 meters (0.25 mile) and cross the Chilliwack River over a sturdy wooden bridge. Just beyond is a major T-junction. From this point you have a choice to drive up Nesakwatch Creek to the right (easier) or Centre Creek to the left (harder).

Of the two, the Nesakwatch Creek Road is better maintained and more easily traveled in regular vehicles. Keep in mind that the condition of these roads varies year to year, even month to month, so don't be surprised if the roads are in great shape and be even less surprised if they are totally washed out. To follow Nesakwatch Creek, stay right and follow the wide and gentle logging road as it bends around and travels due south toward the border. Four kilometers (2.4 miles) up the road, the first real views are reached of the high, glaciated summit of Crossover Peak and the immense avalanche slope below it. In summer, this slope is laced with numerous waterfalls while in the fall, it puts on a showy display of color.

At about the 5-kilometer (3-mile) mark, the road roughens, so park at the Y-junction here (just before the old gate) and walk up the main road for anywhere from 1 to 3 kilometers (0.6 to 1.8 miles) to see the spectacle of the 3,500-foot east face of Slesse Mountain (which means "fang" in the local native language) and the hanging glaciers clinging to its base. There is no more spectacular mountain wall in all of southwestern BC.

For those with outdoor experience and a willingness to follow a some- times faint path up an old logging road, a trail to the base of Slesse leaves the main road at the 5-kilometer (3-mile) Y-junction. Park alongside the road here and walk up the side road to the right for about 100 meters to a decay- ing wooden shack. From here, the Slesse Memorial Trail (usually signed) crosses Nesakwatch Creek on an old bridge and climbs to a memorial plaque for the Slesse crash victims in about one and a half hours of easy hiking. From here, the view of the east face of Slesse and its chaotic hanging gla- ciers is outstanding.

The Center Creek Road is far more challenging and definitely four- wheel-drive terrain. Another obstacle is that the beginning of the road is gated. They key to the gate is available from the Chilliwack River Hatchery

*The northeast face of Slesse Mountain as seen from the Nesakwatch Creek Road.*
*The Northeast Buttress is the prominent rock ridge falling to the right of the summit.*
*Glaciers cling to the base of the 3,500-foot wall of rock.*

(open 8 A.M. to 4 P.M.), discussed above. Once past the gate, the road gently follows the banks of the Chilliwack River past a salmon enhancement facility before sharply curving into the valley of Centre Creek. From the gate the total distance one-way into the valley is 10 kilometers (6 miles). The road is rough in spots but easily manageable in an SUV or four-wheel-drive vehicle. Never steep or exposed, the only real obstacles are the deep waterbars dug across the road and the occasional low-hanging tree.

Once past the 7-kilometer mark (4.2 miles), the peaks of the Illusion and Rexford group come into view. The Yosemite-like granite rock faces here, 2,000 to 3,000 feet high, are among the biggest in the Pacific Northwest. Once deep within the valley, the soaring peaks, buttresses, and glaciers will leave you awestruck as the height and ruggedness of these mountain walls is outstanding and matched in few other places. Several hanging glaciers cling to the base of these rock walls, seemingly within arms reach and looking like they are ready to avalanche away at any moment.

Beyond 10 kilometers (6 miles) the road gets rougher but can be walked right to the US border where the road ends in a rugged cirque of green meadows, rock walls, and snowy peaks. Along the road, several places allow for comfortable camping, especially near the end where a large clearing makes for a good campsite. By hiking up the logging roads on the east side (left) of the valley, the views of the towering mountain walls improve even more.

After seeing these valleys, carefully retrace your route back out to the main road and then continue eastwards towards Chilliwack Lake through lush forests. In the next stretch, the perfectly symmetrical pyramid of 6,900-foot Williams Peak looms above the highway to the north. Through here, the road turns to good gravel, bends to the south, and climbs steadily towards Chilliwack Lake which is reached at 41 kilometers (24.6 miles). Where the maintained road ends, the access road to the campground and boat launch in Chilliwack Lake Provincial Park branches off to the right. This well-maintained and popular campground has 100 sites set in deep forest. From the beach at the end of the road, witness the sharp peaks of North Cascades National Park reflected in the still waters of the lake.

To continue deeper into the mountains and toward the border, stay straight (instead of turning into the park) and drive down the well-maintained and gentle logging road (usually fine for any vehicle) along the eastern shore of Chilliwack Lake. The views get better and better and soon grow to include the massive summits that dominate the southern end of the lake. Mount Lindeman, marked by a 3,500-foot granitic north face, is one of the most spectacular sights in the entire Chilliwack Valley and is easily seen from the road.

At the end of the drive, a gate bars access to Sapper Park on the very southern tip of the lake. The park is named after the surveyors (sappers) who camped here while surveying the Canadian/US border in 1850. Not

*The northeast face of Mount Lindeman in the spring
as seen from the southern end of Chilliwack Lake.*

only is it filled with some of the largest old-growth trees in the lower mainland, it also has several fine sandy beaches. By walking the last 2 kilometers (1.2 miles) of the road, the park can be reached in about a half-hour. From here a trail leads through an ecological reserve to the international border which is only about 2 kilometers (1.2 miles) south of Chilliwack Lake.

The mountains of North Cascades National Park located to the south and east are thought of by many to be the most spectacular and untouched wilderness left in the Continental US. The famed Picket Range lies just south, while the fierce Mount Redoubt group rises on the eastern skyline. As they lie deep in protected areas, these peaks are often reached via Chilliwack Lake and an illegal border crossing.

Once you have seen Chilliwack Lake, the only way to exit the valley is to head back out the same way you came.

# Okanagan/Similkameen
## 10

## The Okanagan
### *Kelowna to Osoyoos*

**General description:** This easy and relaxing 122-kilometer (73-mile) drive travels southbound through "sun and fun" country in BC's arid Southern Interior and features some of the best desert-like scenery in the province. Far from being in the wilderness, this drive passes through the largest communities in the Okanagan and has plenty of opportunities to enjoy the California-like ambiance and numerous recreational activities in the area.

**Special attractions:** As the whole region is geared to tourism, there are numerous opportunities for fun and excitement including water-skiing, power boating, sunbathing, swimming, and snow skiing near Kelowna or Penticton. Other attractions include the scenery alongside Okanagan Lake, the Bighorn Sheep herd at Vaseux Lake, and the fruit orchards and wineries found along the whole route.

**Location:** The Southern Interior of BC from Kelowna south to the US border at Osoyoos.

**Drive route numbers:** Highway 97 the entire way.

**Travel season:** All year long. The area is heavily geared to the summer tourist season so if you go in the off-season, expect to find a lot of the tourist-oriented businesses closed.

**Camping:** Numerous places to camp along the way, both commercial and public. Okanagan Lake Provincial Park, south of Peachland, is the best spot as it has over 150 sites right along the lake.

**Services:** Services are easily found the entire drive as it runs though numerous cities and towns along the way.

**Nearby attractions:** Myra Canyon and the old Kettle Valley Railway, Okanagan Mountain Provincial Park, Big White ski area east of Kelowna, Apex Alpine ski resort west of Penticton, the Okanagan region in Washington state just south of Osoyoos.

 ## The drive

Traveling through the driest area in BC, this route features stark, dry desert-like scenery, picturesque resort towns and beautiful views of Okanagan Lake, the focal point for much of the Southern Interior of BC. The Okanagan is

# Drive 10: The Okanagan
## Kelowna to Osoyoos

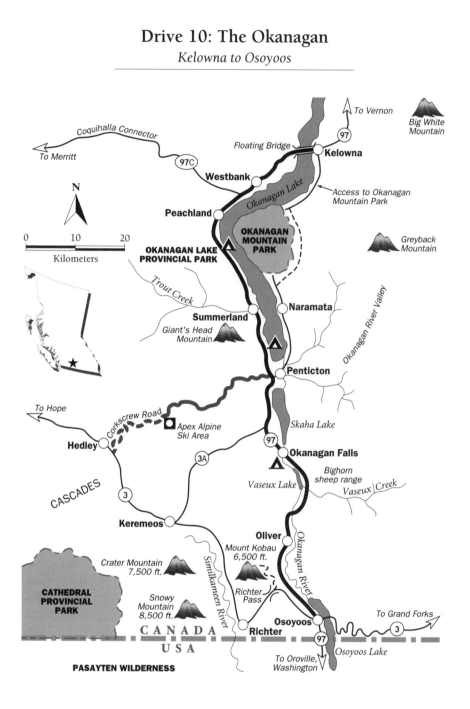

well known as both a retirement and recreational hotspot. For Vancouverites seeking an escape from endless clouds and rain, the Okanagan is an oasis of sunshine, warm water, and fun. This route passes though the major population centers in the Okanagan so don't come here expecting wilderness or solitude. In summer, this area is very hot, with temperatures often topping 35 degrees C (95 degrees F). Although this drive can be done anytime, the optimal times are in early or late summer. Not only will the temperatures be more moderate, the crowds will be thinner. The whole Okanagan is a very busy place in mid-summer, especially on the weekends, when sun-worshippers flock here from all over southern BC.

The drive begins on the western outskirts of Kelowna on Highway 97 at the start of the long floating bridge across Okanagan Lake. Set your trip odometer here. The bridge is situated at a traditional crossing point used by both natives and early settlers at the point where the lake is at its narrowest. Kelowna, with a population of nearly 100,000, is one of the most populous cities in BC and is growing rapidly with a large influx of retirees and urban-ites fleeing the big city life and cold winters in the rest of Canada. Kelowna is dealing with the transition to a major city and the headaches that go along with it. The city, situated near the midpoint of 128-kilometer- (76.8-mile-) long Okanagan Lake, was founded in 1892 as a embarkation point for steam-boat travel up and down Okanagan Lake. The name Kelowna originates in the Okanagan Indian name for "grizzly bear."

Kelowna has traditionally been known as a summer getaway destina-tion but is quickly maturing into a well-rounded city, rated by one Canadian magazine as one of the ten best paces to live in Canada. With the opening of the Okanagan Connector Highway in 1990, Kelowna is now only a four hour drive from Vancouver, a fact that has certainly helped to increased its growth. In summer, lake-based activities are the focal point, with water-skiing, jet skiing, and houseboating all being very popular. In winter, the emphasis shifts to skiing on nearby Big White ski resort and snowmobiling in the forested mountains that ring the city. For golfers, Kelowna is paradise with at least a dozen courses around the city.

Just before the bridge is the signed turnoff to Okanagan Mountain Provincial Park on the left. Situated across from Highway 97 on the east side of Okanagan Lake, this park is one of the only large protected areas in BC's driest area. Of all the different natural environments in BC, the landscapes of the Southern Interior are the least well-represented in the park system, largely due to large private land holdings and decades of development. The park can also be accessed from the south via Penticton and Naramata.

The first 60 kilometers (36 miles) of the drive travel along the west side of Okanagan Lake and feature excellent views of the deep blue lake. The first community encountered past Kelowna is Westbank at 12 kilometers (7 miles). Also fast growing, this community has a seen a lot of new development in recent years, with much of it focused on retirement living. Westbank has become a virtual suburb of Kelowna but is also highly geared to tourism with numerous waterfront parks and resorts. Along here, the orchards that line nearly this entire drive are encountered for the first time. From the town center, located high above the lake on a plateau, turn left and proceed to the waterfront area where most of the tourist facilities are located.

Just beyond Westbank at 16.4 kilometers (10 miles), Highway 97C, the Okanagan Connector, branches off to the right. When it opened, this side route off the Coquihalla Highway cut travel time by over an hour on the Vancouver to Kelowna drive. Highway 97C connects with Highway 5A and then to the Coquihalla Highway at Merritt after passing over a high plateau ringed with dry meadows and expansive views.

Past the turnoff, the highway traverses hundreds of feet above Okanagan Lake, cut out of the steep, dry mountainsides that cradle the lake on its west side. Peachland is reached on the waterfront at 22 kilometers (13 miles) where Okanagan Lake bends to the south. Peachland is an exceptionally parklike town with several waterfront parks on the lake to enjoy the beaches and soak up some summer sunshine. Peachland looks right across the lake to the dry wilderness of Okanagan Mountain Provincial Park. From here, boats can be launched to travel across the lake to the water-accessible-only campsites on the park's western shoreline. Closer to the highway, two parks, Hardy Falls and Antlers Beach (both in Peachland), are excellent places to see the dry ecology of the area.

Okanagan Lake is the supposed home of the legendary Ogopogo, an elusive serpent that some believe to be a remnant from prehistoric days. While most dismiss the occasional sightings as pure fantasy, others have dedicated a good part of their lives to looking for the creature. Whatever the case, the publicity has certainly helped put the Okanagan on the map.

The stretch of Highway 97 between Peachland and Penticton is the most beautiful part of the drive as the highway weaves alongside shimmering Okanagan Lake for the entire distance. At the big bend in Okanagan Lake there are panoramic views both down the lake towards Penticton and back up the lake to Kelowna. The drive along Okanagan Lake in this section is reminiscent of desertlike Sea to Sky highway (Drive 7) with its combination of water and mountain scenery. Through here, several pullouts on the left allow for stopping to take in the scenery. On the steep hillsides to the right, fences run continuously for many kilometers in an effort to keep wildlife from straying onto the highway.

As the route travels south, the surrounding countryside grows drier in appearance with scattered forests giving way to sagebrush and dry, open meadows. Erosional formations also become more apparent as the earth's surface is revealed by the lack of vegetation. For many, this dry scenery is a novelty in rain-soaked BC and a prime reason for the Okanagan's popularity.

*Sunrise on Okanagan Lake as seen from Highway 97 near Peachland.*

At 34.5 kilometers (20.7 miles) the large and busy Okanagan Lake Provincial Park campground is reached on the left. This campground, located right beside the warm waters of the lake, is the largest on the drive with 168 sites and has complete facilities including showers.

If you look across the lake, it is apparent that the hillsides are drier and more barren near the bottom and wetter and more forested near the top. This is due to the fact that increased elevation brings cooler temperatures and more precipitation. The hottest and driest areas in BC are all near sea level and in the bottom of river valleys or alongside lakes in the rainshadow of higher mountains.

Summerland, at 46 kilometers (27.6 miles), is a large, bustling community carved out of a plateau high above Okanagan Lake. The town is located at a point where the mountains that rim Okanagan Lake are pushed back, replaced by a wide, furtive valley. The name of the town says it all and is very descriptive of the whole area. Summerland has its roots in the agricultural and fruit growing industries although it is now increasingly focused upon recreation and tourism. Much of the architecture in the Okanagan has a Spanish look to it, appropriate given the climate. Fruit stands and vineyards are passed seemingly every few hundred feet through here. Places to see here include the easily-reached vantage point from 2,700-foot Giant's Head Mountain on the southern outskirts of town and the Summerland Research Station, where new methods of growing the over 100 types of fruits and vegetables harvested in the area are tested.

Past Summerland, the highway returns to the lake and runs along its shores through an interesting area of arid, sandcastle-like formations above the highway to the right. The distinctive red barked ponderosa pine is found throughout this area as well. This tree only grows in the hottest and driest regions of BC and needs fire to reproduce. Wildfires, most caused by lightning strikes, are a common occurrence in the Okanagan but most are put out quickly due to the proximity of towns and people. Many scientists feel that the quick fire suppression is having a negative impact on the ecosystems of the region.

Sun-Oka Park at 51.5 kilometers (31 miles) is a popular swimming beach with a boat launch and picnic tables. Okanagan Lake here is filled with power boats and is more suitable to high speed fun rather than the quiet contemplation. Paddling can be dangerous here with all the adrenaline junkies whizzing by at mach speed. If you want to paddle in the area, wait until Vaseux or Osoyoos Lakes further south, or head to any number of the quiet lakes found in the hills both west and east of the main Okanagan Valley.

At 60.5 kilometers (36 miles), turn left and follow the signs into downtown Penticton and to the waterfront before continuing the drive south. The city, on a narrow strip of land between Okanagan and Skaha Lakes, has always been the main recreational center in the Okanagan. Green, well groomed, and gardenlike, Penticton is an extremely desirable place to live and visit. Even though it is the second largest city in the Okanagan it still retains a small town feel. The place to be is along the waterfront with a huge stretch of sand and plenty of sun worshipers lying about. Penticton means "place to stay forever" in the language of the nomadic Salish Indians who inhabited the area.

Along with Kelowna, Penticton is rated as one of the most desirable communities in Canada to live. The town itself has plenty of recreation opportunities from golfing to swimming to jet skiing. In all, Penticton is about as close as you can get to California while still being in BC. The city is also a major fruit growing and processing center. During the spring, the blooms on the thousands of fruit trees light up the whole place. One of the most popular things to do in town is to float lazily down the 7-kilometer (4.2-mile) man-made channel that connects Okanagan Lake with Skaha Lake. Dinghies and tire-tubes can be rented on the beach for the trip. Skaha Bluffs, a popular rock climbing center, is located in the hills above town and boasts over 400 routes. Climbers flock here in the spring and fall when the granite cliffs in Squamish, BC's most famous climbing center, are cold, wet, and "out of condition."

Once done in Penticton, carefully follow the signs for Highway 97 to Osoyoos as it makes several turns on the southern outskirts of town. A few minutes past Penticton is the signed turnoff to the Apex Alpine ski area, situated high in the mountains to the southwest. The ski area and resort are 32 kilometers (19 miles) up the access road and are becoming popular as a summer destination as well, featuring both hiking and mountain biking. By turning here, those driving four-wheel-drive vehicles and trucks can take an adventurous backroad past the ski area, into the subalpine, and down the infamous Corkscrew Road to Highway 3 near Hedley (see Drive 11). The earliest this side trip could be accomplished is in July as late lying snow blocks the road before then. Having the *BC Recreational Atlas* (new edition to be retitled *The BC Road and Recreational Atlas*) is essential for locating the various backroads there.

About 8 kilometers (4.8 miles) south of Penticton is the Okanagan Game Farm, home to more than 100 species of animals, including zebras, lions, and camels. With the dry scenery, the 650-acre farm provides habitat not unlike what many of the African creatures are used to.

Just south of Penticton is deep blue Skaha Lake, popular with water skiers and other thrill seekers. The highway runs along the western shores of the lake before climbing inland about halfway down its length. At 75 kilometers (45 miles), Highway 3A, a shortcut to Highway 3 (Drive 11) and Vancouver, heads off to the right and passes through the eastern Cascade Mountains on its way to Keremeos. Stay straight here. About 1 kilometer (0.6 mile) beyond is the turnoff to the Dominion Radio Astrophysical Observatory, located high in the mountains to the west. This astronomical facility is located here to take advantage of the best weather and the clearest night skies anywhere in BC. It is open for tours on Sunday afternoons in summer and self-guided tours year-round. Call for details (see Appendix).

A few minutes further the small and beautifully-situated town of Okanagan Falls (known locally as OK Falls) is seen below, nestled at the south end of Skaha Lake and hemmed in by rock walls and arid mountainsides. Skaha Lake runs for 20 kilometers (12 miles) from here to Penticton and was once connected to Okanagan Lake until sediment cut it off from the larger lake. Okanagan Falls Provincial Park is located on the western outskirts of town and has 20 campsites.

After passing through downtown Okanagan Falls, the highway weaves its way through an increasingly dry and rugged area on the way to Osoyoos in the last half of the drive. In this earth-colored landscape, the only real dashes of color are the bright greens of the irrigated slopes that are the source of the Okanagan's plentiful fruit and vegetable crops. At 85.5 kilometers (51 miles), the highway enters the Vaseux Lake Conservation Area with its large population of California bighorn sheep. The herd located here is the second biggest in the province, smaller in number only to the one living near Farwell Canyon. The craggy, barren cliffs that descend down to the highway are prime habitat for these acrobatic creatures. Numerous signs in the area warn motorists to slow down and help protect the sheep from the perils of traffic as they have little fear of vehicles and are often seen alongside the highway.

In addition to sheep, Vaseux Lake is also known as one of the best bird-watching areas in the province, with some species being found nowhere else in BC. This area is among the best places to admire dry scenery in BC with a few spots giving a good impression of true desert, particularly along the sun-baked cliffs above the highway to the east. Unlike in Washington state to the south, the arid regions of BC give way quickly to the interior wet belt so the extent of dry country in the province is rather limited in comparison.

The aridity of the Southern Interior is due to the rainshadow effect. As wet Pacific storms roll across the province, the uplifting by the mountain ranges to the west causes the clouds to rise and spill their precipitation, mostly on the west side of the Coast and Cascade Ranges. By the time the weather systems arrive in the Southern Interior, they are mostly devoid of measurable precipitation. This area is in the Bunchgrass Biogeoclimatic Zone and is the hottest and driest area in Canada, receiving less than 30 centimeters (12 inches) of precipitation a year. To put this in perspective, the outer west coast of Vancouver Island has about 20 times the annual precipitation as this area. In the summer, the daytime heating of the land often causes dramatic thunder and lightning storms, the source of many of the wildfires that break out in the hot, dry summer months.

Where the highway crosses the Okanagan River just south of Vaseux Lake is the turnoff on the left to small Inkaneep Provincial Park as well as the start of backroads that cross the Inkaneep Indian Reservation. These roads can

*An old wagon at an abandoned farm near Vaseux Lake, southern Okanagan Valley.*

be used to reach Highway 97 just north of Osoyoos and provide for a quieter route through a picturesque landscape dotted with old pioneer-era buildings. On Highway 97 south of Vaseux Lake, a prominent cliff known as McIntyre Bluff towers above the highway and resembles the prow of a ship.

By now the highway is well away from the holiday crowds and more into a working agricultural area. Oliver, met at 101 kilometers (60.6 miles), is a the local hub of the fruit and vegetable industry and literally dozens of fruit stands along the highway through here tempt the driver with mouth-watering fruit and produce. This entire area is heavily cultivated and the best fruit growing area in the entire country. Although much older and more traditional looking than the fast growing cities to the north, Oliver is still a worthwhile stop. The town is strung out along the highway but is quickly left behind as the highway heads south towards Osoyoos and the Canadian/US border.

As the highway traverses south of Oliver, the views up and down the Okanagan Valley are excellent and take in a panorama of parched, near-desert landscapes. Osoyoos, 122 kilometers (73 miles) from the start of the drive, is an attractive town set on the shores of Osoyoos Lake with the US border being minutes away to the south. The town is well-known for its sunshine, searing temperatures, deserts, and Spanish-style architecture. The immediate area is often Canada's hotspot on any given summer day, with temperatures sometimes exceeding 40 degrees C (104 degrees F) during the peak of summer. Osoyoos Lake, which runs well into Washington state, boasts the warmest lake waters in Canada and is well suited to sunbathing and boating.

The famous Pocket Desert, the only one of its kind in Canada, is reached by following Highway 3 east from Osoyoos and then turning left on Forty-fifthth Street and heading to the Inkaneep campground. You may have to ask permission here to cross the Indian reserve to the desert. Although small in size, this parched area receives less than 8 inches of precipitation a year, the magic cutoff line for a true desert. This is the northernmost extension of the Great Basin Desert that encompasses almost all of Nevada and much of eastern Oregon and Washington. In this area the cactus, rattlesnakes, sagebrush, and sand all make it very unlike anywhere else in BC, or Canada for that matter. The Pocket Desert area also has the highest concentration of birds of prey in Canada. In all, it's a very unique place.

The drive ends where Highway 97 intersects Highway 3 on the western outskirts of Osoyoos. If heading back to Vancouver on Highway 3 (Drive 11), turn right and start the long climb into the Cascades. Before heading this way, try and make the time to drive Highway 3 eastward (to the left) for about 20 kilometers (12 miles) to where it climbs a series of prominent switchbacks up Mount Anarchist and yields excellent views of Osoyoos, the Okanagan River valley, and the eastern edge of the Cascade Mountains in the far distance. During the climb, Highway 3 ascends from 900 feet in the arid valley bottom to 4,000 feet in a noticeably wetter and cooler environment.

# *11*

# Crowsnest Highway
## *Hope to Osoyoos*

**General description:** The Crowsnest Highway is a 250-kilometer (150-mile) drive through the Cascade Mountains from the coast to the interior along one of BC's principal west-east routes. The drive passes through a whole range of scenery from low to high and from wet to dry in this cross-section of BC along the Canadian/US border. The Crowsnest quickly travels from the bustling Fraser Valley into the "real" BC—a land of endless forests, jagged summits, and raging white-water rivers. History is a big part of the drive which retraces traditional routes that used to link several gold rush communities.

**Special attractions:** The Cascade Mountains, Manning Provincial Park, the Blackwall Peak Road into the alpine, the ghost towns in the Tulameen River near Princeton, the mining ruins near Hedley, the Pocket Desert, and Osoyoos Lake.

**Location:** The Southern Interior of BC between Hope and Osoyoos.

**Drive route numbers:** Highway 3, the Crowsnest Highway the entire way.

**Travel season:** Any time of year. Where the highway passes through Manning Provincial Park, the road might be snow-covered during winter storms but on the whole the highway is well maintained.

**Camping:** Numerous campsites along the way, most in the various parks. The best camping is in Manning Park near the beginning of the drive or at one of the provincial parks along the Similkameen River later on.

**Services:** Full services in Hope, Princeton, Keremeos, and Osoyoos. The biggest gap with no services is through Manning Park.

**Nearby attractions:** The Skagit River Recreation Area south of Hope, the Sumallo River valley and its fierce summits, the Skagit River Trail from Sumallo Grove, the Corkscrew Road near Hedley, and the mountain wilderness of Cathedral Provincial Park south of Keremeos.

# The drive

The Crowsnest Highway (Highway 3) begins on the eastern edge of the Fraser Valley and quickly enters the mountain, forest, and river scenery that is the hallmark of BC. During the course of this drive the land changes slowly but surely from the rainforests and mist-shrouded peaks of the coast to the parched and sun-baked desert country around Osoyoos. Being mere hours from Vancouver, this is a popular recreational drive for urbanities seeking a weekend escape in the Manning Park area as well as points farther east. Along the way there is a wealth of scenic side trips for those interested in mountain scenery, history, and quiet backroads.

The drive starts on the edge of Hope where Highway 1 becomes Highway 3 just after passing the main turnoff for Hope. Set your trip odometer here. There are no services (except a gas station just before Sunshine Village) until past Manning Park so stop and fill up in Hope. Be sure to follow the signs for Highway 3 and for Osoyoos through here as three routes branch off in Hope—the Trans Canada (Highway 1) north through the Fraser Canyon (Drive 16), the Coquihalla Highway ( Highway 5), and this drive, Highway 3.

This route, known as the Crowsnest Highway, is the initial stretch of a torturous and winding route that runs along the southern border of BC, crosses the Rockies, and ends in Alberta. Despite being slow to drive, Highway 3 is the fastest way to reach the southernmost towns in BC from the Vancouver area. Most of the drive follows the Dewdney Trail, a route pioneered by Edgar Dewdney to access gold finds in the Southern Interior well over 100 years ago. As most of the mountain ranges in BC run north-south, this west-east route has to cross and contour mountain range after mountain range on its way east, thus accounting for the wearisome nature of this drive.

Six kilometers (3.6 miles) past Hope on Highway 3 is the turnoff for the Coquihalla Highway, the fastest route to the growing cities of the Okanagan. Past this major turnoff, Highway 3 starts its long and steady rise up the Nicolum River valley toward its headwaters near the Hope Slide. The mountain uplift at the eastern end of the Fraser Valley tends to collect incoming clouds from passing storms, accounting for the often cloudy and wet conditions found here. From this point on, the weather generally gets better the further you travel east toward BC's arid interior.

The 7-percent grades on this stretch are steep enough that truck runaway lanes exist for those descending the highway toward Hope. Nicolum Creek Provincial Park, just past the Coquihalla turnoff, is a popular spot for Hope residents. With only a few campsites, be here early if you wish stay for the evening. If these are full, the next campsites are in Manning Park, about an hour ahead.

The infamous Hope Slide is reached at 17.5 kilometers (10.5 miles) where a short road climbs up to a good viewpoint. In the winter of 1965, a minor earthquake triggered a tremendous landslide from 6,600-foot Johnson Peak and unleashed more than 100 million tons of rock that buried the valley below to a depth of 1,000 feet. Highways crews struggled for weeks afterwards to clear the debris and build a temporary route through the slide path. Four people died in the slide, two of whom were never found. The

# Drive 11: Crowsnest Highway
## Hope to Osoyoos

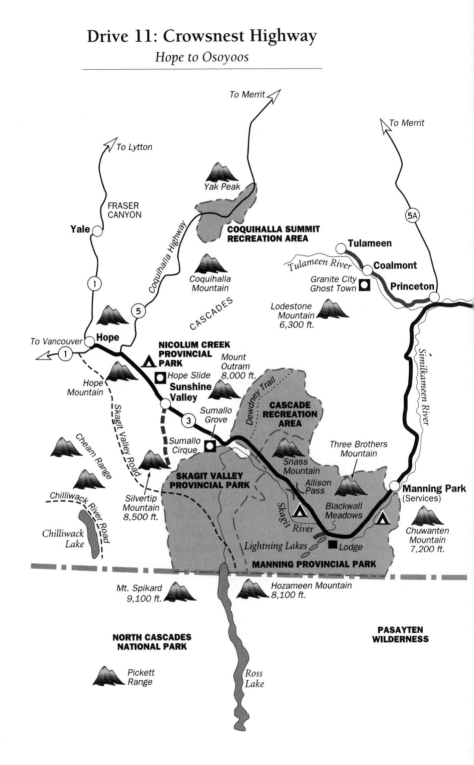

To Merrit

To Merrit

To Lytton

FRASER CANYON

Yak Peak

**Yale**

Coquihalla Highway

5A

**COQUIHALLA SUMMIT RECREATION AREA**

Tulameen River

**Tulameen**

**Coalmont**

Coquihalla Mountain

Granite City Ghost Town

**Princeton**

CASCADES

Lodestone Mountain 6,300 ft.

To Vancouver

**Hope**

**NICOLUM CREEK PROVINCIAL PARK**

Similkameen River

Hope Slide

Mount Outram 8,000 ft.

Hope Mountain

**Sunshine Valley**

Skagit Valley Road

Sumallo Grove

Dewdney Trail

**CASCADE RECREATION AREA**

Three Brothers Mountain

Sumallo Cirque

Snass Mountain

Cheam Range

**SKAGIT VALLEY PROVINCIAL PARK**

Allison Pass

**Manning Park** (Services)

Chilliwack River Road

Silvertip Mountain 8,500 ft.

Blackwall Meadows

Skagit River

Chuwanten Mountain 7,200 ft.

Chilliwack Lake

Lightning Lakes

Lodge

**MANNING PROVINCIAL PARK**

Mt. Spikard 9,100 ft.

Hozameen Mountain 8,100 ft.

**PASAYTEN WILDERNESS**

**NORTH CASCADES NATIONAL PARK**

Pickett Range

Ross Lake

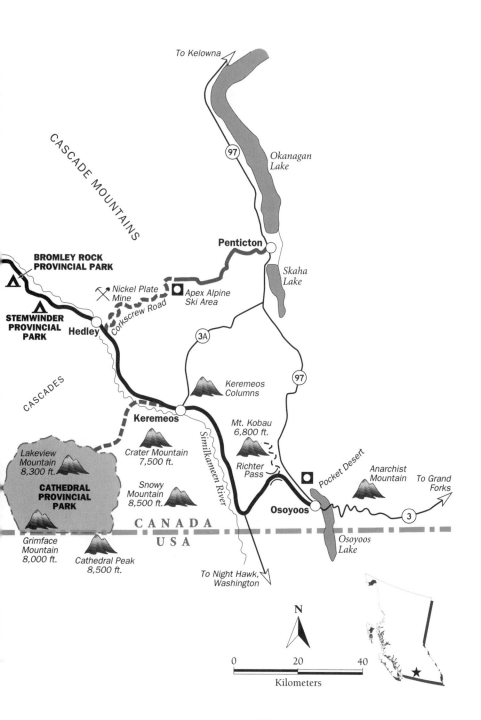

To Kelowna

CASCADE MOUNTAINS

97

Okanagan Lake

Penticton

Skaha Lake

BROMLEY ROCK
PROVINCIAL PARK

Nickel Plate
Mine

Apex Alpine
Ski Area

Corkscrew Road

STEMWINDER
PROVINCIAL
PARK

Hedley

3A

97

CASCADES

Keremeos
Columns

Keremeos

Mt. Kobau
6,800 ft.

Lakeview
Mountain
8,300 ft.

Crater Mountain
7,500 ft.

Richter
Pass

Pocket Desert

Anarchist
Mountain

To Grand
Forks

CATHEDRAL
PROVINCIAL
PARK

Snowy
Mountain
8,500 ft.

Similkameen River

Osoyoos

3

C A N A D A

Grimface
Mountain
8,000 ft.

Cathedral Peak
8,500 ft.

U S A

Osoyoos
Lake

To Night Hawk,
Washington

N

0        20        40

Kilometers

103

slide path is easily recognized by the wide scar that stretches almost all the way across the dark mountainside.

By now the highway has entered the Cascade Mountains, the northernmost part of Washington state's North Cascades that extend into BC to the Merritt area. Although gentler here than the climax of the range just south of the border, there are several peaks along this drive as spectacular as any in the range. The best mountain views from the highway are near Sumallo Grove, on the Blackwall Peak Road, both in Manning Park, and near the end as the highway contours along the dry eastern edge of the range. Several environmental organizations are pushing for Canada to preserve more of its land base in the Cascades to form a large international wilderness area that would link existing protected areas on both sides of the border.

Just beyond the slide, the highway enters a broad pass filled with wetlands just across the highway from the resort community of Sunshine Village. In summer, the Sumallo Valley, backing the resort, makes for an adventurous and scenic side trip off this drive. At the back of the Sumallo River, about an hour from the resort, the magnificent Sumallo Cirque is reached. With some of the biggest mountain faces in southwestern BC, the peaks here are an outstanding sight, more reminiscent of the Rocky Mountains than the Cascades.

The Sumallo Valley is reached by following the main road through the resort and into the obvious valley behind. The logging road here is signed as

*Driving up the Sumallo River Road toward Sumallo Cirque,*
*a side trip off the Crowsnest Highway at Sushine Village.*

the Sumallo River Forest Service road. Continue up the road and deeper into the mountains. Where the Silvertip ski area road branches off left, you can see some of the cirque straight ahead. To get closer, drive as far up the main road as possible, park, and then walk up the last section of decaying road right to the base of Silvertip, Rideout, and Payne, the big three peaks of the cirque. Even in midsummer, this steep-sided valley is cool as the sun is mostly hidden behind the 3,500-foot-high mountain faces. Plan on at least a half day for this side trip, especially if you plan to walk up the road. As with any side trip off the main highways, the *BC Recreational Atlas* (new edition to be retitled *The BC Road and Recreational Atlas*) is a big help in identifying this backroad.

The west gate of Manning Provincial Park is soon reached and is marked by a large carving of a marmot. The parking area here is the trailhead for Mount Outram, a strenuous hike leading up 8,000 feet on the dominating peak of the immediate area. From here on, the drive is much more torturous as it becomes confined by the rugged topography. In the next stretch the highway travels through a deep canyon between perpendicular mountainsides and is one of the highlights of the entire drive. Lushly green, this valley is reminiscent of BC's north coast with its waterfalls and steep walls of rock rising out of a flat valley bottom. The Sumallo River here meanders through a series of turns as it descends alongside the highway toward the Skagit River.

Sumallo Grove, a must-see grove of trees, is reached on the right at 33 kilometers (20 miles). Turn here and follow the short road through stately forest to the parking area. This grove of trees is one of the best and most easily accessible stands of old-growth forest anywhere near Vancouver. Located where the Sumallo and Skagit Rivers meet, the grove has an abundance of huge Douglas-fir, western red cedar, and western hemlock to marvel at. Although forests like this were once common, extensive logging in this corner of the province means that trees this size are seldom seen anymore. The spindly lodgepole pine forests encountered later in the drive will seem scrawny and unattractive in comparison to the spectacle of this grove.

This area is known as Rhododendron Flats as it is one of the only places in the province where wild rhododendrons grow in their natural state. A trail leaves from here and runs alongside the Skagit River all the way to Skagit Valley Recreation Area. Although the Skagit is one of Washington state's biggest rivers, through here it is small and unassuming as it descends towards Ross Lake on the Canadian/US border. Although this is a one-way hike, you can walk as far upriver as you like and then return back to your vehicle at Sumallo Grove. The trail is known for its untouched scenery, flowering rhododendrons (in June), and its nonstop encounters with majestic old-growth forests. See *103 Hikes in Southwestern BC* for a description of the trail. On the whole, the trail is easy and gains little elevation, making for a soothing break from the highway.

Beyond the grove, the highway turns a prominent corner and begins to climb steeply up to the headwaters of the Skagit River. The Cascade Recreation Area, reached on the left just before Allison Pass, was created to protect the mountain wilderness on the northeastern flank of Manning Park. It is best known for the Dewdney and Whatcom Trails, two routes used by miners to cross the Cascades in the early part of the century. These trails are now more popular with horsepackers than hikers as they are long and comparatively dull in comparison to the more striking mountain scenery nearby.

On the way to Allison Pass, the highway crosses the canyonous Skagit River at least five times and gives frequent views of the misty gorge through which the river flows. Allison Pass at 58 kilometers (34.8 miles) and 4,400 feet is the climax of the entire drive. As the treeline is quite high here, the pass doesn't seem nearly as high as the elevation would suggest. From here on through Manning, the Crowsnest passes through cool, moist forests with only the occasional glimpse of the surrounding mountains. Manning is heavily forested and far more gentle than the rugged areas to the south and west. Through the park, signs indicate the locations of the campsites (snow free from mid-May to mid-October), which are all beautifully situated right alongside the Skagit or Similkameen Rivers. The main campsites are Hampton, Mule Deer, Coldspring, and Lightning Lakes.

The main center of the park is reached at 63 kilometers (37.8 miles) where several worthwhile side trips branch off the highway. On the right is the commercial center of the park with a lodge, gift shop, and restaurant. By following the signs, the Lightning Lakes chain is reached in a few kilometers on the same road. These three lakes are linked by small, easily navigable creeks and are popular with fishermen and canoeists. Also found further along is the Gibson Pass ski area and the start of the Skyline Trail, a premier one-way ridge walk across Manning with panoramic views to the jagged peaks of the North Cascades across the border. Strawberry Flats, just east of the downhill ski area, is one of the main cross-country skiing destinations in southwestern BC.

Located across Highway 3 from the lodge is the signed turnoff to the Cascade Lookout and Blackwall Meadows. If you make only one stop in Manning, be sure to drive up this 21-kilometer (12.6-mile) road into the alpine at over 6,000 feet. Most of the road is paved and easy except for the last few kilometers where the surface turns to good gravel. This is the best place in all of BC to view extensive alpine wildflower meadows. From the top of the road, easy loop trails pass through vast meadows with panoramic views in all directions. Those who tackle the easy Three Brothers Trail are treated to the best of the flower displays on the ridge north of Blackwall Peak. This trail is a long one (20 kilometers, 12 miles round trip) but even walking a short part of it is worthwhile for the views of Manning and the showy displays of color. Generally the month of August is the best for seeing the flowers in full bloom but this depends upon the depth of the snow pack and the weather in any given year.

One kilometer (0.6 mile) east of the Lightning Lakes Road is the Manning Park Visitors Center on the left. This is the best place to book campsites, see the nature exhibits, or talk to the park rangers about the conditions of the trails. This area of Manning is the northern end of the 4,000-kilometer- (2,480-mile-) long Pacific Crest Trail that starts on the California/Mexico border and heads north all the way to Canada, passing though numerous western mountain ranges along the way.

At 83 kilometers (50 miles), the east entrance of Manning is reached alongside the Similkameen River where a gas station and several cabins are located. The next point of interest comes at 88.7 kilometers (53.2 miles) where the wide Similkameen River is pinched through a rock gorge beside the highway on the right. If you want to see it, pull off with care as the shoulders are narrow.

From here to Princeton, the highway descends almost the entire way in a series of long traverses and steep, tight corners. Most of the views along here are of the extensive forests on the vast interior plateau east of Manning. Princeton, reached at 137 kilometers (82.2 miles) at the junction of the Similkameen and Tulameen Rivers, is the supply center for the surrounding areas and the biggest community between Hope and Osoyoos. This town of 3,000 is also the turnoff for Highway 5A which travels north to meet the Coquihalla Highway at Merritt. Princeton has its roots in the historic mines just northwest of the town center. For a scenic but optional side trip, drive up the Tulameen River on a paved backroad to these old mining towns that now lie in lonely isolation. To reach the area, turn left into the town center from Highway 3, cross the Similkameen, and follow Highway 5A to a point just north of town where the signed turnoff for Tulameen is found on the left.

In less than a half-hour of driving from Princeton, the partially resorted ghost town of Coalmont is reached. Pass through town towards the mountain wall behind, cross the bridge over the Tulameen River, and then turn left at the T-junction. Only a few kilometers past the bridge is a Forest Service campsite on the river as well as the site of Granite City, a once-booming pioneer town. The remains of the town, one of the biggest in the province in the late 1800s, is marked by several old wood buildings slowly succumbing to the elements. The town of Tulameen, a little farther up the paved road, is larger than Coalmont and is noted for being one of the main stops on the old Brigade Trail from Hope to Kamloops, one of the historic paths from the coast to the interior used in the early part of the century.

Beyond Princeton, the highway runs southeast alongside the gentle and wide Similkameen River through increasingly dry country. As the highway descends, the thick forests slowly but steadily give way to sagebrush meadows and open stands of ponderosa pines. The mountain slopes also become more jagged, barren, and colorful as the highway begins to travel east along the outer edge of the Cascades. Bromley Rock Park, not far past Princeton, is named after Bromley Rock, a prominent rock bluff on the Similkameen. The highway crosses the north side of the Similkameen at 166 kilometers (100 miles) just before Stemwinder Provincial Park is reached, a kilometer (0.6 mile) farther. This small park alongside the river has 29 campsites in a picturesque setting in dry, open forest.

Hedley, population about 300, is reached at 173 kilometers (104 miles) and is a worthwhile stop. The town is closely associated with the Nickel Plate Mine, one of the best preserved ghost town structures in the province. Over 4,000 feet above the town and perched on the edge of a cliff on Lookout Mountain, the remains of the mine are marked by the jumble of buildings steeply arrayed on a cliff face. If you can't see the mine, ask at the gas station and they will point it out to you. Founded in 1904, Nickel Plate was worked until the 1950s and yielded gold, copper, and silver. A tramway was erected from the mine site to Hedley and the swath down the mountainside is still visible.

Just above Hedley, the remains of the lower tramway station and several old buildings are visible on the hill backing the town. In the heyday of the mine, the population of Hedley blossomed to 5,000 people, a far cry from its present population. The Nickel Plate Mine is being slowly restored and long term plans call for a passenger tram from the town to the mine site.

Past Hedley, the thinning forests give way to barren slopes of contorted and colorful rock on both sides of the highway. About 4 kilometers (2.4 miles) past Hedley, a white church on the right marks the Chuchuawaa Indian Reserve and the turnoff to the Corkscrew Road which can been seen switchbacking up the dry mountainside on the left.

This road is one of the most exciting backroads in the province as it quickly climbs to dizzying heights above the Similkameen River valley. From the top of the switchbacks the view down to the Similkameen and towards the distant peaks of Cathedral Park is breathtaking. The road is well-maintained but steep and best suited to four-wheel-drive vehicles. Beyond the top of the switchbacks, the road enters deep forests before coming across a working mine. This mine blocks access to the Nickel Plate Mine while its restoration is underway. Within a few years, visitors will hopefully either be able to drive up the Corkscrew Road to the restored mine or take a tram directly from Hedley itself. The Corkscrew Road continues high over a plateau and eventually reaches Apex Alpine ski area and then connects with the paved road to Penticton in the Okanagan. This adventurous route to the interior is open only in midsummer as snow blocks this high backroad for most of the year.

The remainder of the drive takes in some of the best desertlike scenery in the province, with the section between Keremeos and Osoyoos being especially beautiful. Although the banks of the Similkameen are often green

*The remains of the lower tramway for the Nickel Plate Mine above Hedley.*
*These remains sit on a steep hillside about 200 feet above the town.*

from irrigation, the rest of the landscape is barren and desolate looking with browns, grays, and dull greens being the dominant colors. Between Hedley and Keremeos, watch for the herd of mountain goats that are often seen on the dry cliffs above the highway.

At 197 kilometers (118.3 miles), the signed turnoff to Cathedral Provincial Park is seen on the right. This wilderness park, situated right on the Canadian/US border, protects a magnificent alpine area of lakes and towering granite peaks, and is filled with interesting formations like Stone City and the Giant Cleft. Although some hikers choose to travel on foot into the park, most opt to pay for a vehicle shuttle up the park road to the private Cathedral Lakes Lodge in the heart of the park at over 6,000 feet. Even for non-hikers, the lake and mountain views from the lodge are worth the fare for the drive up the access road. Reservations on the shuttle can be made by calling the lodge (see Appendix). The BC Parks office responsible for Cathedral can be reached by phone as well (see Appendix). This area melts out before almost anywhere else in southwestern BC and offers good early-season hiking in an alpine setting.

Just beyond the park turnoff, the town of Keremeos is reached. Keremeos has a wealth of old wooden buildings and has an outback feel to it, despite being less than five hours from Vancouver. The town has its roots as a Hudson Bay Company trading post, founded in 1860. Today ranching and fruit growing are the two big industries in the area. Keremeos is set in a dry gorge with steep cliffs rising on both sides of town. In summer, this area is often as hot as any place in BC so be prepared for sun and heat. To the south, the high peaks in the Cascades are snowbound for much of the summer, an interesting contrast to the sun-scorched slopes of the valley floor. Just past Keremeos is the agricultural community of Cawston, noted for its heavily cultivated orchards.

The drive between Keremeos and Osoyoos is the nicest part of the entire drive as the easy and wide highway travels in the shadow of massive peaks on the very eastern scarp of the Cascades. The vertical relief in the area is over 7,000 feet in several places, especially in the vicinity of 8,500-foot Snowy Mountain, the highest peak in the area. The colors of the landscape here are endlessly fascinating with the pastel hues of the barren land set against the dark greens of the deep forests higher up on the mountains. Although cultivated in places, the Similkameen River valley here is generally pristine looking and gives a good insight into what most of the Southern Interior must have looked like before its extensive development.

Just west of Osoyoos, the Similkameen River turns away from the highway and runs due south into Washington state. A signed turnoff here leads to Nighthawk, just across the border. Past here, the highway bends northeast and climbs towards 2,200-foot Richter Pass, the divide between the Similkameen and Okanagan River valleys.

*Sunrise near Richter Pass on the Crowsnest Highway.*

Near the pass is Spotted Lake (visible but off-limits), said to be amongst the most highly mineralized lakes on earth and used for centuries by native peoples to heal all sorts of ailments. The backroad that begins beside the lake climbs to an old fire lookout on the summit of 6,000-foot Mount Kobau (best for four-wheel-drive vehicles) and has panoramic views of the great sweep of land from the dry Okanagan Valley to the Cascades.

After Richter Pass, the highway starts a steep descent into Osoyoos. From the marked viewpoints on the left, Canada's only true desert can be seen on the parched flats east of Osoyoos Lake. The desert is reached by following Highway 3 east from Osoyoos and then turning left on Forty-fifth Street and heading to the Inkaneep campground. Ask permission here to cross the reservation lands.

Osoyoos, often Canada's hot spot in summer with temperatures up to 40 degrees C (104 degrees F), is the end of the drive at 248 kilometers (149 miles). The town, like so many others in BC, was the site of a long-gone fort from which furs where traded in the early 1800s. Osoyoos Lake, yet another of the popular lakes in the Okanagan, boasts the warmest lake waters in Canada and is the focal point of town and a popular swimming and boating spot.

From Osoyoos, the options are to travel north up the Okanagan Valley (Drive 10) and loop back to Vancouver via Highway 97C or to continue east on the Crowsnest Highway toward Grand Forks and points beyond.

# Kootenay/Boundary
## *12*

## Silvery Slocan Tour
### *Nelson to Nelson*

**General description:** The Silvery Slocan Tour is a 224-kilometer (134-mile) loop trip through the West Kootenay that travels alongside two mountain-rimmed lakes and links together some of the oldest and most picturesque towns in BC. The area also has the province's greatest concentration of ghost towns and other reminders of its past gold rushes. Although the loop is described from Nelson, it can be entered at several places depending upon the direction you are coming from.

**Special attractions:** Excellent mountain scenery; historic buildings in all the towns; the ghost towns of Sandon, Kootenay and Slocan Lakes; Ainsworth Hot Springs.

**Location:** The West Kootenay area of southeastern BC.

**Drive route numbers:** Nelson to just past South Slocan on Highway 3A, Highway 6 from there to New Denver, New Denver to Kaslo on Highway 31A, Kaslo to Balfour on Highway 31, and finally Balfour back to Nelson on Highway 3A.

**Travel season:** Spring, summer, or fall. If you want to boat on any of the lakes or visit Sandon, be sure to come in summer. The optimal time to drive this loop trip is from mid-September to mid-October when the fall color throughout the area is at its peak. In winter, the highways are often treacherous, especially between New Denver and Kaslo.

**Camping:** The only designated park campsite is at Kokanee Creek Provincial Park just east of Nelson near the end of the drive. This is a large lakeside campground with 132 sites. There is commercial camping in Nelson, New Denver, and Ainsworth Hot Springs.

**Services:** Regular tourist services in the small towns along the loop. There are no services between New Denver and Kaslo.

**Nearby attractions:** Two rugged mountain parks, Valhalla and Kokanee, both excellent hiking and climbing destinations; the side trip from New Denver north to the Nakusp Hot Springs; Cody Caves; the ferry ride across Kootenay Lake; and the scenic drive south to Creston and back.

 # The drive

This scenic drive is a clockwise loop trip from Nelson back to Nelson and is known as the "Silvery Slocan Tour," named after the area's gold rush of the late 1800s. Although the loop is described starting in Nelson, the major town on the route, the drive can be entered from several places. From Revelstoke to the north, the route is met at New Denver. From Castlegar to the west, the loop is joined near South Slocan, and from the east, the drive is joined at Balfour, just east of Nelson.

The West Kootenay is a distinctive region within BC and is home to an abundance of scenic drives, picturesque towns, and beautiful lakes and mountains. Most of the Kootenay is set under the towering flanks of the Monashee, Selkirk, and Purcell mountain ranges, all just west of the Rocky Mountains and collectively known as the Columbia Mountains. Long, fjord-like lakes such as Arrow, Kootenay, and Slocan are also a hallmark of the West Kootenay. Within BC, this area is well-known as a hotbed of environmentalism and a last refuge of the hippie culture from the 1960s.

The towns here have a distinctly different feeling from anywhere else in BC, witnessed by their significant artistic and outdoor recreation-oriented populations. Although some logging has occurred, environmental groups have worked hard to preserve the wilderness character found throughout the region. Hikers from all over BC are drawn to the area by the presence of both Valhalla and Kokanee Glacier Provincial Parks, two exceptionally scenic mountain parks laced with trails past towering rock faces, exquisite lakes, and lush wildflower meadows.

The beginning of the drive is in downtown Nelson and the corner of Vernon and Ward, across the street from the historic city hall. Facing Kootenay Lake and backed by forested mountains, Nelson is one of BC's most scenic towns. Baker Street, one block up the hill, is the main street and is well worth a walking tour. Founded in 1887, Nelson was once the third largest town in BC. Today, over 350 of its buildings have designated heritage status, many of them styled in the Victorian-era theme so popular in the early part of the century. Unlike most BC towns which exist primarily to service the surrounding resource industries, Nelson, with a population just over 9,000, has an artistic flair and caters to the traveler looking for more than just the basic services.

Known for its steep streets, wealth of historic buildings, and laid-back atmosphere, Nelson has always been a popular tourist destination. While in town, be sure to see the brick city hall, the Nelson museum, and the restored streetcar that runs along the lakeshore. Nelson is also well-known for its nearby skiing, hiking, canoeing, river kayaking, and mountain biking

# Drive 12: Silvery Slocan Tour
## *Nelson to Nelson*

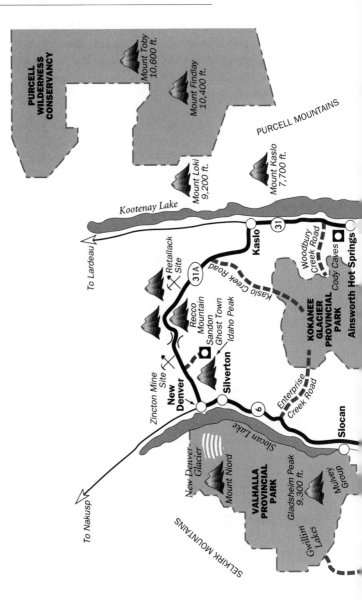

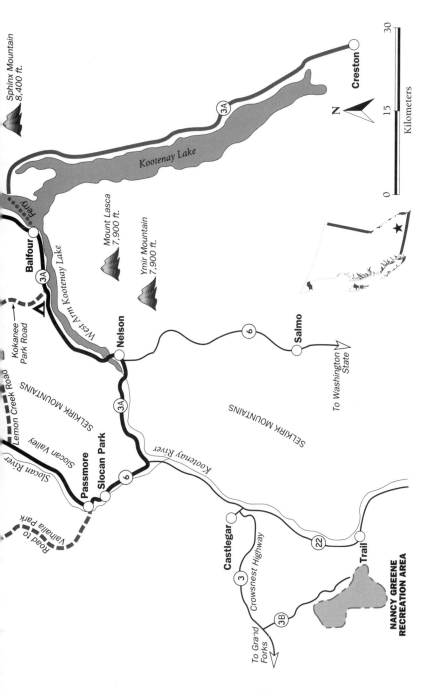

opportunities. With ample lakes, rivers, and mountains, and two stunning mountain parks situated nearby, the Nelson area has become a mecca for outdoor adventure. Red Mountain and Whitewater ski areas, both just outside Nelson, are known across North America as a home to hard-core skiers looking for steep and extreme runs.

When you leave Nelson, follow the signs west out of town on Highway 3A toward Castlegar, the nearest big population center to the west. At first, the highway passes scattered residential and commercial development on the outskirts of town. Only 3 kilometers (1.8 miles) into the drive is the Kootenay River Dam, easily seen below the highway.

At 23.4 kilometers (14 miles), take a right turn onto Highway 6 at the well-signed junction. Now into the Slocan Valley, the scenery begins to perk up as the highway travels northwards and deeper into the mountains. The lower Slocan Valley is pastoral and the driving is relaxing as the highway passes though sleepy communities set below green mountainsides. At 39 kilometers (23.4 miles) is the settlement of Passmore and the main access point to Valhalla Provincial Park. From here, the 50-kilometer (30-mile) drive to the park is rewarding scenically as it climbs into the granite world of the Valhallas. Once on the gravel access road, follow the signs to the parking area at the southeastern edge of the park. Even for those not planning on hiking, this backroad drive is worthwhile to gain a more intimate and close-up view of the southern Selkirks. Valhalla Provincial Park was created in the 1980s by the BC government after years of lobbying by the Valhalla Wilderness Society based in New Denver.

Even from the end of the road at the Gwillim Lakes trailhead, the surrounding area is a spectacular combination of meadows and sweeping granite walls reminiscent of Yosemite National Park in California. From here, hikers trek to Drinnon Pass and the stunning Gwillim Lakes in a few hours and witness some of the best mountain scenery in BC. For those who have the time, experience, and energy, this trip is highly recommended. Consult the book *100 Hikes in the Inland Northwest* or call BC Parks for details (see Appendix). Be aware that this is grizzly country and most hikers are equipped with bear bells and bear spray. Both Valhalla and Kokanee are occasionally closed due to bear encounters so try to call ahead to see if there are any warnings or closures you should know about.

The Slocan Valley is in the interior wet belt and the lush scenery feels almost coastal throughout this area. The weather is very changeable so expect anything from cold rain to searing heat within a span of several summer days. Even if the weather is poor, there is so much to see along this drive that you should still venture out despite the weather.

The scenery grows even better near 67 kilometers (40.2 miles) where the highway passes high above the small town of Slocan, seen below on the southern shore of Slocan Lake. Looking west, several granitic peaks in the Valhalla Range are readily visible and give a hint as to the rugged beauty of this mountain cluster. The Mulvey Group, partially seen from here, is renowned by mountaineers as having some of the best alpine rock climbing in North America. Many of the peaks have Nordic names like Asgard, Gimi, and Thor, or more sinister names like the Devil's Couch and Lucifer Peak.

From here all the way to New Denver, the highway is etched into the mountainsides on the east side of Slocan Lake with good views of the sinuous, fjord-like lake for much of its distance. As the west side of Slocan Lake is protected in Valhalla Park, much of the view is very pristine. Alongside the lake, the highway becomes more tortuous as it winds in and out of side valleys. Near 76 kilometers (46 miles), the highway climbs and traverses hundreds of feet above the lake and has excellent views up to the lake's north end. Much of the drive along here was once a hair-raising experience but after millions of dollars were invested in improvements in the 1980s, this section has lost its reputation as an intimidating drive. This part of the highway is reminiscent of the Sea to Sky Highway from Horseshoe Bay to Squamish (Drive 7) with its combination of water and mountain scenery.

On all four of the connecting highways that form this loop, the blue signs marking the road access points for Kokanee Glacier Provincial Park are easily spotted. As the park sits dead center inside the confines of this drive, each of the highways intersect gravel roads leading the various trailheads in the park. Kokanee Glacier is a high elevation mountain park known for its alpine lakes, shapely granite peaks, glaciers, and remnants of high elevation mines. Consult the book *100 Hikes in the Inland Northwest* for details on the access points and trails for Kokanee.

Beyond 92 kilometers (55 miles), the highway descends steeply to the level of the lake on the way to Silverton. Historic, quaint, and well-maintained, Silverton is an excellent stop. The colorful and historic buildings here date back to 1891 when a mining boom swept the whole region. Today Silverton is a well-preserved example of an early mining town set in a scenic lakeside location. Be sure to stop and see the Silverton Art Gallery and Mining Museum beside the highway in an old schoolhouse dating back to 1919.

Just past Silverton is the bigger town of New Denver, a sleepy place known for its artists, environmentalists, and laid-back ambiance. Although New Denver is also known as a historic mining town, it has the rather dubious distinction of also being the home for Japanese Canadians forcibly interned during World War II. Today the Nikkei Internment Memorial Center in New Denver focuses upon this difficult period in Canadian history. Also worth seeing here is the Silvery Slocan Museum, which displays artifacts from the early days of New Denver in the late 1800s. The town is situated on Slocan Lake and is a popular departure point for boat trips up and down the lake as well as for the New Denver Glacier Trail which climbs steeply into the mountains across the lake from the town.

In the center of New Denver at 102 kilometers (61 miles), turn right onto Highway 31A and begin to climb steeply toward Sandon. By staying straight, Highway 6 reaches Nakusp and its hot springs within the hour. This route serves as the entry point for this loop drive for those coming from the north via Revelstoke or Vernon. Be sure to gas up if you're running low as there are no more services until Kaslo.

Once on 31A, the highway climbs up a V-shaped valley with high peaks ahead in the distance. Logging trucks are often encountered on this section of road so be patient if caught behind one of these slow-moving behemoths. At 110.5 kilometers (66 miles) you see the marked turnoff to Sandon, an excellent side trip off the tour. This well-groomed gravel road reaches Sandon in 5 kilometers (3 miles).

Sandon, one of the best preserved true ghost towns in BC, is seeing a bit of a revival as local history buffs attempt to preserve many of the creaky buildings at the former mine site. Founded during the Silvery Slocan gold rush in 1894, Sandon quickly grew into a bustling mining town complete with 24 hotels, 23 saloons, and a thriving red-light district, all carved out of the wilderness in this narrow valley. Home to 5,000 in its heyday, it even had electrical power before Vancouver. There's lots to see here, so park your vehicle and walk around for a while. The museum is the main source for information and has a well-stocked gift shop.

*The side of an old mine building in the ghost town of Sandon.*

**Previous Page:** *A faint trail winds through the rainforest near Port Renfrew (Drive 1).*

**Left:** *A sea kayaker enjoys beautiful calm water at Sechelt Inlet Marine Park, Sunshine Coast (Drive 6).*

**Below:** *Sunrise on Saltspring Island, looking east from Mount Tuam (Drive 4).*

**Facing Page:** *Lighthouse Park is located near the start of the Sea to Sky Highway (Drive 7).*

**Facing Page:** Gwillim Lakes in Valhalla
Provincial Park (Drive 12).

**Above:** Spectacular Mount Robson, seen here
from Berg Lake, attracts mountaineers from all
over the world (Drive 18).

**Right:** A fishing boat glows in the evening sun
near Tofino (Drive 2).

**Following Page:** Lush north-coast canyons such
as this can be found along the Yellowhead
Highway (Drive 22).

Right on the edge of Sandon is the beginning of the Idaho Peak Road which climbs steeply for 12 kilometers (7.2 miles) to an old fire-lookout at 7,500 feet. The views and the wildflower meadows are spectacular on the top. The 360-degree view takes in much of the southern Selkirk Range, Slocan Lake, and New Denver. In most years, the road is open in early July, however in deep snow years it might be inaccessible well into August. Be sure to ask in the museum about the condition of the road before heading up. Although cars do make the trip, the road is more suitable to four-wheel-drive vehicles as it is steep and narrow.

Heading out on the same road, turn right on 31A to continue the tour. Looking back from the turnoff toward New Denver brings views of the gentle New Denver Glacier sprawling above the town it was named after. The next stretch of highway is known as the "Valley of the Ghosts" for its wealth of ghost towns and old mining structures. Many of the buildings and mine sites are barely visible on the hillsides above the highway so be sure to drive slowly and watch carefully for them.

On both sides of the highway at 115 kilometers (69 miles) is the remains of the Zincton Mine. Not much is left today but you will still see mine shafts, old timbers, and debris scattered about through here. This area is the very core of the Silvery Slocan mining boom that occurred just over 100 years ago. By 1892, there were over 750 mining claims staked out in the area and the K&S Railway was developed to haul the ore down to Kaslo on Kootenay Lake. Today, much of Highway 31A follows the route of this long-gone railway.

Just past Zincton, the highway enters a broad and gentle pass surrounded by high peaks rising to over 9,000 feet. In the pass, both Bear and Fish Lakes are surrounded by marshy areas that provide ideal beaver habitat. Fish Lake has a designated rest area with washrooms. A highlight of the trip, the remains of Retallack, is reached at 122 kilometers (73 miles). This collection of old red buildings is set against a rugged backdrop and makes for an excellent photograph. Once past the ruins, the highway begins to gradually drop into the Kaslo River valley. The descent to Kaslo is not nearly as steep as the climb up to Sandon from New Denver. From the pass, the raging torrent of the Kaslo River accompanies the highway all the way to Kootenay Lake and is almost always within sight.

Kaslo, reached at 148 kilometers (89 miles), is the most scenic town on this loop. Situated on the shores of Kootenay Lake and surrounded by both the Selkirk and Purcell Mountains, the town calls itself "the Switzerland of the Americas." Kaslo is one of the oldest towns in the province and celebrated its 100th anniversary in 1994. Still home to many of the original buildings, the town site is a popular tourist destination as well as a main access point to boating on the 100-kilometer- (60-mile-) long Kootenay Lake. So large is the lake that sailboats are seen tacking back and forth on its

*The remains of the Cody mine, found just up the valley from Sandon.*

surface on windy days. The town is also well-known as the home of the *SS Moyie,* a restored sternwheeler that used to ply the waters of Kootenay Lake, transporting goods and people up and down the lake. In Kaslo, be sure to see the magnificent old city hall, the St. Andrews Church, and the court-house, all concentrated in the historic downtown area.

Following the signs to Nelson, turn right in Kaslo and proceed south-wards along the west side to Kootenay Lake on Highway 31. From here to Balfour the lake is almost constantly in view, resembling a larger version of Slocan Lake seen earlier on the drive. Like other mountain lakes in the area, Kootenay Lake is also long and narrow and rimmed by mountains on both sides of its entire length. Looking across the lake yields views of the south-ern end of the Purcell Mountains that lie between the Selkirks and the Rock-ies. Eastern BC is a rugged place with range after range of mountains merging together to form a great mass of peaks from the Interior Plateau to the Rock-ies. Although the extent of the mountain ranges is not readily visible from the roads below, hiking in Kokanee Glacier Provincial Park or flying over the area reveals the true nature of this vertical landscape.

At 167 kilometers (100 miles) is the signed turnoff to the right for the Cody Caves Provincial Park, 13 kilometers (7.8 miles) off the highway on a gravel access road. These caves, only seen with the aid of an experienced guide, form the most accessible cave system in BC with over a kilometer (0.6 mile) of narrow passages to explore. For information on access to the caves, call BC Parks (see Appendix).

*The old city hall in downtown Kaslo dates back to 1898*
*and is the only wooden city hall left in British Columbia.*

Just past the turnoff to the caves is Ainsworth Hot Springs. Situated in an old mine site, these hot springs are reported to be the hottest in Canada at 45 degrees C (113 degrees F). Several resorts here cater to those wanting to stay and enjoy the hot springs, the scenery, and the boating on Kootenay Lake.

At 185 kilometers (111 miles) is the tiny settlement of Balfour and the Kootenay Lake ferry terminal. Taking the ferry across Kootenay Lake and then driving south to Creston and back is a great side trip off this loop. In addition to the novelty of the longest free ferry ride in the world, the winding road along the east side of the lake is every bit as scenic as the loop just traveled. Allow at least a half day for this drive and don't be surprised if you have to wait a few hours for the ferry in mid-summer.

Past Balfour, Highway 31 becomes Highway 3A for the final leg of the tour and follows closely the shores of the west arm of Kootenay Lake back to Nelson. Along this stretch, waterfront homes and cottages and boats dot the lakeshore for almost the entire distance.

At 197 kilometers (118 miles) is the main access point for Kokanee Glacier Provincial Park. This well-maintained winding gravel road climbs to near treeline on the edge of the park and allows for the easiest approach to the alpine in the Nelson area. Just a few hundred meters past the turnoff is Kokanee Creek Provincial Park on the shore of Kootenay Lake. Popular with Nelson residents, this camping and boating-oriented park is often full so be sure to arrive early if you want to camp. The drive ends at 224 kilometers (134.4 miles) where the highway crosses back into Nelson at the metal bridge across Kootenay Lake.

# Rocky Mountains
## *13*

## Kootenay Parkway
### *Bow Valley to Radium Hot Springs*

**General description:** The Kootenay Parkway is a 100-kilometer (60-mile) drive through Kootenay National Park, one of BC's two Rocky Mountain national parks. Although lesser known than Banff National Park to the east, Kootenay is every bit as beautiful. Along the way, Highway 93 passes through the western edge of the Rockies alongside two major rivers and beneath scores of towering peaks. The entire route is downhill from the heights of the Continental Divide all the way to the hot and dry Columbia River valley.

**Special attractions:** Mountain peaks; the famed Rockwall; numerous day hiking, backpacking, and climbing opportunities; wildlife viewing; Radium Hot Springs; and less congestion than the other Rocky Mountain parks.

**Location:** In BC's Rocky Mountains southeast of Golden along the BC/Alberta border.

**Drive route numbers:** The Kootenay Parkway, Highway 93 the entire way.

**Travel season:** Any time of year. The vast majority of visitors come in mid-summer. The other seasons are quieter but a lot of the facilities are closed. Winters are cold and snowy but the highway is open and is a beautiful drive on clear days.

**Camping:** There are several highly organized campgrounds in the park so be sure to book ahead if possible. There is also commercial camping in Radium Hot Springs at the end of the drive.

**Services:** Stock up at either Lake Louise or Banff. There are no services along the drive.

**Nearby attractions:** The other Rocky Mountain national parks, the Columbia River valley, the Purcell Range to the west of Radium Hot Springs, and Highway 95 north to Golden and south to Cranbrook.

 The drive

Kootenay National Park, the second smallest of the Rocky Mountain parks at 1,400 square kilometers (543 square miles), protects a long and narrow swath on the western edge of the Rockies and is bordered by Yoho National Park to the north, Banff National Park to the east, and Mount Assiniboine

# Drive 13: Kootenay Parkway
*Bow Valley to Radium Hot Springs*

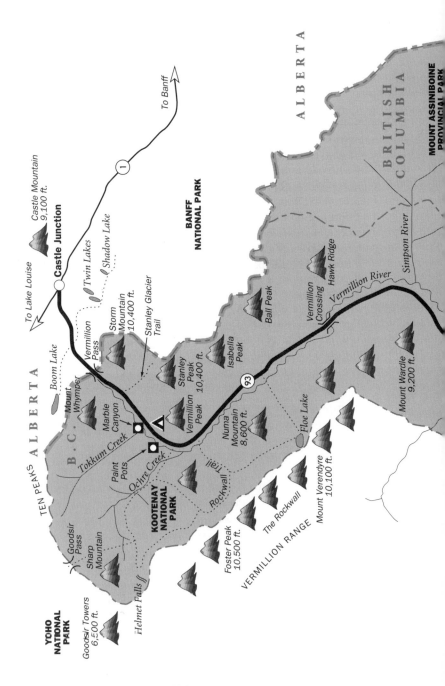

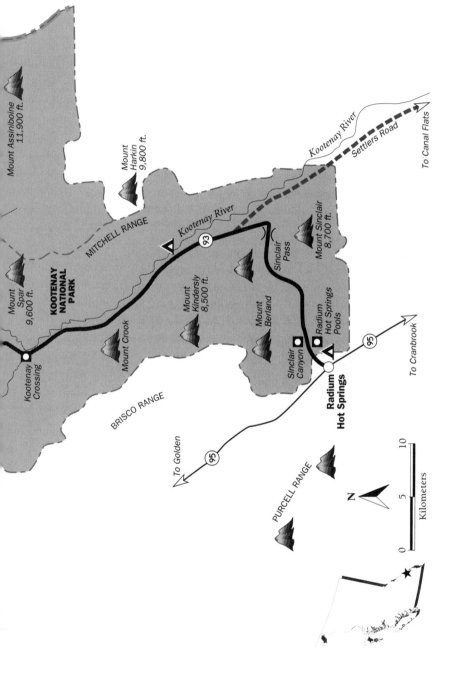

Mount Assiniboine 11,900 ft.

Mount Harkin 9,800 ft.

Kootenay River

Settlers Road

To Canal Flats

Kootenay River

MITCHELL RANGE

93

Mount Spar 9,600 ft.

KOOTENAY NATIONAL PARK

Sinclair Pass

Mount Sinclair 8,700 ft.

Mount Kindersly 8,500 ft.

Mount Berland

Mount Crook

Radium Hot Springs Pools

Kootenay Crossing

Sinclair Canyon

BRISCO RANGE

Radium Hot Springs

95

To Cranbrook

To Golden

95

PURCELL RANGE

N

0   5   10
Kilometers

125

Provincial Park to the southeast. The main feature of the park is two major river valleys, the Kootenay and Vermillion, and the mountain crests paralleling them. The park encompasses a wide variety of landscapes from the glacier-clad peaks near Vermillion Pass to the arid canyons near Radium Hot Springs.

Kootenay has been used for centuries by natives as a travel corridor through the Rockies. In 1858 a party of white explorers discovered Vermillion Pass on the northern end of the park and forged an important new trade route. The last of the Rocky Mountain parks to be created, Kootenay is also lightly visited in comparison to Banff and Jasper National Parks. The park was created in 1920 when, in exchange for building a road through here, the provincial government gave Canada the land to create a national park. Indeed this highway was the first road across the Rockies, preceding the Yellowhead and Kicking Horse Passes more commonly used today.

Set your trip odometer at the junction of Highway 93 and the Trans Canada Highway (Highway 1) in Banff National Park, 28 kilometers (16.8 miles) from either Lake Louise of Banff. From the junction, the most notable view is eastwards to the symmetrical form of Castle Mountain, an isolated, craggy peak that is one of the most recognizable sights in the Rockies and the subject of more postcards that almost any other place in the entire range.

Once on Highway 93 heading south and climbing out of the wide Bow Valley, the view straight ahead is of 10,400-foot Storm Mountain on the left and massive 11,700-foot Mount Temple on the far right. Several popular hiking trails are accessed in this stretch, including Boom, Egypt, and Shadow Lakes (see the *Canadian Rockies Trail Guide* for details on hikes along this drive). The scenery through here is among the best of the drive with sky-piercing summits lining the highway on both sides as you cross the main spine of the Rockies.

Vermillion Pass, the high point of the drive at 5,400 feet, is reached at 10 kilometers (6 miles). From here the drive is downhill for most of the way, first following the Vermillion and then Kootenay River valleys through the mountains and into the Columbia River valley. At the pass, the highway crosses the Continental Divide into BC at the northern entrance to Kootenay National Park. Not only is the pass a major geographic boundary, it also divides water flowing toward the Pacific Ocean from water flowing to Hudson Bay in Canada's Arctic. It's fascinating to think that snowflakes that fall mere feet from each other can eventually end up in different oceans thousands of kilometers away from each other.

Located at the pass is the short Fireweed Trail, an interpretive walk through the burn site of a forest fire that occurred 30 years ago. Far up ahead, the distant ridge of barren, grey summits is the stupendous Rockwall, an almost unbroken 30-kilometer- (18-mile-) long cliff face that averages over 3,000-feet high its entire distance. The Rockwall, who's 10,000-foot summits are part of the Vermillion Range, is one of the most famous natural features in the Rockies.

The parking lot for the Stanley Glacier Trail is reached at 13.4 kilometers (8 miles). Although 10,400-foot Stanley Peak and its glaciated flanks can been seen from the highway, a rewarding 8-kilometer (4.8-mile) round-trip hike trail switchbacks up into this hanging valley for better views of the impressive mountain faces and gives a close-up glimpse of a cascading icefall.

At 16.9 kilometers (10 miles) is both the trailhead for Marble Canyon as well as the Marble Canyon campground, one of the three major campgrounds in the park. Marble Canyon is an easy 800-meter (0.5 mile) trail that crisscrosses a deep gorge to a pounding waterfall set in a deep, grey canyon. This spot is also the start of the long backpacking trail to Kaufmann Lake, situated on the backside of the famous Valley of the Ten Peaks.

Only 3 kilometers (1.8 miles) farther is the Paint Pots parking lot where a short walk leads to the Paint Pots, a unique geological feature where an iron-rich mineral spring boils to the surface to stain the ground in a deep ochre color. Aboriginal peoples used this place as a source of paint as well as an important gathering place. The Paint Pots parking area is also the starting point for treks into some of the most spectacular places in the Rockies. Located here is not only the northernmost access point for the classic multiday backpack beneath the Rockwall but also the starting point for the trek to Helmet Falls, one of Canada's highest waterfalls, and Goodsir Pass, a

*Peaks of the Rockwall in the Vermillion Range as seen from the Kootenay Parkway.*

narrow cleft on the divide between Kootenay and Yoho National Parks that features breathtaking views of the sheer 6,500-foot north face of the Goodsir Towers. Be aware that all of the hikes from here are strenuous and best suited for experienced and fit hikers.

By now it's obvious that this route through the Rockies is much less busy than the other national parks to the east. Kootenay has only a quarter of the annual visitors that Banff gets, meaning that both its trails and highways are much quieter and solitude is easier to find.

In the next stretch, the highway curves slightly eastwards and runs along the forested base of the Rockwall. Although it is not seen in its full glory from the highway (you have to hike the Rockwall Trail to really experience it), glimpses of it can be seen up through the side valleys that descend to the valley bottom. Along here, the highway runs alongside the turquoise Vermillion River and has sweeping views from the river to the high summits of the Rockwall, making for a memorable scene and a great picture.

Between 23 and 30 kilometers (13.8 to 18 miles), the Rockwall is often seen above the forested shoulder. Although the peaks vary from flat-topped to spirelike, the color of all the peaks is consistently dark grey and even from far below, the height and verticality of the cliffs is astounding. At 32.8 kilometers (19.7 miles) is the trailhead for Floe Lake, the southern entrance to the Rockwall Trail. Floe Lake itself, reached after a stiff 10-kilometer (6-mile) one-way hike, is one of the classic beauty spots in the Rockies, featuring a turquoise lake with floating icebergs below a sheer 3,000-foot cliff. The Rockwall Trail, revered as one of the most beautiful (and most strenuous) backpacking trails in the Rockies, runs for 55 kilometers (34 miles) one-way along the base of the wall. It travels though vast meadows, over two major passes, and is almost always within sight of the fractured glaciers and soaring cliffs that have made this chunk of the Rockies famous.

Seven kilometers (4.2 miles) beyond the trailhead is Vermillion Crossing, the commercial center for central Kootenay National Park. Here you will find a park information center, Kootenay Lodge, restaurant, gift shop, and the access for the rugged and little-used trail up Verdant Creek, part of Hawk Ridge which parallels the highway to the east.

Beyond here, the highway crosses to the west side of the Vermillion River and does a high traverse with sweeping views across the river to a long series of barren, multicolored peaks. At sunset, this long mountain ridge glows brilliantly in the low-angled light and makes for a long-remembered sight. Several pullouts on the left allow for easy stopping to take a look at the river-to-mountain views. The wide side valley cutting through the mountains to the east is the Simpson River valley, a little-used route to 11,900-foot Mount Assiniboine, known as the "Matterhorn of the Rockies," which rises just to the east but can't be seen from the highway.

Bending around a prominent corner, the Kootenay Parkway passes between Mount Wardle on the right and Split Peak on the left. Both peaks are composed of grey limestone and have pocket glaciers clinging to their flanks. Mount Wardle is home to a large herd of mountain goats that occasionally descend from their high mountain world to the roadside to use a salt lick. As is the case in all of the Rockies, "animal jams" may be found here as drivers pull off the road to have a better look at the goats.

After passing between the two mountains, the highway descends steadily toward Kootenay Crossing where the Vermillion and Kootenay Rivers meet. A sign here details the history of the highway. It originated as a commercial route to transport the crops of the Windermere Valley (just south of Radium Hot Springs) to markets in Alberta. After the present route was surveyed, construction began in 1911 but money for the project soon ran out with only 22 kilometers (13.2 miles) being finished. It wasn't until 1922 that the route was fully completed, two years after the creation of the park.

Now beside the swiftly flowing Kootenay River, the highway has superlative views across the river to a long series of summits on the eastern edge of the park. Unlike the last part of the drive, the valley here is wide open and the scenery is in full view. Although the most prominent mountain in view is 9,800-foot Mount Harkin, numerous others compete for attention in the long row of peaks in the Mitchell Range to the east. To the west, the Brisco Range is seldom seen from the highway. The Kindersly Pass Trail, starting from the highway 9.5 kilometers (6 miles) east of Radium Hot Springs, climbs to a high summit in the Brisco Range and has panoramic views of much of the southern half of the park.

At 77.7 kilometers (46.6 miles) is the McLeod Meadows campground, the second largest in the park. Just a few minutes past the campground, gravel Settlers Road branches off to the left and continues to follow the Kootenay River for over 50 kilometers (30 miles) to where it enters the Columbia River valley at Canal Flats, making this an adventurous and alternative way out of the park.

Beyond 87 kilometers (52 miles), the highway begins to climb out of the Kootenay River valley toward Sinclair Pass. Near the pass, the views from the signed Kootenay River viewpoint are superlative and well worth the stop. Once you are into Sinclair Creek, the scenery closes in and the distant views disappear. Being on the wet western edge of the range, this area more resembles BC's interior ranges than the main core of the Rockies found to the east.

In the last part of the drive, the highway is narrow, twisty, and descends steeply enough to have truck runaway lanes on the corners. Olive Lake, a pleasant picnic area, is passed at 92.4 kilometers (55.4 miles) on the left as the highway sweeps around a steep corner. Rocky Mountain bighorn sheep are commonly seen through here so scan the hillsides carefully.

Where the grade lessens, it enters Sinclair Canyon and its colorful rock walls that line the highway. After passing through a tunnel, the Radium Hot Springs pools (operated by the park) are reached at 102 kilometers (61 miles). These hot springs were used by aboriginal peoples for hundreds of years before the park's creation and have a water temperature of 40 degrees C (104 degrees F). Several hundred thousand people soak in the pools every year so expect lots of company in the summer months. The main park information center is located beside the pools and is the best place to contact for information on the park's hiking trails and campground availability.

Just past the hot springs is a string of motels lining both sides of the highway, many with a Bavarian theme in light of the mountain setting. Just before the drive ends, it passes through the narrowest part of Sinclair Canyon. Park at the small lot on the right just at the entrance to the prominent canyon section and walk through the gorge to a viewpoint with views into Radium Hot Springs and the wide Columbia River valley as well as back toward the highway where an impressive engineering feat allows the highway to pass over a waterfall and through the narrow chasm on a bridge.

The view toward the Columbia River valley is interesting in that it is noticeably drier than the areas just to the east that were seen along the drive. The valley lies in the rainshadow of the interior ranges to the west, a wide series of mountains that steal eastbound precipitation before reaching the valley. Some of the scenery here is reminiscent of the Okanagan, with dry, rolling sagebrush-covered hills seen just below the viewpoint. A small pocket of the Columbia River trench is actually in the same biogeographic region as the Okanagan despite being far east of BC's dry Southern Interior.

Redstreak campground, the largest in Kootenay, is situated on a bench above the highway and is accessed via Highway 95 on the outskirts of town. This campground with nearly 250 sites is a busy and popular place. From Redstreak, a 30-minute hike takes you to the hot springs.

At 104 kilometers (62.4 miles), the highway leaves the park and enters Radium Hot Springs. This unique resort community of a few hundred residents swells in the summer months as a key gateway to the Rockies as well as being a destination in itself. Although the town is famous for its hot springs, the adventure possibilities in the area are virtually limitless. The town looks across the Columbia Valley toward the Purcell Range and yet another set of wilderness mountains.

From here head back the same way you came or continue farther into BC. To reach Highway 1, turn right on Highway 95 and reach Golden in about two hours of driving.

# *14*

# Icefields Parkway
## *Lake Louise to Jasper, Alberta*

**General description:** The Icefields Parkway, stretching 230 kilometers (138 miles) between Lake Louise and Jasper through the heart of two world-famous Rocky Mountain national parks, is one of the premier mountain drives on earth. Once you've completed this drive it will be forever etched into your memory and most likely you'll dream of returning again and again. As a bonus, the drive is easy and relaxing, unlike most mountain drives elsewhere in BC.

**Special attractions:** Nonstop postcard-like scenery, the Columbia Icefield, Bow Summit, Peyto Lake, Mount Edith Cavell, frequent wildlife sightings, fully protected wilderness, and an excellent network of hiking trails and campgrounds.

**Location:** Between Lake Louise and Jasper along the very western edge of Alberta. Although not in BC, this drive follows the Continental Divide and is often within sight of peaks right along the BC/Alberta border.

**Drive route numbers:** The Icefields Parkway, Alberta Highway 93.

**Travel season:** Any time of year. Summers are high season and crowded, but all the trails and facilities in the parks are open. Spring is pleasant and less crowded but the trails are still snowed in. Fall is a magical time to drive the parkway to see the fall colors and the mountains dusted in snow. The parkway is open in winter but blizzards and extreme cold can make the drive somewhat hazardous.

**Camping:** Numerous highly organized, full-facility campgrounds along the parkway. Be sure to book ahead if possible.

**Services:** Limited services in Lake Louise, full services in Jasper. Saskatchewan Crossing at the halfway point has the only gas and basic supplies along the parkway.

**Nearby attractions:** Almost too many to list. The area has many parks and protected areas in all directions. The main attractions are of course natural—the mountains, glaciers, lakes, rivers, forests, and the unlimited outdoor recreation possibilities. The town of Banff, just south of Lake Louise is *the* classic Rockies tourist town and well worth a visit.

 The drive

The Icefields Parkway begins in Lake Louise, Alberta, just north of town where Highway 23 leaves the Trans Canada Highway. The easiest way to

# Drive 14: Icefields Parkway

*Lake Louise to Jasper, Alberta*

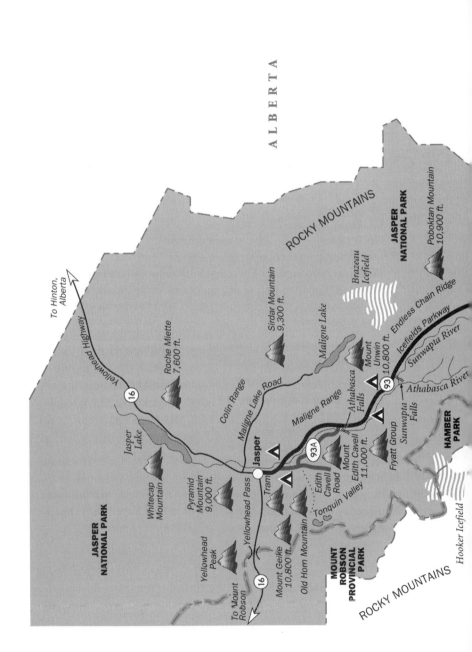

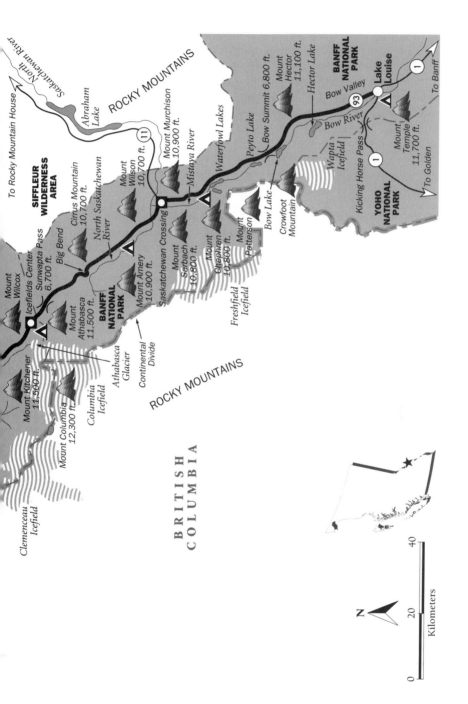

North Saskatchewan River

To Rocky Mountain House

Abraham Lake

ROCKY MOUNTAINS

SIFFLEUR WILDERNESS AREA

11

Mount Murchison 10,900 ft.

Mount Wilson 10,700 ft.

Cirrus Mountain 10,700 ft.

Mistaya River

Waterfowl Lakes

North Saskatchewan River

Big Bend

Sunwapta Pass 6,700 ft.

Icefields Center

Mount Wilcox

Mount Athabasca 11,500 ft.

BANFF NATIONAL PARK

Saskatchewan Crossing

Mount Amery 10,900 ft.

Mount Sarbach 10,800 ft.

Mount Chephren 10,800 ft.

Mount Patterson

Freshfield Icefield

Mount Kitchener 11,500 ft.

Columbia Icefield

Athabasca Glacier

Columbia Icefield

Mount Columbia 12,300 ft.

Continental Divide

ROCKY MOUNTAINS

Clemenceau Icefield

BRITISH COLUMBIA

Peyto Lake

Bow Lake

Crowfoot Mountain

Bow Summit 6,800 ft.

Mount Hector 11,100 ft.

Hector Lake

Bow Valley

Bow River

Wapta Icefield

Kicking Horse Pass

YOHO NATIONAL PARK

Mount Temple 11,700 ft.

BANFF NATIONAL PARK

93

Lake Louise

1

To Banff

To Golden

ROCKY MOUNTAINS

N

0      20      40

Kilometers

reach the village from BC is via Highway 1 over Kicking Horse Pass (Drive 15). Lake Louise is an excellent introduction to the Rockies having two must-see destinations—Lake Louise (the lake) as well as Moraine Lake. These are two of the most famous and popular spots in all of the Rockies so expect crowds. Lording over Lake Louise is 11,700-foot Mount Temple, often refered to as the "Eiger of the Rockies" because of its foreboding 5,000-foot north face.

In all of the Rockies, the Lake Louise area is one of the best centers for both hiking and sightseeing. The village has its basic services grouped near the mall in its small center. Be sure to stop in at the Lake Louise visitors center, the best place for information on the park as well as the place to book campgrounds along the Banff stretch of the parkway. If the forecast looks poor, it's worth waiting here or in Banff (about 45 minutes south on Highway 1) for the weather to clear up before driving the parkway as there is nothing more frustrating than driving through some of the best scenery in the world and not being able to see anything.

Banff National Park was created in 1885 and was Canada's first national park. Combined with the other surrounding parks, this area is designated as the Rocky Mountains World Heritage Site as it forms one of the largest protected areas on earth. Although aboriginal use of today's mountain parks stretches back thousands of years, the modern day exploration in the Rockies started in the early 1800s but didn't really pick up momentum until the early 1900s. Luckily, politicians early on decided to preserve the Rockies for future generations to marvel at—truly one of the most far-sighted decisions in Canadian history. Banff was created to help to promote both the Rockies and the new Canadian Pacific Railway which ran through the area long before any roads where built. Unlike newer national parks, Banff has a lot of commercial development like towns, roads, and ski areas. Because of this, visitors to the Rockies range from hard-core mountaineers to pampered luxury travelers. Although both see similar scenery, their experiences here are a world apart.

The way to the Icefields Parkway is well signed from Lake Louise. At the beginning of the parkway is a toll booth where park day passes must be purchased before continuing north. For those staying more than seven days in any of the national parks, the $35 annual pass is worthwhile. Be sure to get your free copy of the National Parks visitors guide which is revised annually and is the best current source of information for the six national parks along the BC/Alberta border. Listed are points of interest, campgrounds, wildlife tips, facts about the parks, and other information useful to visitors.

Once on the parkway itself, the crowds of Lake Louise are quickly left behind as the route travels deeper into the mountains. For the most part, the parkway is an easy drive with most who venture here coming for the scenery. In the initial stretches, the parkway climbs out of the wide Bow

Valley and into its narrow headwaters where the mountain walls grow ever closer. Mount Hector, at 11,100 feet one of the highest summits along the parkway, rises to the east and is an awesome sight. Even near the beginning, the views of peaks and glaciers to the west are excellent. Tiny Herbert Lake at 3 kilometers (2 miles) has near-perfect reflections of the peaks looming over Lake Louise, including massive Mount Temple.

The Icefields Parkway climbs gently throughout this section with ever improving views as it nears the treeline. At 16 kilometers (10 miles) is the Hector Lake viewpoint and the sight of the first big lake along the drive. Rising behind the lake is the Waputik Icefield, the first major glacier system encountered. Just beyond here is Bow Lake, a vast turquoise gem set in front of multi-summited Crowfoot Mountain and its hanging glacier. There is a large pullout here to take in one of the classic views in the Rockies. To the northeast, a prominent red-roofed lodge marks the trailhead to powerful Bow Falls which can be seen cascading over bare rock in the distance.

The land through which the parkway now travels was used as far back as the early 1800s by fur traders and natives who traveled up the same valleys and over the same passes. Back then the early travelers referred to it as the "wonder trail," quite a compliment in those days when all of Canada was still true wilderness. A road was first punched through these mountains in the 1930s as a make-work project during the Depression. Soon after the present highway was opened in the early 1960s, word soon spread of its natural wonders and right from the start it has been a very popular drive.

Bow Summit, at 6,800 feet the high point of the drive, is reached at 40 kilometers (24 miles). Here the parkway is nearly above treeline with only a thin band of forest separating the road from the alpine tundra and barren, rocky slopes all around. The pass is broad and gentle but lined with cathedral-like summits on both sides. Just beyond the crest is the turnoff on the left to Peyto Lake. If you only make one stop along the drive, make it this one. This side road climbs in a few minutes to a parking lot from which a short path leads to a viewing platform high above the turquoise expanse of Peyto Lake and its ring of craggy grey summits. This viewpoint has yielded countless postcards over the years. In the distance, the parkway can be seen threading its way north through the classic U-shaped valley of the Mistaya River.

After Bow Summit, the parkway gradually descends all the way down the Mistaya River valley to Saskatchewan Crossing, passing almost continuous mountain walls on both sides. Mount Patterson (10,500 feet), the rugged peak above Peyto Lake, is now seen from its east side with the incredible Snowbird Glacier cascading precipitously over its nearly vertical cliffs. By now many hikers will have realized that the roadside scenery on this route is better than what they struggle to see by trail in other places. The dominating feature in this middle section is pyramidal Mount Chephren, 10,800 feet high and easily one of the most prominent summits along the parkway.

The east face of Mount Patterson and the Snowbird Glacier
as seen from the Icefields Parkway just north of Bow Summit and Peyto Lake.

Its nearly flawless symmetry and massive bulk make it one of the great peaks of the Rockies, no small accomplishment in this range of wonders. When passing beneath its towering east face, try to imagine climbing it in winter, something that was accomplished just a few years ago.

Although Banff and Jasper National Parks are highly developed and host millions of visitors a year, over 90 percent of these parks is still true wilderness. All throughout the Rockies, the trail network is well developed and maintained and ranges from easy strolls to demanding multiday back-packing routes. By setting foot on any of the dozens of trails that start on the parkway, remote and lightly visited high alpine areas brimming with peaks, glaciers, lakes, and meadows are easily reached. The *Canadian Rockies Trail Guide* is the best reference for all the hikes in the range.

Near the base of Mount Chephren and other giants like Howse Peak, the Waterfowl Lakes are passed on the left at 56 kilometers (34 miles). The Waterfowl Lakes campground found here is one of the biggest along the parkway with 116 sites. All through this stretch, the castle-like layered mountains are impressive, with cliffs up to 4,000 feet high falling away from the summits which range from 10,000 to 11,000 feet. As the BC/Alberta border runs right through the Continental Divide, the peaks visible to the west are half in BC and half in Alberta.

The Rockies are mainly sedimentary mountains and were actually part of a massive sea bed. Continental drift and plate collisions forced the Rockies to rise slowly out of the sea over 70 million years ago and the ocean slowly drained west to expose the ever-growing peaks. The Rockies were once much higher than today but erosion over millions of years has worn several thousand feet off their summits. Typically, the nature of sedimentary rock is that large cliffs and massive fortress-like summits are common. With all the impressive summits it's no wonder that the Rockies are known around the world for their technical and spectacular climbing routes. Unlike the Colorado Rockies where most of the high peaks can be hiked to the summit, these mountains are generally summited only after hard, exposed, and technical climbing. Peaks like Mount Robson and Mount Alberta are among the world's great mountains and are always high on international climbers' lists for their challenging and spectacular scenery.

At 77 kilometers (46 miles) is Saskatchewan Crossing, the only commercial development along the route. Here the North Saskatchewan River turns east and slowly flows into the plains of Alberta. At the crossing are a lodge, gas station, and gift shop, all set beneath the multipeaked Mount Wilson, a landmark in the central section of the parkway. From this point, Alberta Highway 11, the David Thompson Highway, branches off to east and toward Rocky Mountain House.

When driving the parkway, particularly at dusk or dawn, you will hopefully be rewarded with a wildlife sighting. In the numerous times I have driven the parkway I've seen grizzlies, moose, mountain goats, black bears, and Rocky Mountain bighorn sheep among others. Wildlife sightings like these are common and a big reason why people from around the world make the pilgrimage to the Rockies. Some visitors see so much wildlife they begin to disregard it while others never even glimpse a deer. Obviously luck plays a big part in seeing wildlife. Most often you'll know there's wildlife on the road when you see an "animal jam"— a bunch of cars pulled over and people milling about. Near the major centers like Banff, the sight of wildlife on the highway can lead to major delays as everyone slows down to take a picture.

Traveling north from Saskatchewan Crossing, the neck-stretching height of Mount Wilson to the east (right) is an outstanding sight. On sunny days, pull off the highway just south of the Rampart Creek campground and look for rainbows formed by the sun hitting the veil-like waterfalls pouring down the immense cliffs. As an added attraction, the display of fall color at the base of Mount Wilson is one of the best in the Rockies.

Through the next stretch, the parkway travels alongside the turquoise North Saskatchewan River for many kilometers with almost constant picture-perfect scenery to the west with the river, forest, and sky-scraping peaks making for a memorable combination. Near the head of the Saskatchewan River, the flanks of 10,700-foot Cirrus Mountain plunge to the very edge of the parkway where the aptly-named Weeping Wall is encountered at 105 kilometers (63 miles). In winter when these waterfalls freeze, ice climbers from around the world flock here to test both their skill and their luck in what many regard as an almost suicidal sport.

Immediately after the Weeping Wall, the parkway bends around a prominent corner toward the headwaters of the North Saskatchewan River and then loops back and begins to climb steeply toward Sunwapta Pass and the cold, severe world of the Columbia Icefield. From the top of the switchback, the view back down the parkway to the south reveals the extent to which the route is confined by its mountainous terrain.

The signed Parker Ridge Trail, reached just before Sunwapta Pass, is the easiest trail along the entire parkway to access the alpine. From the 7,400-foot ridge crest, reached in about 2 kilometers (1.2 miles) of easy hiking, the views include the long tongue of the Saskatchewan Glacier as well as the spirelike summits backing the Athabasca Glacier. The Wilcox Pass Trail, a little closer to Sunwapta Pass, is also one of the best short trails in the Rockies and rewards hikers with an aerial view of the Columbia Icefield.

Sunwapta Pass, the second highlight point (6,700 feet) on the parkway and the boundary between Jasper and Banff National Parks, is reached at 122 kilometers (73 miles). Jasper, created in 1907, is the larger of the two national parks even though it receives only half of Banff's estimated 4.7

million visitors per year. Of the two parks, Jasper is more glaciated, rugged, and remote. The north end of the park in particular sees very little visitation and is almost as wild today as it was when the first explorers passed though the area over 100 years ago.

Although the weather in the Rockies is often better than the coastal and interior mountains of BC, the weather is statistically poor here at least one in every three days in summer. The weather varies from year to year, with some summers being sunny for weeks, while in others, it seems to rain every day. Depending upon the weather, the elevation of the area, combined with the massive glaciers, can make for a refreshing change or a miserably cold and windy experience.

The famed Columbia Icefield, the most scenic part of the drive, is reached at 127 kilometers (76 miles). Through here the parkway travels through a high-mountain environment usually only seen by hikers and mountaineers. Although the Icefields Interpretive Center is a worthy stop, the real attraction is the Athabasca Glacier which flows from the heart of the icefield to within easy walking distance. Towering above the glacier are the distinctive twin summits of 11,500-foot Mount Athabasca and 11,400-foot Mount Andromeda, a worthy backdrop to such a magical place.

The Athabasca Glacier is retreating year after year and markers along-side the access road show its slow but steady backward movements. From the parking lot, the glacier is only a few hundred feet away on an uphill

*View from the Icefields Parkway along the Sunwapta River toward the Athabasca Glacier and the Columbia Icefield. The prominent glaciated peak on the left is Mount Andromeda.*

gravel path. For those who have never experienced a glacier before, this may be the highlight of the entire trip to the Rockies. The best way to see the glacier is to take one of the snowcat tours onto the glacier (booked at the interpretive center). The lumbering snowcats travel up an ice road high on the glacier and allow visitors to get out and explore the glacier on foot. Except for a couple of other locations in BC and Alaska, this is the easiest glacier-viewing in North America.

Glaciers are formed where more snow falls every year than melts. As the snow falls and accumulates over the centuries it is compressed into a dense layers of ice that flow plasticlike downhill, pulled by gravity. The prominent icefalls on the slopes of Mount Andromeda are formed when glaciers flow over cliffy terrain which causes the ice to wildly break up. Active icefalls are sometimes more easily heard than seen, being noted for their thunderlike claps as ice breaks free and hurtles downwards.

The Columbia Icefield, straddling the Continental Divide, is considered the hydrological apex of North America, with its ice melting and flowing into three oceans—the Pacific, Atlantic, and Arctic. Although only the outermost edges are seen here, the icefield itself is a massive plateau of ice over 300 square kilometers in size. Ringing the icefield on all sides are some of the grandest peaks in all the Rockies, including the spires of North Twin, Mount Alberta, and Mount Kitchener, all around 12,000 feet high and well-known to mountain-lovers worldwide.

Beyond the awesome environs of the icefield, the parkway descends alongside the braided Sunwapta River to where the river dives into a deep canyon. Throughout this section, the sheer edge of the Columbia Icefield can be seen high above where it abruptly ends at the top of massive cliffs. There are several pullouts along here to see both the canyon and the last view of the Athabasca Glacier in the distance. Immediately beyond these viewpoints the parkway drops sharply and views of the menacing north face of 11,500-foot Mount Kitchener are gained. On this 4,000-foot wall of rock and ice lies one of the hardest and most extreme mountaineering routes in the Rockies, the Grand Central Couloir.

Slowly and surely, the parkway leaves the austere landscapes of the icefield area behind for the forests and lush riverside scenery of the Sunwapta River. At 175 kilometers (105 miles) is the parking lot for Sunwapta Falls which is a 15-minute walk away. Just beyond is the Athabasca Valley viewpoint, a good place to get out the binoculars and try to identify the famous peaks like Mount Alberta that line the upper Athabasca where it turns inland from the highway. From here to Jasper, the parkway passes six campgrounds—be on the lookout for the signs if you plan to camp. Most of the campsites are just south of Jasper with the Whistler and Wapiti campgrounds alone having over 1,000 sites.

*The edge of the massive Columbia Icefield as seen from the Icefields Parkway.*

The next stretch of the parkway is exceptionally scenic as it runs alongside the turquoise Athabasca River and features views into the Fryatt Group. This compact group of summits is most notable for the sharp twin summits of Mount Christie and Mount Brussels. To the right of the highway is the Endless Chain Ridge, a series of sharp summits that are remarkably similar looking.

At 199 kilometers (119 miles), a prominent turnoff to Athabasca Falls is reached. This road (Highway 93A) is an alternative route to the Jasper area and a shortcut for those heading to Mount Edith Cavell. Staying on the parkway, the turnoff to Marmot Basin ski area and Mount Edith Cavell is reached just before Jasper at 223 kilometers (134 miles).

The drive up the winding road to the Cavell Meadows area is absolutely a required side trip and one of the most breathtaking spots in all of the Rockies. Turn left here and follow 93A back to the south and traverse high above the Athabasca River. The Cavell Road turnoff is on the right at the 5 kilometer (3 mile) mark and is well-signed. Despite being paved, this road is narrow, winding, and rough. It is kept this way to decrease the traffic and the speed in this extremely busy area. Trailers should be dropped off at the designated lot at the start of the road. This side trip is not included in the distance markers.

The road winds and climbs for 14 kilometers (8.4 miles) to the Cavell parking lot, virtually at the base of 11,000-foot Mount Edith Cavell which towers like a skyscraper 5,000 feet above. Be sure to take the easy and short Path of the Glacier Trail to the small glacial lake at the foot of the peak to gain a better viewpoint for the Angel Glacier icefall which clings to the north face of the mountain. Two kilometers (1.2 miles) back from the main parking lot and across from the youth hostel is the wide trail down to Cavell Lake (reached in a few minutes) and the start of the trail into the Tonquin Valley and the Ramparts, one of the finest backpacking trips in the Rockies. A part of the famed Ramparts can be seen from the small viewpoint (marked by a cairn) about a kilometer (0.6 mile) past the hostel at the point where the road turns a prominent corner and descends toward the parkway.

Back on the parkway, Jasper is only minutes away. Along this stretch, the barren looking Maligne Range dominates the skyline to the east and is much more desolate and dry-looking than the environs around Edith Cavell. Just south of Jasper at 228 kilometers (137 miles) is the turnoff to the Jasper Gondola and an opportunity to attain a 360-degree panorama without breaking a sweat. From the top of the gondola, the view includes the Ramparts, Mount Edith Cavell, and Jasper lying in the midst of a ring of peaks.

Jasper, reached at 230 kilometers (138 miles), is the end of the parkway and a worthwhile place to soak up some Rocky Mountain ambiance. While much smaller and less touristy than Banff, Jasper is still a busy place and home to dozens of lodges, restaurants, gift shops, outdoor stores, and other services. Before heading off on further driving adventures, be sure to stop in at the historic Jasper visitor center, especially if you need information or reservations for the rest of the park.

The driving options from here are to head back down the Icefields Parkway to see a different perspective of it, or to head west along the Yellowhead Highway (Drive 22) past the monarch of the Rockies, Mount Robson.

# 15

# Trans Canada Highway

## *Golden to Lake Louise*

**General description:** This 82-kilometer (49-mile) drive, starting where the Revelstoke to Golden drive (Drive 17) leaves off, is a spectacular mountain drive through BC's gateway to the famous Canadian Rocky Mountain national parks. From the recreation-oriented town of Golden, the Trans Canada quickly enters the foothills of the Rockies before reaching the main divide of the range in Yoho National Park. Most of the awe-inspiring scenery on this drive is in the second half as the highway climbs to Kicking Horse Pass in the shadow of towering, cathedral-like peaks. The drive ends in Lake Louise in Banff National Park, the hub of several more scenic drives.

**Special attractions:** One beautiful, postcard-like view after another; Emerald Lake, Yoho, and Lake O'Hara Valleys; the fascinating history of the Kicking Horse Pass.

**Location:** On the very eastern edge of BC where the Trans Canada enters Alberta in Banff National Park.

**Drive route numbers:** Highway 1, the Trans Canada Highway the entire distance.

**Travel season:** Any time of year. The highway can be treacherous in winter due to snow storms. Summer is busy but the best time to come as everything is open and the hiking trails are free of snow.

**Camping:** Commercial camping in Golden and public camping in both Yoho and Banff National Parks. The campsites in the parks are in high demand in the summer months, making booking ahead a wise decision.

**Services:** Full tourist services in Golden, limited services in Field and Lake Louise, both of which are in national parks.

**Nearby attractions:** Endless hiking and backpacking opportunities, rafting on the Kicking Horse River, the Icefields Parkway (Drive 14), the Purcell Range south of Golden which includes the world-famous Bugaboo Spires.

 # The drive

Set your trip odometer in downtown Golden where most of the services for travelers are found grouped along the Trans Canada Highway. As is the case with Revelstoke, Golden grew with the completion of the Canadian Pacific Railway (CPR) railway in the late 1800s. Although the present population is small, Golden is a busy place filled with travelers passing through on their way to or from the Rockies. Although the Rocky Mountain towns like

# Drive 15: Trans Canada Highway
## *Golden to Lake Louise*

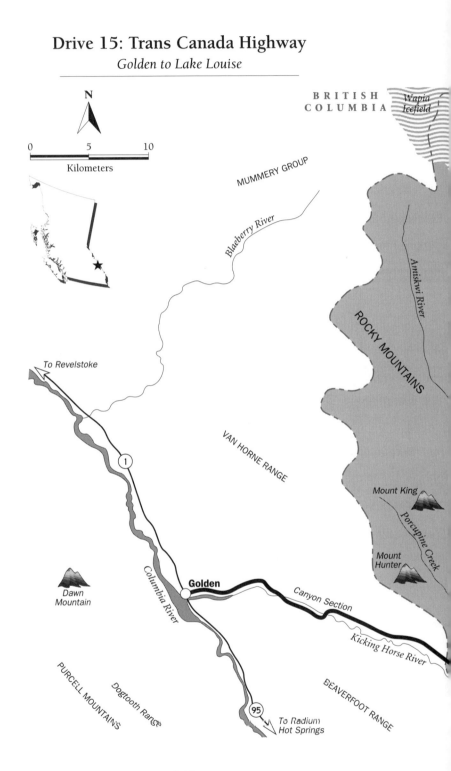

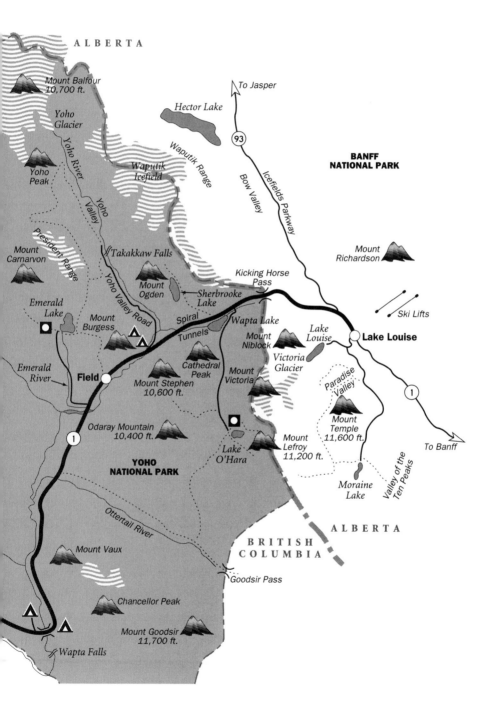

ALBERTA

Mount Balfour
10,700 ft.

Yoho
Glacier

Hector Lake

To Jasper

93

BANFF
NATIONAL PARK

Yoho River

Yoho
Peak

Waputik
Icefield

Waputik Range

Bow Valley

Icefields Parkway

Mount
Richardson

President Range

Mount
Carnarvon

Yoho Valley

Takakkaw Falls

Emerald
Lake

Mount
Ogden

Sherbrooke
Lake

Kicking Horse
Pass

Ski Lifts

Emerald
River

Mount
Burgess

Yoho Valley Road

Spiral
Tunnels

Wapta Lake

Mount
Niblock

Lake
Louise

Lake Louise

Field

Cathedral
Peak

Mount
Victoria

Victoria
Glacier

Paradise
Valley

1

Mount Stephen
10,600 ft.

Odaray Mountain
10,400 ft.

Lake
O'Hara

Mount
Lefroy
11,200 ft.

Mount
Temple
11,600 ft.

To Banff

Valley of the
Ten Peaks

YOHO
NATIONAL PARK

Moraine
Lake

Ottertail River

ALBERTA

BRITISH
COLUMBIA

Mount Vaux

Goodsir Pass

Chancellor Peak

Mount Goodsir
11,700 ft.

Wapta Falls

145

Jasper and Banff are much more famous, Golden is trying to attract its share of tourists, many of whom rush through here on their way elsewhere. Few other places have access to as many natural wonders as Golden, which boasts four national parks within day-trip distance. One main advantage of the area is that it's less crowded and lacks the rules and regulations of the national parks, which to many seem onerous and overly restrictive. Keep in mind that Golden is the start of the Mountain Time Zone so set your watch ahead an hour here.

In every direction, mountains stretch away for as far as the eye can see, making Golden a perfect base for all types of outdoor pursuits. The town actively promotes itself as an adventure destination, with all types of activities possible in the surrounding area from whitewater rafting to nature study. Golden is in a good position to capitalize on the booming ecotravel industry that has become a large part of the overall tourism business in BC.

For mountaineers there are few other places in North America that have the sheer quantity of climbing challenges that are found here. In addition to the well-known peaks of the Rockies, the legendary Bugaboo Spires in the Purcells as well as the vast bulk of the incredibly rugged Selkirks are all within easy striking distance. Additionally, numerous high alpine lodges have been built nearby to serve heli-hikers and heli-skiers who flock here to try these expensive but thrilling activities.

Golden is situated in the Rocky Mountain Trench, one of the most notable features in North America. In its 1,600-kilometer (960-mile) length from here to Montana, the flat-bottomed trench varies between 3 and 16 kilometers wide. In this northern section, the Columbia River runs north through the trench and forms the divide between the Rocky Mountains to the east and the Columbia Mountains to the west. Although Golden is seemingly far from the semi-deserts of the Southern Interior, the scores of peaks to the west create a rainshadow effect over the valley and give Golden a hot, sunny climate for much of the summer. Many summer travelers are surprised just how hot it gets here after being in the cool, high elevation valleys of the surrounding mountains.

Although the two ranges are very different, when looking out to the peaks on both sides of the town it might be hard to differentiate between the Rockies and the Purcells. The Rockies are formed from sedimentary rocks like limestone and shale that once were the bottom of a long-gone ocean floor. Plate tectonics forced the Rockies to thrust upwards about 100 million years ago, exposing the sedimentary layers and creating the mountains you see today. It is these layered rock formations that give the Rockies their distinctive appearance. The Purcells, on the other hand, are much older than the Rockies (1.5 billion years) and are composed of metamorphic rocks with a good amount of granite and quartzite, the type of rock that climbers seek out. The climate of the two ranges is also different with the Rockies having a much more continental influence (hot summers, cold winters) while the Purcells lie in the milder interior wet belt.

Golden takes only a few minutes to pass through on the way east. Once on the outskirts of town, the highway quickly leaves behind all vestiges of civilization as it climbs into the gorge of the Kicking Horse River. Although challenging enough in summer, this twisty and narrow part of the Trans Canada Highway is notorious in the winter months when heavy snowfalls and icy conditions make driving here a real challenge. In an attempt to increase interprovincial trade, the federal government is talking seriously about spending millions of dollars on an ambitious project to straighten out this section of the highway. Rocky Mountain bighorn sheep are frequently seen alongside the road in this section, often causing "animal jams," a common occurrence in the Rockies.

The highway enters Yoho National Park, one of the two Rocky Mountain national parks in BC, at 26 kilometers (16 miles). If you plan to stop in the park, park passes must be purchased at either the manned or self-pay station. The name "Yoho" is derived from the Cree word for "how magnificent." The park was created in 1886, about the same time as the other Rocky Mountain parks. Together, the mountain parks are designated by the United Nations as the Canadian Rockies World Heritage Site by virtue of the fact that they form one of the biggest continuous protected areas on earth. The Rockies are easily seen from the highway so visitors here, unlike other places in BC, don't have to lace up their hiking boots to actually see the scenery they are driving through.

Yoho, although smaller than the other Rocky Mountain parks, packs a great deal of beautiful scenery into its 1,300 square kilometers (507 square miles) of land just west of the Continental Divide. The park is bordered by Banff National Park to the east and Kootenay National Park to the south. The main valley in the park, the Kicking Horse, was named by James Hector who was scouting routes across the Rockies in 1858 when a horse kicked him in the chest. Hector discovered the pass, one of the easiest places to cross the backbone of the Rockies, which was destined to be a major causeway.

Once in the park, the highway travels along the banks of the swift Kicking Horse River before crossing to the east side and turning north for its ascent toward Kicking Horse Pass and Lake Louise. Driving eastward, the majestic peaks in the core of the Rockies begin to rear their heads above the lower peaks to the west. Just 4.5 kilometers (2.7 miles) past the park gate is the turnoff to Wapta Falls, a good introduction to the many scenic waterfalls found throughout the Rockies. This 100-foot-high waterfall is an easy 2.5-kilometer (1.5-mile) walk on a well-groomed path. Just beyond the waterfall parking area are two of the biggest campgrounds in the park, Chancellor Peak and Hoodoo Creek, on opposite sides of the highway where it bends sharply north.

As the highway through the park is divided for most of the distance, a few of the pullouts on the opposite side of the highway are not accessible. The turnoff to beautiful and popular Emerald Lake is at 53 kilometers (32 miles). The access road to this aqua-green lake is 9 kilometers long (5.4 miles) and passes Natural Bridge, where the Kicking Horse River travels under a natural rock arch. Emerald Lake is one of the most recognizable scenes in the Rockies with its backdrop of jagged peaks soaring high above the lake. Canoes can be rented at the historic Emerald Lake Lodge to paddle its placid waters.

Back on the highway, the peaks looming above Field soon reveal themselves. Most notable is 10,600-foot Mount Stephen, a Rocky Mountain icon that rises over 6,000 feet above the town. Reached at 55 kilometers (33 miles), Field, elevation 4,100 feet, is the commercial center of the park and offers full tourist services as well as an interesting and informative visitors center.

While Field is closely associated with both Yoho and the construction of the CPR, it is now also known as the center of research into the Burgess shale, a unique fossil bed found on a mountainside nearby. The fossils of the shale date back over 530 million years and this site is only one of three on earth where the creatures of the Cambrian Period can be studied. In the period from 1910 to 1917, Dr. Charles Wescott, the discoverer of the fossils, found over 65,000 fossils, many of which ended up in the Smithsonian Institution in Washington, DC. Access to the fossil beds is restricted and the only way to see it is as part of a guided hike. Call the Yoho Burgess Shale Foundation for information (see Appendix).

Traveling east of Field, the highway begins to rise steadily toward Kicking Horse Pass. Four kilometers (2.4 miles) farther is the marked turnoff to the Yoho Valley, a must-see area of peaks, glaciers, and waterfalls. Although the Yoho Valley is the domain of the hiker and has numerous trails (which include Iceline, Twin Falls, and Whaleback—see *The Canadian Rockies Trail Guide* for details) striking out for the high alpine, drivers are treated to the sight of Takakkaw Falls, 15 kilometers (9 miles) up this major side valley. On the way to the falls, the Yoho Valley Road passes two campsites, Monarch and Kicking Horse, before rising in several steep and exceptionally tight switchbacks (unsuitable for most RVs and trailers) to the end of the road and the parking area. The falls, the second highest in BC and an easy 10-minute walk away, originate from an out-of-sight glacier and pour 1,300 feet over a rock face to come crashing down very near the viewing platform.

Heading east, the highway climbs beneath the towering walls of Mount Stephen to the Spiral Tunnels viewpoint at 63 kilometers (38 miles). This is a mandatory stop, not only for the history of the railroad but as a magnificent viewpoint for the Yoho Valley, Mount Stephen, and Cathedral Peak which soars just behind. The viewpoint is named after the spiral tunnels blasted out of the base of the mountains here to lessen the grades of the railway track as it approaches Kicking Horse Pass. After the construction of the tunnels, the original 4.5 percent grades that caused so many accidents were reduced to 2.2 percent, still steep, but much easier than before. Display boards here show the history of the railroad and the trains can be seen entering the tunnels far below if you're here at the right time.

Climbing again, the highway passes the turnoff to Lake O'Hara at 69 kilometers (41 miles), just past turquoise Wapta Lake. This classic alpine valley of jewel-like emerald lakes set beneath forbidding peaks has always been the heart of Yoho and has one of the greatest concentrations of high-impact scenery in all the Rockies. Lake O'Hara is known as the "flipside" of Lake Louise as it is set below the opposite side of the same peaks. From Lake O'Hara, numerous trails branch out to the numerous lakes tucked into the very bases of giant peaks like Mount Hugabee and Mount Lefroy, both nearly 11,500 feet high. With the overwhelming popularity of the valley and the resulting impacts, the park closed the access road to private cars and now runs a shuttle bus up the road several times a day. Not only do the campsites in the valley need to be reserved, so does a spot on the bus, making Lake O'Hara difficult to visit on short notice. Contact the park office for more details (see Appendix).

The drive crosses the Continental Divide at 74 kilometers (44 miles) and into both Alberta and Banff National Park. From here, descend into the wide Bow Valley and follow the signs to Lake Louise at the end of the drive

*The majestic summit of Mount Stephen as seen from the Spiral Tunnels viewpoint near Kicking Horse Pass in Yoho National Park.*

*Cathedral Peak as seen from the Yoho Valley Road on the way to Takakkaw Falls.*

at 82 kilometers (49 miles). From Lake Louise, there are many scenic driving options. Travel south to the busy commercial center of the Rockies, Banff, or north up the incomparable Icefields Parkway (Drive 14). Another option is to loop back to Golden via the Kootenay Parkway (Drive 13) and the Columbia River valley via Highway 95. Before leaving the village, be sure to visit both Lake Louise (the lake) and Moraine Lake, two of the most famous sights in the Canadian Rockies.

# High Country
## *16*

## Fraser Canyon
### *Hope to Lillooet*

**General description:** A challenging and historic 170-kilometer (102-mile) drive through the legendary Fraser Canyon just northeast of Vancouver. Traveling from the lush environs of Hope to the scorching, near-desert conditions of Lillooet, the drive up the Fraser Canyon provides a glimpse into the startling variety of landscapes and environments of southwestern BC and retraces the route of one of BC's most famous gold rushes.

**Special attractions:** Thrilling driving, the Fraser Canyon itself, the history of the route, the opportunity to drive the "Coast Mountain Circle" tour, the "meeting of the waters."

**Location:** Southwestern BC due north from Hope along the eastern edge of the Coast Mountains.

**Drive route numbers:** Highway 1 (Trans Canada Highway) from Hope to Lytton and then Highway 12 from Lytton to Lillooet.

**Travel season:** All year. This dry area seldom gets hit with snow so it's generally easy to drive in winter as well. Summers can be exceptionally hot here.

**Camping:** Any of the provincial parks along the way, most notably at Emory Creek, Alexandria Bridge, and Skihist (just east of Lytton on Highway 1) Provincial Parks.

**Services:** Numerous in the first half of the drive along Highway 1 and then none between Lytton and Lillooet.

**Nearby attractions:** Numerous opportunities for backroad exploration off the main route, rafting opportunities on the Fraser and Thompson Rivers, the Coquihalla Canyon east of Hope, the wildlife and limestone formations north of Lytton, the reaction ferry across the Fraser, hiking up the lower Stein River canyon to view Indian pictographs, other scenic drives starting in Lillooet.

 ## The drive

This scenic drive starts in Hope, a historic gold rush town on the very eastern edge of the Lower Mainland where the flatness of the Fraser Valley abruptly ends amongst the mountain walls that loom above the town. Hope is the gateway to three scenic drives in this book and is the place where the "real" BC begins. This small community has its roots as a trading post on the Fraser (Fort

# Drive 16: Fraser Canyon

*Hope to Lillooet*

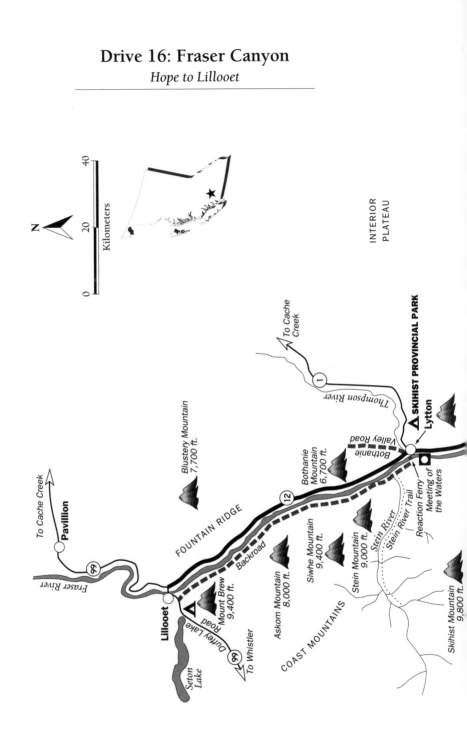

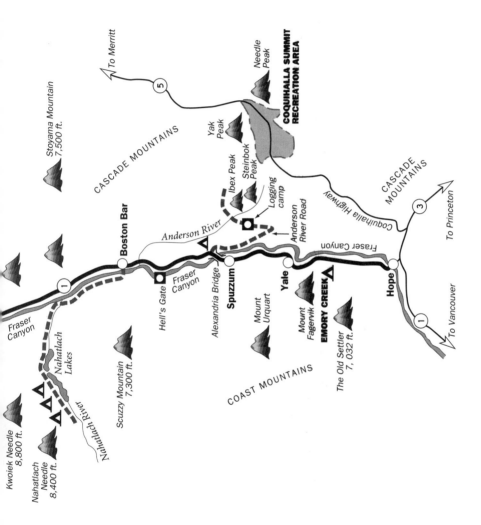

Hope) that was established by the Hudson Bay Company in 1848. With the coming gold rushes, Hope grew quickly to rival upriver Yale as the main town and supply center for miners heading north to the interior. Hope's prospects were further boosted by a stop on the transcontinental railway in 1866.

Today Hope is the gateway to almost all travelers in BC leaving the mega-cities in southern BC bound for points east and north. Whichever way you approach Hope, be sure to follow the signs for Highway 1 north to Lytton and Kamloops. Pass through downtown Hope and alongside the Fraser where a long and scenic waterfront park is situated. The distance markers for this drive start at the bridge over the Fraser on the northern outskirts of Hope. From here north, the drive is steeped in both history and beautiful canyon scenery, making for one of the most popular and widely known scenic drives in BC.

The Fraser River was named for the famous Canadian explorer Simon Fraser who traveled down almost its entire length in 1808, following the original native Sto:lo inhabitants of the area who have been using the river for centuries as a source for food and spiritual inspiration. In the Fraser Canyon itself, archeologists have concluded that there has been continuous occupation by native peoples for at least 9,500 years. In 1858, gold was discovered north of Hope on the Fraser and like many other places in North America during this period, a frenzied gold rush began. As miners poured into the area, clashes soon erupted with the local natives and nearly caused a local war.

Along this drive you'll be hard-pressed to admire the scenery without pulling off the highway periodically. The drive on this twisty, tunnel-riddled

*Misty mountainside in the lower Fraser Canyon near Hope.*

highway up the deepest canyon on BC's largest river takes a lot of concentration. Until the 1940s much of the road was a hair-raising single track where two cars traveling in different directions had a hard time passing each other. Starting in the rain-soaked environment near Hope, this drive winds it way for 170 kilometers (102 miles) with the Fraser River in almost constant sight.

Despite being close to Vancouver, this area feels left behind by time and is much quieter today than it was even 20 years ago. With the opening of the Coquihalla Highway, much of the Southern Interior-bound traffic has abandoned this route in favor of a more direct and relaxing drive along that highway. As part of the Trans Canada Highway (Highway 1), this stretch of road is considered one of the most challenging sections in the whole country, matched only by the section of the highway between Golden and Lake Louise in the Rockies.

Past the bridge, the first few kilometers are straight and narrow through low, forested mountains. Through this section, scattered residential and commercial development is located on both sides of the highway. Lake of the Woods, near the beginning, is a pleasant stop before traveling north and is a popular swimming and boating spot for Hope residents in the summer. At 16.8 kilometers (10 miles), Emery Creek Provincial Park is reached, the site of an old mining camp, and has 34 campsites in the deep forest.

Much of the traffic on this route is either industrial (logging and trucking) or British Columbians headed to northern BC via Prince George. While the Coquihalla for most drivers is a "foot to the floor" affair, this drive is tailor-made for a more laid-back approach. Allow time to stop at the old-fashioned diners, read the historical markers, marvel at the peaks and icefields high above, and pull out along the way to look over the edge to the Fraser River far below. In fall, the canyon is at its prettiest when the vine maples lining the river turn golden yellow and contrast sharply with the dull greys and browns of the cliff-lined gorge.

Historic Yale and the real start to the Fraser Canyon is reached at 23 kilometers (13.8 miles). Here you will find the standard services including gas, food, and accommodation. Yale, home to about 200 people, was one of BC's most important towns during the gold rush period. During those heady days, Lady Franklin Rock, just upstream on the Fraser, blocked access for steamships plying the river northbound, so miners and their supplies were unloaded in Yale in order to continue the journey toward the Cariboo via the Cariboo Wagon Road. Over 30,000 miners passed through Yale on their way to the rich Cariboo gold fields in the late 1850s. The Yale museum located downtown in a historic old home is the best place to relive the past of this frontier town.

Just beyond Yale is the first of the tunnels that allow passage through the rock-walled canyon ahead. The tunnels along this route were named for nearby camps on the Fraser used by the miners during the gold rush period. Here the true character of the canyon is revealed—cliffs dropping sheer into the churning brown river lined by high peaks on both sides. A pullout to the right beside the beginning of the first tunnel allows for a good view of the river below and possibly native fishermen working on the far bank.

In the next section care is required due to the winding nature of the highway and numerous dark and narrow tunnels. Only pull off the road where there are signs indicating viewpoints as there are no shoulders wide enough anywhere in the deepest portions of the canyon. From here to Boston Bar the highway has almost nonstop river views although you might be too focused on the road to be able to see them. Not far past Yale is the Saddle Rock Tunnel, named after Saddle Rock, an important native fishing site on the river. At 35.5 kilometers (21.3 miles) the Sailor Bar Tunnel is located, named after a mining camp on the Fraser.

The blink-and-you-miss-it town of Spuzzum is quickly passed at 41 kilometers (24.6 miles) on the right. Spuzzum has a reputation in BC as being in the middle of nowhere, although in reality, given the vast distances in the province, it's really not that remote, being only three hours from Vancouver.

At 43 kilometers (25.6 miles) the large Alexandria Bridge is reached where the highway crosses the Fraser to the east side for the remainder of the drive. The bridge itself affords good views both up and down the river.

Immediately after the bridge the Anderson River Road, a wide logging road, cuts back steeply to the right. This road leads to some of the most spectacular mountains in BC in about 25 kilometers of backroad driving best suited to four-wheel-drive vehicles. Once past the major logging camp at about 16 kilometers (9.6 miles), stay left at the major fork just after the major bridge over the Anderson River and curve around into the north Anderson River for a few more kilometers to an excellent viewpoint for the Steinbok Group, a series of dramatic granite spires. This drive can be done July to September but only travel here on the weekends as the road can have heavy logging-truck traffic. Call Cattermole Timber for an update on the road and detailed directions (see Appendix).

Just past the bridge is Alexandria Bridge Provincial Park, an exceptionally pleasant campsite along the banks of the Fraser. Here, the old Alexandria Bridge across the Fraser (now a footbridge) allows for thrilling views of the river surging below.

In the stretch north of the park, look west (left) and see a logging road etched high into the mountainsides across the river. Despite its improbable location, the road is used to haul timber out of the side valleys off the Fraser. As more accessible timber is cut over time, logging companies are forced to work harder and harder to find valuable wood.

At 51.5 kilometers (31 miles) the twin tunnels of Hell's Gate and Fairabee are reached, separated by only a few feet. Past the tunnels, Hell's Gate, the most infamous section of the canyon, is easily spotted in the distance up ahead, marked by the red tram station perched above the gorge. Be sure to stop here and take the tram down into the rocky depths of the canyon to see firsthand the narrowest and more harrowing spot for those trying to navigate downriver. Located at the bottom terminal is a series of interpretive displays, a restaurant, and a gift shop. The Fraser runs swifty through here in a 100-foot-wide, rock-walled gorge. During peak flows, almost a billion liters of water pass through here per minute.

In Simon Fraser's journey down the river that now bears his name, this was his most frightening stretch. He was helped by a series of ladders and wooden scaffolding erected along the canyon walls by natives. Simon Fraser University, named after the explorer, has a series of large paintings in its halls to commemorate this historic passage through Hell's Gate. During the construction of the CPR in 1913, a massive rock slide here almost severed the river and blocked access upstream for millions of migrating salmon. As a result, a series of fish ladders now allow the salmon to bypass Hell's Gate. Although many think of this event as one of BC's worst environmental disasters, the Fraser is still the largest salmon-producing river in the world.

Past Hell's Gate, the highway traverses high above the river and the views are magnificent up and down the canyon in this next section. At 55 kilometers (33 miles) the China Bar Tunnel is encountered, almost a full kilometer (0.6 mile) long. It's always a memorable experience to meet an oncoming rig in one of these narrow tunnels! The tunnels are not lit so headlights are a must and caution is required as this highway is infamous for its nasty accidents.

The small logging town of Boston Bar appears a few minutes after the tunnel. Narrow and sprawling, Boston Bar is a classic resource town, pure function, little style. If you want to experience trucker-sized meals, this is the place to do it. Boston Bar is the gateway to the Nahatlach River, popular with all sorts of outdoor recreationalists, especially whitewater rafters who enjoy the almost continuous rapids on this wild and fast mountain river. The Nahatlach is reached by crossing the major bridge over the Fraser behind town and heading north on the west side road for about 20 kilometers (12 miles) to the signed turnoff for the valley. The road leads past the three Nahatlach Lakes and is laced with numerous popular Forest Service campsites. The road can be rough but is traveled by everything from lifted four-wheel-drive trucks to Honda Civics.

From here on, you become increasingly aware that the mountain walls to the west are growing in height. As the highway travels north, it closely follows the eastern escarpment of the Coast Mountains. Although the peaks here are dry and barren for the most part, they are high enough to be pocked with snow and ice all year long.

North of Boston Bar, the highway becomes more relaxing as it travels in a straighter line toward Lytton. For the most part the highway climbs high above the Fraser with the river being less visible than was the case south of Boston Bar. Several pullouts on the left along this next stretch allow for views down to the now-hidden Fraser. By 90 kilometers (54 miles), the land has grown noticeably drier and barren-looking due to the rainshadow effect. As the highway travels north and deeper into the interior, BC's Pacific coast angles away to the northwest meaning that more and more land is put between the Fraser and the coast. Because of this, most of the storms that rake the Coast Mountains are spent by the time they reach this parched area. Lytton, just ahead, often competes with Osoyoos as Canada's hotspot in summer with temperatures often rising to over 40 degrees C (104 degrees F).

Near 100 kilometers (60 miles), the first views are gained of the Fraser/ Thompson Divide, where the prominent wedge-shaped Bothanie Mountain divides the Fraser, on the left, from the Thompson, a tributary, on the right. As you near Lytton, the peaks to the west grow higher and bolder. These peaks along the very eastern edge of the Coast Mountains are the highest in southwestern BC, with Skihist Mountain (not visible) almost reaching 10,000 feet.

Lytton, at 108 kilometers (65 miles), is a small town of 400 at an important river junction. Lytton is famous for two reasons—the "meeting of the waters" and the fact that it's promoted as the "river rafting capital of Canada." Several rafting companies based here take adventurers on thrilling rides down the turbulent stretches of both the Fraser and Thompson through rapids with sinister names like "Devil's Kitchen" and "Jaws of Death."

Turn left into downtown Lytton, following the signs for Highway 12 and Lillooet. The road drops down and passes through the rustic town before coming alongside the confluence where the green Thompson mixes with the silty brown Fraser. The Fraser River, 1,388 kilometers (833 miles) long and draining a quarter of the province, has its source just south of Mount Robson in the Rocky Mountains. The Thompson River, named after explorer David Thompson, is nearly 500 kilometers (300 miles) long and drains much of north-central BC. At the confluence, cross the one-lane metal bridge over the Thompson and proceed north on Highway 12 toward Lillooet.

From here on, the road is seemingly empty in comparison to the first stretch as the Trans Canada Highway forks at Lytton and then follows the Thompson on its way to Cache Creek and Kamloops. Within a kilometer (0.6 mile) of the bridge, two important junctions are reached. The road dropping to the left leads shortly to the reaction ferry across the Fraser, while the road to the right signed "Bothanie Valley" leads steeply uphill into a hanging valley east of the spine of Bothanie Mountain. Both are worthwhile and scenic side trips.

The reaction ferry is free as it's considered part of the provincial highway system. It crosses the river every few minutes using the current as its propulsion. The primary reason for drivers to use the ferry to is access the Stein Canyon, found several kilometers north of the crossing. The Bothanie Valley Road is a worthwhile side trip to see the colorful limestone cliffs above the Thompson, the long view back down the Fraser Canyon southward, and the chance to spot the herd of California bighorn sheep that live in the area. Although most of the far end of the road is best for four-wheel-drive vehicles, this first stretch is fine for almost any vehicle.

Traveling north on Highway 12 from here is beautiful with the high, shapely peaks to the west and the dry barren slopes of Bothanie Mountain to the east. The gash of the Stein River valley is very apparent to the west with its unmistakable V-shaped gorge. This valley, the largest untouched wilderness river valley in southwestern BC, was the source of a large environmental battle in the 1980s and 1990s. With the strong support of local natives, the entire length of the Stein from the alpine peaks in its headwaters to its lower canyon is now protected in a provincial park.

By taking the reaction ferry across the Fraser and traveling about 5 kilometers (3 miles) north, the trail access for the Stein Canyon is reached. The Stein Valley Heritage Trail travels for 70 kilometers (42 miles) upriver and then over its mountainous western rim. Despite BC's wealth of scenery, this rugged trail is one of the few designated multiday backpacks in southwestern BC. The most rewarding part of the trail is the first few kilometers up the lower canyon where the turquoise Stein roars through a granite canyon of boulders and scattered ponderosa pines with Indian pictographs dotting the canyon walls. For more information on this hike, consult BC Parks (see Appendix).

Continuing on Highway 12, the route curves in and out of dry side valleys draining into the Fraser. This area, part of the hottest and driest biogeoclimatic zone in BC (the Interior Bunchgrass Zone), is extremely arid and stricken by forest fires almost every summer. Much of the sun-baked land here is within sight of snowcapped peaks that tower over 7,000 feet above. The east side of the river is noticeably drier than the west side due to increased sun exposure. Through here you will pass several ranches alongside the Fraser as well as bright green ginseng farms irrigated with water from the river.

In several stretches halfway between Lytton and Lillooet, the highway is blasted out of buff-colored cliffs and has a sheer drop into the Fraser mere feet away (with no guard rails). Hang on to the wheel tightly and slow down through these sections. Rockfall is a constant problem on Highway 12 so keep an eye out for it and avoid this section in the dark.

Just before reaching Lillooet at 170 kilometers (102 miles), the high white and grey limestone peaks of Fountain Ridge come into view to the right. It is readily apparent by now that Lillooet is set amongst giant peaks, 7,000 to 9,000 feet high, and is dwarfed by its surroundings. Where Highway 99 intersects Highway 12, turn left and cross the major bridge into Lillooet at the end of the drive.

Lillooet, population around 2,000, is also a gold-rush era town with a wealth of historic sights. The town once had a population of over 15,000 during the Cariboo gold rush in the mid to late 1800s, which made it the most populous town north of San Francisco. Lillooet is the starting point for two more scenic drives, the Carpenter Lake Road (Drive 19) and the Chilcotin Backroads (Drive 20), and the end point for the Duffey Lake Road (Drive 8), making it an important hub for a number of beautiful areas. The town itself is pleasant and clean and well worth a visit. Be sure to fill up on supplies here as it's the major center for a large stretch of empty country in all directions.

# 17

# Trans Canada Highway
## *Revelstoke to Golden*

**General description:** This 150-kilometer (90-mile) section of the Trans Canada Highway is arguably the most spectacular part of its entire length across the country. East of Revelstoke it passes through two national parks in the Selkirk Mountains and features views of whitewater rivers, deep forests, forbidding peaks, and extensive glaciers. Highlights of the drive include the optional side trip to the 6,000-foot summit of Mount Revelstoke as well as the drive through peak and glacier-lined Rogers Pass.

**Special attractions:** Excellent mountain views, glacier viewing, easy access to alpine terrain, far-ranging views and wildflowers on Mount Revelstoke, the history of Rogers Pass.

**Location:** Southeastern BC in the Selkirk Mountains between Revelstoke and Golden on Highway 1.

**Drive route numbers:** Highway 1, the Trans Canada Highway the entire distance.

**Travel season:** The highway is well maintained and easily traveled all year long. Midsummer gives the best chance to actually see the mountains and go hiking. In this interior wet belt, the weather can be miserable for much of the fall, winter, and spring. Winter snowstorms can make the Rogers Pass section difficult.

**Camping:** There are several commercial campgrounds in both Revelstoke and Golden. Mount Revelstoke National Park has no camping facilities but Glacier National Park has two excellent campsites just south of Rogers Pass.

**Services:** Revelstoke and Golden both have a full range of tourist services with nothing in between, except for Rogers Pass which has a gas station, lodge, and restaurant.

**Nearby attractions:** Upper Arrow Lake, Highway 23 along Lake Revelstoke, world-class hiking and mountaineering, heli-skiing in the surrounding mountains based out of either Revelstoke or Golden, backroads along massive Kinbasket Lake, the Rocky Mountains just east of Golden (Drive 15).

 The drive

This mountain-lined section of the Trans Canada Highway passes beneath the towering ramparts of the Selkirk Mountains and links together two communities, Revelstoke and Golden, well known for their outdoor adventure

# Drive 17: Trans Canada Highway
*Revelstoke to Golden*

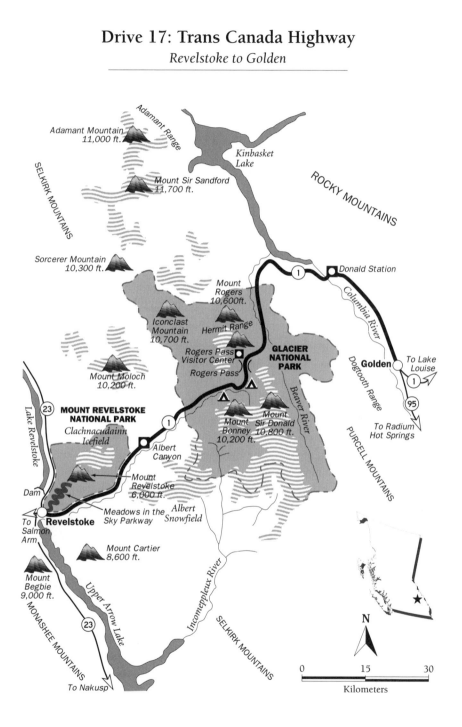

possibilities. The scenery along the way ranges from close-up views of wild-flowers to far-ranging views of rugged granite peaks buried in glacial ice. As this drive is along the Trans Canada Highway, Canada's major cross-country route, it is always busy day and night. Although most drivers rush through on their way somewhere else, the two national parks crossed are worthy of a few days stay to enjoy one of the most beautiful stretches of roadside scenery in Canada.

The drive begins in the northern part of Revelstoke where the typical services for travelers are located, such as gas, food, and lodging. Set your trip odometer here. The main part of town is reached by exiting off Highway 1 and heading south into the pleasant, tree-lined downtown. Revelstoke has an interesting mix of residents that range from heli-ski guides to loggers, all living in the shadow of the Monashee and Selkirk mountain ranges. Like many of the towns along the Trans Canada, Revelstoke was founded in the late 1800s as a railway stop on the newly completed Canadian Pacific Railway.

The town is situated between dammed Lake Revelstoke to the north and Upper Arrow Lake to the south. Revelstoke is of course closely associated with Mount Revelstoke National Park which forms its eastern skyline. Although the resource industries have been having a hard time in the last few years, the increasing interest in the town as an adventure center coupled with its situation on a major highway ensures that Revelstoke has a bright future. Skiing is big business in these parts, especially the heli-skiing

*The view looking north from Mount Revelstoke*
*to Lake Revelstoke and the northern Selkirk Range.*

which is considered to be the best in the world. Numerous high alpine lodges in the nearby mountains cater to die-hard skiers who spend thousands of dollars for the ski vacation of a lifetime.

Try to drive this route on a clear day, otherwise the mountain views will be hidden and the drive might be disappointing. Even in summer, the weather can be poor for days on end as low pressure systems collide with the massive uplift of the Interior Ranges. In winter, the snowsheds at Rogers Pass are a good indication of the immense snowfall that the area receives from November to March. In a stormy winter, up to 60 feet of snow can fall on the pass, making snow removal and avalanche control a major job.

Leaving Revelstoke, the exit off Highway 1 to Mount Revelstoke National Park is only 1 kilometer (0.6 mile) east of town. Although the "Meadows in the Sky Parkway" is an optional side trip off this drive, it is highly recommended (it is not included in the distance markers for the drive). The paved parkway climbs over 4,000 feet in 26 kilometers (16 miles) to the 6,000-foot level on Mount Revelstoke and is usually snow-free and accessible from early July to late September. The parkway is narrow and steep in spots but fine for any vehicle except RVs or those pulling trailers.

Within a kilometer (0.6 mile) of the start, a toll booth is reached. All drivers must purchase a Parks Canada pass to continue upwards. The pass can also be used in Glacier National Park if you plan to explore that area as well. Annual passes that are good in all the national parks can also be bought, a good value if you are heading to the Rockies afterwards.

Along the parkway, several viewpoints overlooking Revelstoke show how dominated it is by its mountain surroundings. In the upper stretches, alpine flowers grow in profusion right alongside the road. The most recognizable are lupine and Indian paintbrush. From the top, the views to the south and west are spectacular and take in dozens of high peaks including glaciated Mount Begbie, Revelstoke's signature peak. In few other places in BC (Crowsnest Highway, Drive 11, is one of them) is the high alpine world so easily accessible.

From the parking lot, several trails branch off to marked viewpoints. The easiest one to reach is below the parking area on the far side of the nearby subalpine lakes. Once the snow has completely melted off, a shuttle bus runs up to near the very summit of the mountain where the views open up to the north and into some truly wild country. This area is famous for its wildflower displays. Be here in mid-August for the peak bloom in most years.

In addition to the easy and paved walks to the various viewpoints, several longer wilderness trails leave the top of the road and head east toward Eva and Jade Lakes nestled below the summits of the sprawling Clachnucadainn Icefield in the heart of the park's remote backcountry. With its lakes and meadows, the park can be extremely mosquito ridden in summer so bring bug spray and try to cover up, otherwise you won't stay long enough to enjoy the views.

Central BC is home to several mountain ranges west of the Rockies: the Monashees, the Selkirks, and the Purcells, collectively known as the Columbia Mountains (also called the Interior Ranges). From the top of Mount Revelstoke you'll see a great deal of the Columbias. These ranges are separated from the Rockies by the wide Columbia River trench and although easily confused with their more famous neighbors to the east, they are in fact very different. The Columbias are much older than the Rockies and are metamorphic rather than sedimentary. The firm, granitic rock of these ranges has been sculpted by glaciers over time to create hundreds of jagged, pyramidal summits. Although harder to see from the highways, they are no less rugged or spectacular than the Rockies. Many of the peaks in the Interior Ranges are world-class challenges for experienced climbers and are known throughout the world. The towering summits seen from here and above Rogers Pass are but a tiny fraction of the scenic wonders in this vast sea of peaks.

Back on Highway 1 heading east, the section of Mount Revelstoke National Park through which the highway passes is reached at 17 kilometers (10.2 miles). As is often the case in resource-rich BC, park boundaries are conveniently drawn to exclude prime stands of timber coveted by logging companies. After passing through Mount Revelstoke National Park, a 16-kilometer (9.6-mile) gap exists between it and Glacier National Park and it's only the rugged topography that has prevented the logging from being more noticeable than it is.

Where the highway passes through the extreme southern portion of Mount Revelstoke, the steep mountainsides block views to the peaks above. The park's glaciers are more easily seen when traveling the highway in the opposite direction. Through the Mount Revelstoke part of the drive, several well-signed interpretive trails allow for an easy and relaxed introduction to the ecology of the park. The two most popular trails are the Skunk Cabbage Trail at 24 kilometers (14 miles) and the Giant Cedars Trail at 27 kilometers (16 miles). Both of these short interpretive trails lead through lush scenery more reminiscent of the wet coast than the interior.

After exiting Mount Revelstoke, the highway quickly enters Albert Canyon, named after the 10,000-foot namesake peak that remains hidden from view. The Albert Canyon hot springs resort at 36 kilometers (22 miles) is known not only for its hot springs but also as a base for outdoor adventure. River rafting on the Illecillewaet River (which means "fast water" in the native language) is especially popular here.

Now traveling through increasingly rugged country, the highway reaches the first of the numerous avalanche sheds (tunnels) that protect it from the menacing avalanche paths above. With some of the most avalanche-prone slopes in BC, avalanche control is very important here. Although highway workers use artillery to keep the snow depths from reaching dangerous levels, avalanches are unpredictable and can be triggered at the slightest provocation.

Glacier National Park, entered at 49 kilometers (29 miles), is by far the larger of the two parks. Created in 1886, it protects over 1,350 square kilometers (521 miles) of heavily glaciated landscape in the northern Selkirk Mountains. Although the highway corridor is a busy place, most of the park is remote wilderness and little visited, being too rough for easy travel or development. With the heavy snowfalls nourishing over 400 active glaciers, the park is aptly named. In few other places in BC is it possible to see more scenic mountain country from the comfort and security of a vehicle. The weather in Rogers Pass is often stormy so if you pass through on a clear day be thankful and try to stay long enough to take in the views. Alongside the highway runs the swift Illecillewaet River whose source is the Illecillewaet Glacier.

The two designated campgrounds in the park, Loop Brook and Illecillewaet (by far the bigger of the two), are found just before Rogers Pass about 14 kilometers (8.4 miles) and 17 kilometers (10.2 miles) respectively past the park entrance. Before bending to the north and climbing steeply, the highway has dead-on views of mighty Mount Sir Donald, an imposing 10,800-foot wedge of granite that is rated by climbers as one of the classic mountaineering challenges in North America. The mountain is typical of the horn-shaped peaks in the Selkirks, having been sculpted over time by glaciers wearing at its flanks.

When the Canadian Pacific Railway was pushed through Rogers Pass in 1885, mountaineers from all over the world began to climb these fierce peaks, often in the company of Swiss mountain guides who found the mountains here every bit as challenging as the European Alps. Not long after the railway was finished, a posh mountain hotel named Glacier House was built to capitalize on the ever increasing interest in the scenery as well as the new and thrilling sport of mountaineering. Indeed, the Rogers Pass area is thought of as the birthplace of Canadian mountaineering.

After turning a prominent corner, the highway climbs steadily to 4,500-foot Rogers Pass at 70 kilometers (42 miles) where a prominent arch marks its site. Stop here to take in the views of the Illecillewaet Glacier, also known as the "Great Glacier," to the east as well as the numerous other peaks that all compete for attention on the jagged skyline. With binoculars the numerous crevasses on the tongue of the glacier are easily spotted. Only the snout of the Illecillewaet Glacier can be seen, with the majority of it forming a high plateau of ice, ringed by peaks that soar out of the glacier's gentle surface. Like glaciers all over the world, it has been retreating steadily for decades and someday may not even be visible from the highway.

The Rogers Pass area has numerous trails that steeply head up through the forest and onto the alpine slopes below the glaciers. Despite the fact that most of the trails are strenuous (but short), they provide superlative views not seen from the highway. The visitors center is the best place for information

*The towering summit of Mount Sir Donald as seen from the Trans Canada Highway on the approach to Rogers Pass.*

on the pass's trails, the best of which include Avalanche Crest, Abbott Ridge, and Balu Pass.

Although a deep snowpack covers the park for over seven months a year and makes for poor wildlife habitat, several species of wildlife call the park home including grizzly bears, mountain goats, and a particularly rare breed of mountain caribou. Many of the trails in the park travel through prime bear habitat (Balu Pass is named after the Indian word for bear) and are often posted with warning signs. Proper precautions, such as making lots of noise and carrying pepper spray, are needed if hiking on the trails.

The Rogers Pass visitor center, a kilometer (0.6 mile) beyond the pass, is a must-see for its gorgeous interior, interpretive displays, and well stocked bookstore and gift shop. The center, built to resemble the snow sheds that line the highway, focuses on both the natural history of the park as well as the interesting human history, in particular the building of the railway through here. Located beside it is a gas station, small store, and a luxurious hotel, the Glacier Park Lodge. Other than camping, this lodge is the only place to stay in the park (see Appendix for phone number). Framing the skyline to the north is the Hermit Range, home to numerous summits over 10,000 feet high. The steep Hermit Trail, which starts a few hundred meters north the visitors center, allows hikers and climbers to access this compact group of peaks.

Rogers Pass, one of the only easy places to cross the Selkirks, was discovered in 1882, with the Canadian Pacific Railway soon following. Before much of the railway is located far underground in tunnels free from the dangers of avalanches, the railway was subjected to "white death" on a regular basis. From 1885 to 1916, avalanches killed 250 people, with the worst incident occurring in 1910 when a catastrophic slide buried and killed 63 people. The visitors center has a moving display about this tragedy. Despite the existence of the railway, it wasn't until 1962 that the Trans Canada Highway was finally completed through this challenging hunk of mountain country.

As beautiful as the scenery is in summer, the winter vistas of the surrounding peaks buried under a heavy blanket of snow are even more spectacular. Despite the high avalanche hazard, Glacier is well-used by adventurous backcountry skiers who strike out for the high meadows and glaciers. In short, winter travelers trade the danger of prowling grizzlies in the summer months for the equally terrifying threat of avalanches.

Beyond Rogers Pass, the highway descends into the wide Beaver River valley and passes between towering Mount Tupper and Mount Macdonald before entering a series of snow sheds. These two peaks, almost mirror images of one another, are majestic sights, composed of massive faces of near vertical rock. As the highway curves north, the views grow to include the back side of the Hermit Range as well as the striking northwest ridge of Mount Sir Donald, an even more dramatic view of the peak than from the Illecillewaet River.

The park is left behind at 87 kilometers (52 miles) as the highway travels north before curving back to the east and into the Columbia River trench at the junction of the Selkirk and Purcell mountain ranges. This is also the start of Mountain Time Zone so be sure set your watch ahead an hour. Before bending back south, the Trans Canada passes the southern-most reaches of huge Kinbasket Lake which divides the Selkirks from the Rockies. The Kinbasket Lake Road (a logging road) turns off the highway right where it bends south and then runs along the western rim of lake to give adventurers access to some exceptionally rugged landscapes. The Ada-mant Range, just north of Glacier National Park, has several of BC's most awesome peaks, including the apex of the Selkirk Range, mighty 11,700-foot Mount Sir Sandford.

Donald Station, at 123 kilometers (74 miles), is situated at the first place where the railway crossed the mighty Columbia River in the late 1800s. Through here, the leading western edge of the Rocky Mountains tower on the horizon to the east as the highway heads south toward Golden which is reached at 149 kilometers (89 miles). For more information on Golden and the continuation of Highway 1 to Lake Louise in the Rockies, see Drive 15.

# 18

# Mount Robson Provincial Park

## *Tete Jaune Cache, BC to Jasper, Alberta*

**General description:** The main focal point for this 100-kilometer (60-mile) scenic drive is Mount Robson, the highest peak in the Rocky Mountains. Known as the "Monarch of the Rockies," Mount Robson is an outstanding sight from the Yellowhead Highway which passes beneath its towering south face. Past Mount Robson, the scenery includes the headwaters of the Fraser River and numerous other jagged summits. The drive ends in Jasper, Alberta, a hub of a great number of beautiful drives, especially the unmatched Icefields Parkway (Drive 14).

**Special attractions:** Mount Robson, Moose Lake, the Fraser River, the resort town of Jasper, wildlife sightings.

**Location:** Mount Robson Provincial Park, east of Valemount and west of Jasper, Alberta.

**Drive route numbers:** Highway 16, the Yellowhead Highway the entire way.

**Travel season:** Any time of year. The Yellowhead Highway is well-maintained as a major west-east route through Western Canada. The weather tends to be best both midsummer and midwinter. In the winter months the snow-covered views are beautiful but many of the facilities and services are closed then.

**Camping:** Commercial camping in Valemount and park camping in both Mount Robson and Jasper Parks. The two campgrounds just before the Mount Robson visitors center are the best camping spots on the drive.

**Services:** Valemount, just south of Tete Jaune Cache on Highway 5, has full tourist services. There are no services between there and Jasper.

**Nearby attractions:** Heli-skiing, heli-hiking, and sightseeing flights over Mount Robson from Valemount; the hike to Kinney Lake, the Valley of a Thousand Falls, and Berg Lake, all reached from the Berg Lake Trail on Mount Robson, Jasper National Park; and the Icefields Parkway (Drive 14).

 The drive

Threading below the mightiest summit in the Rockies, the Yellowhead Highway (Highway 16) from Tete Jaune Cache to Jasper is one of the highlights of driving anywhere in BC. Who has driven beneath the south face of Robson and not stared wide-eyed at its sheer height and bulk? While the highlight of the drive comes in the beginning near Mount Robson, there's still a lot to see

# Drive 18: Mount Robson Provincial Park

*Tete Jaune Cache, BC to Jasper, Alberta*

To McBride

ROCKY MOUNTAINS

ALBERTA

B.C.

Fraser River

16

Mumm
Glacier

Berg
Lake

Mount
Robson
13,048 ft.

Whitehorn
Mountain
11,200 ft.

Valley of a Thousand Falls

Kinney Lake

Robson
Glacier

Resplendant
Mountain
11,300 ft.

Visitor center

Tete Jaune
Cache

MOUNT ROBSON
PROVINCIAL
PARK

Rearguard
Falls

Overlander
Falls

RAINBOW RANGE

CARIBOO MOUNTAINS

Mount
Terry Fox

Moose
Lake

Mount Sir
Wilfred Laurier
11,600 ft.

Valemount

Moose
Marsh

SELWYN RANGE

5

To Clearwater

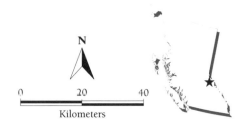

N

0        20       40
Kilometers

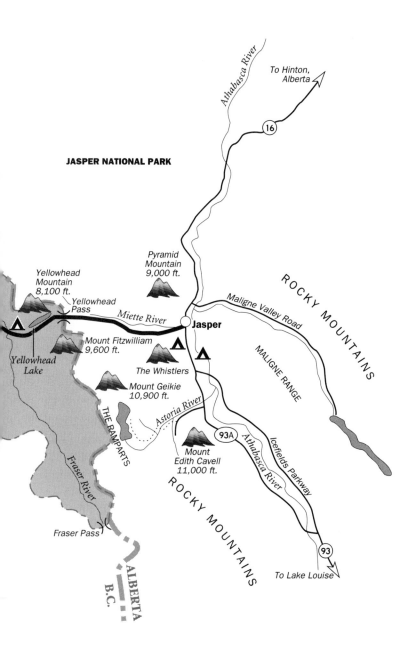

**JASPER NATIONAL PARK**

Athabasca River

To Hinton, Alberta

16

Pyramid Mountain 9,000 ft.

Yellowhead Mountain 8,100 ft.

Yellowhead Pass

ROCKY MOUNTAINS

Maligne Valley Road

Miette River

**Jasper**

Yellowhead Lake

Mount Fitzwilliam 9,600 ft.

MALIGNE RANGE

The Whistlers

Mount Geikie 10,900 ft.

Astoria River

THE RAMPARTS

93A

Athabasca River

Icefields Parkway

Fraser River

Mount Edith Cavell 11,000 ft.

ROCKY MOUNTAINS

Fraser Pass

93

To Lake Louise

ALBERTA

B.C.

beyond it. The problem is that after seeing the stupendous bulk of Mount Robson, the second highest peak in BC, few other sights compare.

Mount Robson, 13,048 feet high, is truly worthy of all the superlatives lavished upon it. Local Indians refer to the peak as "Mountain of the Spiral Road." From any angle it positively dominates the surrounding landscape for a great distance. So prominent is Robson that it's easily seen from the summits of peaks over a hundred miles away. This drive is a grand entrance to the Rockies and leads to Jasper from where the incomparable Icefields Parkway can be driven south to Lake Louise through the core of the Rockies to complete an unforgettable loop trip through the best scenery of the entire range.

Set your trip odometer at Tete Jaune Cache at the junction of Highways 5 and 16. Most people reach Mount Robson from the south by passing through Kamloops and then taking Highway 5 for 340 kilometers (204 miles) north through the Thompson River valley to Valemount, the closest town and supply center for the Mount Robson area. If you make your way to Robson via this route, be sure to take the 100-kilometer (60-mile) round-trip drive to Helmcken Falls in Wells Grey Provincial Park to see one of the world's most captivating waterfalls. To reach the falls, turn off at Clearwater on Highway 5 and follow the signs north into Wells Grey. From the north, Mount Robson is approached via Prince George on the Yellowhead Highway which runs along the Fraser River past the eastern edge of the high and remote Cariboo mountain range.

Tete Jaune Cache was the site of an old railway camp in the early part of the century. Little remains today of the once thriving town of 3,000 and drivers are none too keen to explore the area with much-anticipated Robson views only a few kilometers ahead. Once on Highway 16, the first real point of interest, besides the ever-present Fraser River, is Rearguard Falls at 3 kilometers (1.8 miles). This 30-foot waterfall is the last barrier to salmon migrating up the Fraser, the largest salmon-producing river in the world. The falls are a short walk from the parking lot just off the highway.

Beyond the falls the highway climbs, and if it's a clear day, Mount Robson soon is sighted towering above the surrounding mountains. Even those who pass by here regularly cannot fail to be impressed by Robson's majestic presence. At 7.5 kilometers (4.5 miles) is the Mount Terry Fox rest area, below the peak named for the revered one-legged runner who died while attempting to run across Canada to raise money for cancer research.

Driving east, Mount Robson slowly reveals itself as the highway approaches the base of the mountain. By now the nearly 10,000-foot south face of Robson—the greatest vertical relief of any peak in the Rockies—is fully in view and it appears as if the highway is heading straight into the mountain. To put the view into perspective, the base-to-summit elevation of Robson as seen from here is almost as great as that of Mount Everest.

Many a calendar and postcard shot has been taken here of the Yellowhead Highway gracefully arcing toward Robson.

Much of the time the summit of Robson is lost in the clouds, the mountain being so high that it creates its own weather. The best photographs of the peak are taken near sunset when the last rays of light highlight the south and west faces and reveal colors hidden in the harsh light of midday. Mount Robson Provincial Park is entered at 14 kilometers (8.4 miles). Just before the visitors center, you pass two campgrounds, Robson Meadows (on the left with 125 sites) and Robson Creek (on the right with 19 sites). These two popular campgrounds are often booked up for long stretches at a time, a problem common to all Rocky Mountain campgrounds. Some of the sites can be reserved but most are available on a first-come, first-served basis.

The Robson visitor center is an excellent stop not only for the interpretive displays but also for the best view of Robson along the entire highway. The interesting and informative visitors center is the place to ask questions, book campgrounds, and look at all the displays about the mountain. For those not able to go hiking, a video shows many of the scenic highlights of the park, including Berg Lake, the most popular backpacking objective in the Rocky Mountains.

The 50-kilometer (30-mile) round-trip trek to Berg Lake on the north side of Mount Robson takes in so many powerful sights that it is a justifiably popular trip. Just a few of the highlights are Kinney Lake, a turquoise gem reached after about 4 easy kilometers (2.4 miles); the Valley of a Thousand Falls, the highest concentration of major waterfalls in Canada; mighty Emperor Falls; and finally Berg Lake itself, positioned directly beneath Robson's incredibly sheer 7,500-foot-high north face. Berg Lake is one of the finest spots in the Rockies and is named after the icebergs that float around its emerald green surface.

Mount Robson is a major climbing objective and a coveted prize for mountaineers from around the world. Unlike many peaks, Robson has no easy route to its summit and in some years repulses all climbers who come to master it. From 1939 to 1953, Robson defeated every attempt to climb it. At the minimum, the climb of Robson takes up four full days and many take up to a week to reach the top. Mount Robson was climbed for the first time in 1913 by Conrad Kain, an alpine guide from Austria who became known as one of Canada's great climbers in the first half of the century. So awed was Kain upon his fist visit to Robson that he remarked, "God made the mountains, but good God! who made Robson?" Although Robson looks dry and barren from the south, the northern aspect seen by climbers and hikers is very different and much more dramatic. A great amphitheater of ice pours off the summit to feed the Robson Glacier, a spectacular sight every bit as awesome as the scenery in the high peaks of Alaska or the Yukon.

*The nearly 10,000-foot southwest face of Mount Robson
seen at sunrise from the Mount Robson Visitors Center.*

Actually, before 13,200-foot Mount Waddington in the Coast Mountains was discovered in 1925, Mount Robson was considered the highest mountain in the province. Some controversy still exists as to which is the highest peak in BC. Mount Fairweather, right on the BC/Alaskan border, climbs to more than 15,500 feet but is only half in BC.

Beyond the visitors center, the views of Robson are quickly left behind to be replaced by mountains that would be considered grand elsewhere, but after viewing Robson, seem small and insignificant in comparison. Overlander Falls parking area is reached at 17.8 kilometers (10.7 miles). The falls are an easy 15-minute round-trip walk.

By now the highway is running alongside the muddy Fraser River not far from its headwaters deep in the mountains just to the southeast. The Fraser Valley is one of the wettest in the Rockies and is positively lush in comparison to the rest of the range. As is always the case, the rainshadow effect means that passing clouds are torn open as they hit the leading edge of the Rockies, leaving little for the drier eastern areas near Jasper.

The mountain views along here are mostly to the south (right) of the Selwyn Range with the occasional big peak spotted up the side valleys. Turquoise-colored Moose Lake, the largest in the park, is encountered at 25 kilometers (15 miles), with the highway running along its shores for several kilometers. At the end of the lake is a boat ramp where canoes can be launched for a scenic paddle on the placid waters. Beyond the lake, the highway passes through an extensive marsh-filled wetland, popular with moose. Signs through this stretch warn of moose on the highway so slow down, particularly at night. Through here the mountain views begin to get more exciting again as the road approaches Yellowhead Pass, the climax of the highway.

At 57 kilometers (34 miles) is the first view of the shapely Mount Fitzwilliam which stands alone and dominates much of the remainder of the drive. Just a few kilometers beyond, the road crosses the Fraser to the south side and the views switch over to the mountain wall to the north. In a few more kilometers, the highway crosses the Fraser at the point where it turns inland and away from the highway. The actual source of the Fraser River, BC's longest at 1,388 kilometers (833 miles), is Fraser Pass on the BC/Alberta border. The source is less than 30 kilometers (18 miles) away but deep in the mountains and little visited.

Yellowhead Lake, just ahead, is the next attraction passed by the highway. This narrow lake is set below glorious Yellowhead Peak, a long multi-peaked ridge of colorful rock that has a faint resemblance to the Valley of the Ten Peaks near Lake Louise (without the glaciers). Alongside the lake is the Lucerne campground (32 sites) and a boat launch. Once past the lake, the mountain views temporarily disappear as the highway passes through closed-in forests.

*Indian paintbrush beside the highway in Mount Robson Provincial Park.*

The Yellowhead Highway is a heavily used transportation corridor across BC from Prince Rupert to Jasper. Much of the traffic speeds along, more intent on getting somewhere else fast than in experiencing the scenery. Highways dissect all of the mountain parks and create an obstruction to animals on their traditional migratory routes. Every year, animals are tragically killed, often at night, while trying to cross the highways. Unlike Banff National Park with its wildlife underpasses, no such structures exist here to safeguard the park's wildlife with the result that dead animals are occasionally seen on the side of the highway, an unfortunate result of the battle between development and preservation. A new conservation initiative called Y2Y (Yellowstone to Yukon) is attempting to reduce the impediments to wildlife migration throughout the Rockies by planning wildlife-friendly development and lessening the hazards of preexisting barriers like the Yellowhead Highway.

Yellowhead Pass, 3,700 feet high, is reached at 77 kilometers (46 miles) on the eastern boundary of Mount Robson Provincial Park and at the entrance point to both Jasper National Park and Alberta. This gentle pass, used for centuries as a travel corridor, is the lowest of the major passes through the Rockies. Be sure that your watch is set to Mountain Time, an hour ahead of most of BC. From here the highway descends into the Miette River valley. Toll booths are reached just inside the boundary of Jasper National Park. Anyone stopping in the national parks is required to buy a park pass. As of 1999, the rate was $5 per day for 2 people in a vehicle. Annual passes can be bought for those staying over a week or for those who plan to visit other national parks on their trip.

Driving east, the valley opens up and the vistas expand to include the Athabasca River valley running north-south through the heart of Rockies and the barren-looking Maligne Range, the backdrop to the Jasper townsite. The drive ends at 102 kilometers (61 miles) where Highway 16 intersects with Highway 93, the Icefields Parkway. To the left, Jasper is reached within a kilometer (0.6 mile), while to the right is the beginning of the northern end of the Icefields Parkway (Drive 14).

It's well worth spending a day wandering the streets of Jasper and soaking in the mountain ambiance with the other tourists from around the world. Be sure to stop in at the historic Jasper National Park Visitors Center in the center of town if you need information, want to book campsites, or would like to talk to a park ranger.

# Cariboo/Chilcotin

## *19*

# Carpenter Lake Road
## *Lillooet to Bralorne*

**General description:** Starting in Lillooet, this challenging 110-kilometer (66-mile) drive travels west through a variety of breathtaking scenery from the arid canyons near Lillooet, through the Bridge River Gorge, along turquoise Carpenter Lake, and finally ends deep in the Coast Mountains at the historic settlements of Gold Bridge and Bralorne. Those with a fear of heights might want to avoid this drive as over half of it is on gravel roads, often perched mere feet from sheer edges.

**Special attractions:** Exhilarating driving, a gateway to outdoor adventure, excellent desert-like scenery, a herd of California bighorn sheep, the Bridge River canyon, turquoise Carpenter Lake, the Coast Mountains, the historic buildings in both Gold Bridge and Bralorne, and the chance to drive a loop trip via the Hurley River Road.

**Location:** Due north of Pemberton on the southern edge of the Chilcotin.

**Drive route numbers:** Highway 40, the Carpenter Lake Road.

**Travel season:** Late spring to early fall only. The road is often rough in the spring until the maintenance crews have time to work on it. In winter, the route is open but can be hazardous due to snow and ice.

**Camping:** Most of the camping is at numerous BC Forest Service campsites along the way. Look for the signs or see the *BC Recreational Atlas* (new edition to be retitled *The BC Road and Recreational Atlas*) for all of the locations. There is one BC Hydro campsite along the shores of Carpenter Lake.

**Services:** None between Lillooet and Gold Bridge. Only very limited supplies and services at Gold Bridge and Bralorne—gas (limited hours), lodging, basic food store, and two restaurants.

**Nearby attractions:** Boating on Carpenter Lake, the side trip over Mission Pass to Seton Portage, the Southern Chilcotin Mountains, heli-skiing and heli-hiking, floatplane-based fishing, endless hiking and climbing possibilities, and Tyax Lodge.

 # The drive

The beginning of this adventurous drive is in downtown Lillooet at the Visitor Infocenter, a great place to ask about the condition of the road before you head off. Lillooet is reached by taking either of two scenic drives, the Duffey Lake Road (Drive 8) or Fraser Canyon (Drive 16). For a really complete cross section of scenery, be sure to take the Sea to Sky Highway (Drive 7), Duffey Lake Road, this drive, and then continue back to Pemberton via the mountain-lined Hurley River Road (described at the end of this drive). This loop journey is an excellent introduction to the wide variety of rugged landscapes in southwestern BC.

Few roads in BC pack as much scenery into a such a short drive as the Carpenter Lake Road. In its distance it travels through a variety of stunning landscapes and has almost non-stop views of natural spectacles along the way. The province is slowly paving the road but it will be several more years before the whole project is completed. Caution is required along almost the entire length of this drive as the road travels near precipitous slopes with no guard rails. Additionally, much of the road is tight, twisty, and barely two lanes wide so take extra care on the corners and be sure to stay in your lane at all times. Despite being just north of the mega-resort of Whistler, the area traveled through feels almost as remote as any in the province. It's too far away from the weekend getaway crowd to attract much traffic.

Lillooet is a historic place in a gorgeous setting. On all sides, high, jagged peaks up to 9,400 feet envelop the town. Situated in a dry bowl alongside the Fraser River, the area is in BC's driest zone and has the province's highest ever recorded temperature, a searing 44 degrees C (112 degrees F). Lillooet dates back to the Cariboo gold rush in 1848, with the population then being almost nine times greater then than it is now.

Lillooet, population about 2,000, caters mainly to tourists and the resource industries which still dominate the local economy. Although Lillooet has the potential to be another outdoor mecca like Whistler or Squamish, the fact that it is at least a four hour drive from Vancouver has largely prevented it from being more popular with the adventure crowd. The planned Cayoosh ski resort, just west on the Duffey Lake Road, may provide the needed spark for change away from dependence on traditional resource industries to a more sustainable future.

Be sure to stock up on anything you need before leaving Lillooet as there is only limited gas and food available in Gold Bridge. Follow the main road north from the visitors center for 1.4 kilometers (0.8 mile) to where you reach a major intersection. Turn left here onto Moha Road at the signs for Gold Bridge and begin to curve north toward the Bridge River valley. Along here, the road traverses above the Fraser and passes scattered industrial

# Drive 19:Carpenter Lake Road
*Lillooet to Bralorne*

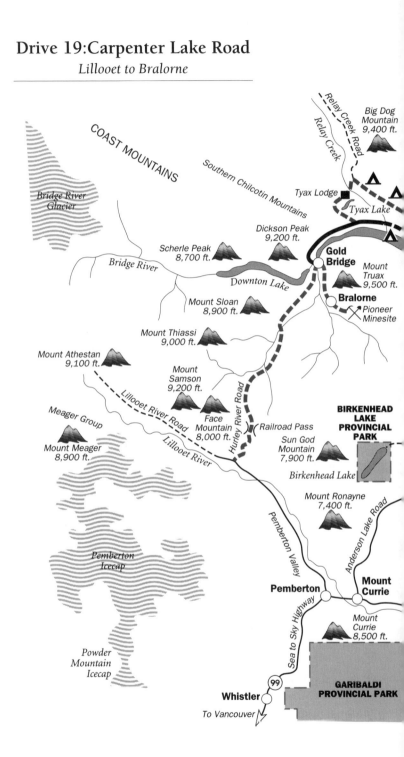

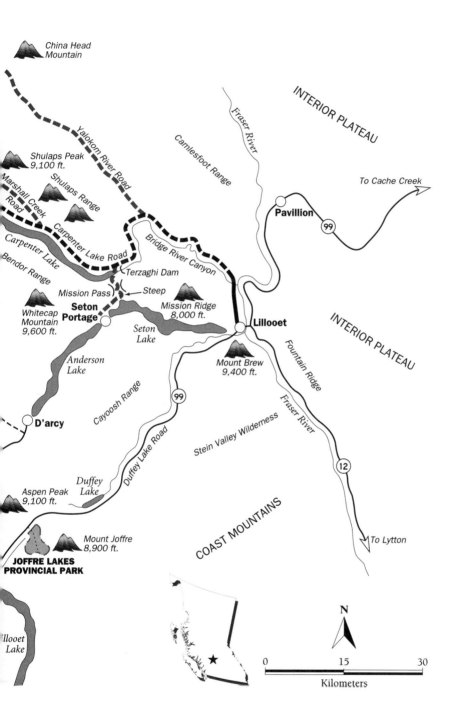

China Head
Mountain

INTERIOR PLATEAU

Fraser River

Yalokom River Road

Camlesfoot Range

To Cache Creek

Shulaps Peak
9,100 ft.

Shulaps Range

Marshall Creek
Road

Carpenter Lake Road

Bridge River Canyon

Pavillion

99

Carpenter Lake

Bendor Range

Terzaghi Dam

Mission Pass

Steep

Mission Ridge
8,000 ft.

INTERIOR PLATEAU

Seton
Portage

Whitecap
Mountain
9,600 ft.

Seton
Lake

Lillooet

Anderson
Lake

Mount Brew
9,400 ft.

Fountain Ridge

Cayoosh Range

99

Fraser River

D'arcy

Duffey Lake Road

Stein Valley Wilderness

12

Duffey
Lake

Aspen Peak
9,100 ft.

Mount Joffre
8,900 ft.

To Lytton

JOFFRE LAKES
PROVINCIAL PARK

COAST MOUNTAINS

lllooet
Lake

N

0          15          30

Kilometers

development. After rising steeply, the road soon reaches the crossing of the Bridge River and a great view into the Bridge River rapids on the Fraser. These rapids are considered the most challenging on the whole length of the Fraser, and as such are closed to commercial rafting.

After crossing the river, the road turns northwest and begins a slow and steady climb up to the Bridge River canyon rim. Through here, the road follows the course of the old Moha Indian trail. Although you wouldn't know it from looking into the dry river gorge below, the Bridge River has its source in one of the biggest icefields in the entire Coast Range far to the west of Gold Bridge. Throughout this high stretch, panoramic views both up and down the length of the river and back toward Lillooet are constantly within sight. At 15 kilometers (9 miles) the pavement ends and the road turns to gravel for most of the remaining distance to Gold Bridge.

Although a designated highway, the maintenance of the road is variable, so expect anything from a relaxing drive on a freshly graded road to a grueling endurance test of potholes and washboard. The condition of the road depends on the severity of the past winter as well as the fluctuating highway budget. Call the Ministry of Highways to inquire about its condition (see Appendix). Any vehicle (except RVs and trailers) can make this journey but make no mistake, this is the Chilcotin, a place where trucks are the norm and everyone is used to the rough roads.

In the next stretch, the road traverses a steep mountainside with the Bridge River over a thousand feet below, deeply entrenched in a rock-walled chasm. Several pullouts along here give an opportunity to stop and gaze into the canyon and its rapid-filled river far below. For those with a fear of heights, this part may be unnerving as the road is narrow and there is a yawning void to the left for many kilometers. At 30 kilometers (18 miles) is a prominent corner of the Bridge River where the best views of the river gorge along the whole drive are seen. The dry scenery here is impressive with open, sun-baked scree slopes on the right and eroded, sandcastle-like formations above the river to the left. California bighorn sheep are commonly spotted through here as they graze alongside the road.

Just beyond the corner, the signed Yalokom River Road branches off to the right, the start of a beautiful but sometimes challenging backroad that traverses along the very eastern edge of the Coast Mountains. In its distance it runs through extensive dry meadowlands and beneath colorful, desert-like peaks before reaching its end near the 70-kilometer (42-mile) mark below the slopes of China Head Mountain. For serious backroad travelers in BC, this area has achieved legendary status due to its wealth of old mining roads that climb high into the alpine for sweeping views of the Southern Chilcotin Mountains.

From the junction of the Yalokom and Carpenter Lake Roads, the views take in several compact mountain clusters. To the south rises Mission Ridge, the 8,000-foot mountain spine that rises from Lillooet's doorstep, while to the west is the dry and remote Shulaps Range which is the last significant range of peaks in the Coast Mountains before the Fraser Plateau. These peaks are high (up to 9,400 feet) but barren and open to hikers long before the snowier areas to the west. To the north, but largely unseen, is the Camelsfoot Range, a high elevation area of forested peaks laced with cattle trails bordering the Fraser.

Almost immediately beyond the junction the road drops sharply to the Bridge River in several tight and narrow switchbacks. The scenery through this section is exciting with high peaks framing the skyline on all sides. Once at the bottom, the road curves into the Bridge River canyon and the most spectacular portion of the drive. Although many roads run through so-called canyons, this is the real thing.

For the next 10 kilometers (6 miles), the road is etched into cliffs that often overhang the road by ten feet or more. So sheltered is the road that even in the middle of a hot summer day, the sun rarely reaches the canyon floor, making for a much cooler micro-climate. Protected from the area's scorching temperatures, the canyon floor is lush and green and unlike anything encountered on the drive so far. Although this short section is paved, the road is broken up due to rockfall and must be driven cautiously. Across the river, colorful cliffs rise in sheer walls 2,000 to 3,000 feet high and form the base of peaks several thousand feet higher. Near 44 kilometers (26 miles), look across the river to a prominent corner in the cliffs (about halfway up the major rock wall) and see a spectacular waterfall billowing out from a tight crack.

The twisty portion of the canyon is left behind just before the Terzaghi Dam and the beginning of Carpenter Lake at 49 kilometers (29.4 miles). This is also the turnoff point for the drive to Mission Pass and the outback community of Seton Portage, nestled between the ramparts of the Bendor and Cayoosh Ranges. The road climbs 2,600 feet from the dam to Mission Pass and then drops 4,000 feet down the other side in a series of steep switchbacks and intimidating corners to Seton Portage which lies on a narrow strip of land between Seton and Anderson Lakes. It is a 40-kilometer (24-mile) round trip from the Terzaghi Dam to Seton Portage and back—plan on three hours minimum for this exciting side trip. There are two Forest Service campgrounds near the dam along the Mission Pass Road.

Carpenter Lake is manmade despite its natural look. The construction of the Terzaghi Dam (named after its chief engineer) in 1958 backed up the Bridge River into a long and narrow lake that filled the valley floor for a great distance. The distinctive turquoise color of the lake is due to suspended sentiment from the many glacier-fed creeks that drain into the Bridge River system. The large elevation differentials between the Bridge River valley and Seton Lake to the south were the impetus for the damming of the

*A view of the Carpenter Lake Road where it emerges from the confines of the Bridge River canyon. Carpenter Lake is reached within minutes of here.*

Bridge River. Water from the lake flows steeply downhill through a tunnel and powers a hydroelectric generating system at Shalath on the shores of Seton Lake.

The first few kilometers along the lake heading west to Gold Bridge are the most intimidating of the entire drive along the lake's 53-kilometer- (31.8-mile-) long shoreline. For several kilometers the road is rough, narrow, and features numerous tight corners where caution is required. Carpenter Lake is always about 100 feet below the road with a sheer drop from the road's edge into the lake.

The scenery from here on is dominated by the lake and its steep-sided backdrop of green forests crowned by snowy summits. Although some logging has occurred here, much of the original forests remain. The sharp peaks that line the lake to the south are part of the Bendor Range which is almost unknown even to the most hard-core mountaineers in the province. One of the tallest summits in southwestern BC, Whitecap Mountain, 9,600 feet high, lies unseen just to the south of here. Other soaring peaks in the range that are visible from the road include Mount Williams and Mount Bobb, both over 9,000 feet high.

At 67.7 kilometers (40.6 miles) is the BC Hydro Bighorn Creek campground, one of the few places where Carpenter Lake is actually accessible. Just past the campground is the turnoff to the Marshall Creek Road to the right. This backroad travels away from the lake and eventually meets up with the Relay Creek Road just north of Tyax Lodge and along the way passes four Forest Service campgrounds. Marshall Creek Falls, a little past the turnoff, spills over a rocky lip and forms a scenic waterfall beside the road.

Driving in this section, the head of Carpenter Lake is soon revealed, as are several of the high summits that anchor its western end. The most notable is pyramidal Dickson Peak, 9,200 feet high, which dominates the view for much of the remaining drive. By now, the lake is wider and the driving much more relaxing than before. Pavement is reached at 83 kilometers (50 miles), much to the delight of drivers who endured the rough gravel to this point.

At 94 kilometers (56 miles), a prominent junction is reached. By turning right and uphill here, Tyax Lodge is reached in 9 kilometers (5.4 miles), located on Tyax Lake near the edge of the Southern Chilcotin Mountains. One of the premier wilderness resorts in BC, Tyax also has the claim to fame of being the biggest log structure on the West Coast. Rather than endure the long five hour drive from Vancouver to the resort, many of its guests choose to fly in via the floatplane docked in front of the resort. Sightseeing flights can be arranged here to fly over the massive glaciers to the west or to be transported to remote lakes for an afternoon of fly fishing. In winter, Tyax is a base for snowmobiling and heli-skiing adventures in the surrounding mountains.

The Relay Creek Road beyond Tyax is one of the main entry points into the Southern Chilcotin Mountains, a series of gentle and colorful peaks in the rainshadow of the Coast Mountains to the west. These mountains are laced with old mining roads that are used by mountain bikers, horse packers, and hikers to access this unique wilderness area. The Forest Service office in Lillooet publishes an excellent map of the area's multitude of trails (see Appendix).

Continuing west on the main road, the end of Carpenter Lake and its grassy estuary is soon reached. Through this section, the shapely spire of 8,900-foot Mount Sloan rises to the southwest. At 104 kilometers (62.4 miles) a key junction is reached. Turn left here at the sign pointing to Gold Bridge and cross over the Bridge River.

The Bridge River area hosted several boom-and-bust gold rushes in the 1800s before finally being established as the site of a successful mine between 1928 and 1948. Gold Bridge, home to about 70 hardy people, is a historic place dating back to a mining boom in the 1930s. Back then it was in competition with Bralorne, just up the road, to be the main supply center for the area. Gold Bridge was built by the miners themselves who found the restrictive and morally-correct rules of Bralorne (no gambling, prostitutes, or alcohol) not to their liking. At present, the town features several businesses, namely a hotel, restaurant, and gas station.

Be sure to continue up the steep (but mostly paved) road for 7 kilometers (4.2 miles) to Bralorne. Along this route, the road climbs over 1,000 feet and has breathtaking views of the mountain panorama to the west in addition to vertigo-inducing views straight down into the Hurley River canyon. In Bralorne, a small hotel and restaurant mark the center of town. The 60 or so residents are drawn here by the wilderness setting and some of BC's cheapest real estate prices. Although not far north of Whistler, Bralorne is a world apart and seems much more remote and isolated than it really is. Behind the town rust-colored peaks loom skyward, a sure indicator of mineralization that must have attracted the first prospectors to the area.

Several kilometers beyond Bralorne is the old mining settlement of Brandian with its rows of abandoned bunkhouses in a picturesque meadow setting. By continuing just past the ghost town on the same road, the decaying Pioneer Mine site is reached a few minutes later where the road dead-ends. Be extremely careful prowling around the old mine as several of the buildings have collapsed in the past few years and there is much hazardous junk lying everywhere. From the mine, the rocky peaks in the Cadwallader Range are visible to the south.

Another short and scenic drive in the area is to Gun Lake which lies just to the west of Gold Bridge. Find the turnoff just south of town on the Hurley River Road. This cabin-lined lake has awesome views of Mount Sloan's forbidding north face to the south and is a popular fishing spot.

*The remains of the Pioneer Mine, found just beyond Bralorne.*

Once you have retraced the route back to the main junction at Gold Bridge, you have the option of going back to Lillooet the way you came or heading south over the Hurley River Road. The Hurley is a highly recommended route back to Pemberton and Vancouver from here. Although it can be rough, it has none of the hair-raising and exposed sections found along the Bridge River canyon or Carpenter Lake. The main hazards are the logging trucks which occasionally use the road and the steep 3,500-foot descent into the Pemberton Valley from Railroad Pass. Call the Ministry of Forests in Squamish to inquire about the condition of the road and the logging activity taking place in the vicinity (see Appendix for phone number).

Overall the road is wide, well-marked, and traveled. It is about 80 kilometers (48 miles) back to Pemberton from Gold Bridge via the Hurley. From there you can connect with the Sea to Sky Highway (Drive 7) south to Vancouver. Keep in mind that the road doesn't open up until June in most years due to deep snow in Railroad Pass. As you travel south on the Hurley, mountain walls rise on both sides of the road. Due to logging the views are almost always good and culminate in the approach to Railroad Pass. Here a series of rugged, glaciated summits tower directly above the road—a breathtaking sight on a clear day. From the 4,400-foot-high point at Railroad Pass, the view of the massive Pemberton Icecap is eye-opening, as is the view down into the narrow Pemberton Valley. The road in the last section is steep (but wide) but is passable to most vehicles. Once at the bottom, turn left and hit pavement within ten minutes on the way to Pemberton.

If you choose to return to Lillooet the way you came, be extra cautious on the way back as you will be driving in the outside, exposed lane. Now traveling east toward Lillooet along Carpenter Lake, the views change to include several mountain ranges that were invisible on the way in to Gold Bridge.

# 20

# Chilcotin Backroads

## *Lillooet to Williams Lake via the High Bar Road*

**General description:** Threading its way through the deepest wilderness left in the entire length of the Fraser River, Chilcotin Backroads is a spectacular introduction to the near-desert landscapes of the eastern Chilcotin and is one of the classic drives in BC. If the optional route down the High Bar Road is included, this 240-kilometer (144-mile) journey is easily the most thrilling in this book. Despite being close to Vancouver (in relative terms), you'll meet more cowboys, miners, and Indians than tourists. This drive description is far more complicated than others so having the *BC Recreational Atlas* (new edition to be retitled *The BC Road and Recreational Atlas*) or another detailed map is a big help as the whole area is laced with backroads.

**Special attractions:** Solitude in the most beautiful sections of the Fraser River, a true sense of accomplishment; arid, near-desert landscapes; excellent weather; adventurous driving; and a shortcut to the Chilcotin and Highway 20 (Drive 21).

**Location:** Along the Fraser River between Lillooet and Williams Lake in south-central BC.

**Drive route numbers:** Highway 99 from Lillooet to Pavillion and then on gravel Forest Service backroads. Most of the roads are well-signed at the junctions.

**Travel season:** Late spring to midfall. For the High Bar Road option, come only in midsummer when the roads are dry.

**Camping:** The only designated camping is at Kelly Lake Provincial Park on the northern side of Pavillion Mountain or at Big Bar Lake northeast of Jesmond. Along the High Bar Road there are several places to camp on Crown land.

**Services:** None between Lillooet and the end of the drive in Williams Lake. See the book's introduction for details on essential equipment for safe backroading.

**Nearby attractions:** Numerous guest ranches in the area, the Southern Chilcotin Mountains that can be accessed by four-wheel-drive vehicles west of the High Bar Ferry, two newly created provincial parks, and the historic Gang Ranch on the opposite side of the Fraser.

# Drive 20: Chilcotin Backroads
*Lillooet to Williams Lake via the High Bar Road*

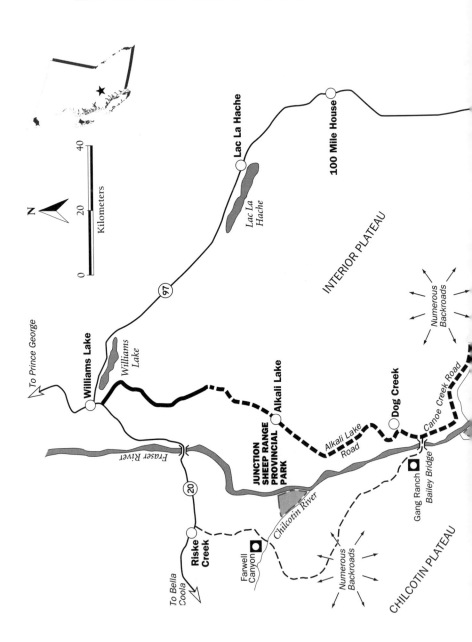

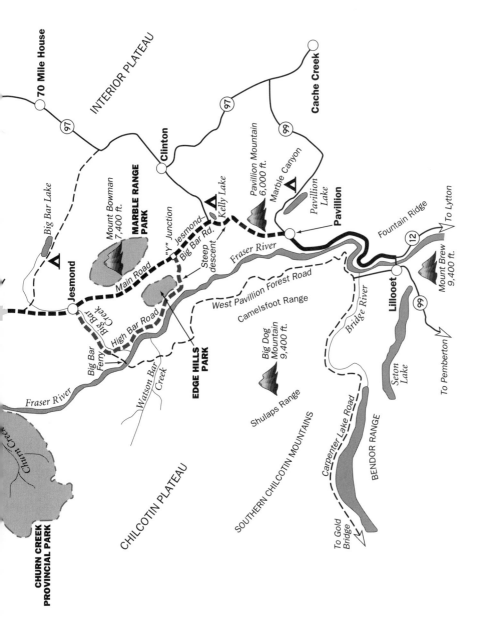

70 Mile House

INTERIOR PLATEAU

97

Clinton

97

99

Cache Creek

Big Bar Lake

Mount Bowman
7,400 ft.

MARBLE RANGE
PARK

Pavillion Mountain
6,000 ft.

Marble Canyon

Pavillion
Lake

Pavillion

"Y" Junction

Jesmond-
Big Bar Rd.

Kelly Lake

Jesmond

Main Road

Steep
descent

Fraser River

To Lytton

Fountain Ridge

12

Big Bar Creek

High Bar Road

West Pavillion Forest Road

Camelsfoot Range

Mount Brew
9,400 ft.

Big Bar Ferry

Lillooet

99

Watson Bar
Creek

EDGE HILLS
PARK

Big Dog
Mountain
9,400 ft.

Shulaps Range

Bridge River

To Pemberton

Fraser River

Seton
Lake

Churn Creek

CHILCOTIN PLATEAU

SOUTHERN CHILCOTIN MOUNTAINS

Carpenter Lake Road

BENDOR RANGE

CHURN CREEK
PROVINCIAL PARK

To Gold
Bridge

191

 # The drive

Although not marked on official highway maps, the road network that makes up this drive through the eastern Chilcotin is a feasible route for adventurous drivers on one of the most memorable backroad networks in the whole province. The drive begins in Lillooet and ends in Williams Lake at which point you can head back south on Highway 97 or continue your Chilcotin adventure on Highway 20 (Drive 21) to Bella Coola. Be sure to fill up in Lillooet as there is no gas along the drive until Williams Lake is reached. The entire drive is approximately 240 kilometers (144 miles), most of which is on gravel backroads. During the drive description, there are two intersections where trip odometers should be reset to zero to follow the route as described.

The start of the drive begins at the bridge across the Fraser River on the eastern outskirts of Lillooet at the junction of Highways 99 and 12. Lillooet, set in a wide, mountain-rimmed valley beside the Fraser, is mile zero on the old Cariboo Wagon Road, which part of this drive follows. Set your trip odometer here and turn left on Highway 99, the northernmost extension of the Sea to Sky Highway. The quickest way to reach this point from Vancouver is up the Fraser River on Highway 1 to Lytton and then Highway 12 to Lillooet (Drive 16). A more scenic and varied (but longer) approach is via Highway 99 to Pemberton (Drive 7) and over the mountainous Duffey Lake Road to Lillooet (Drive 8).

Once heading north out of Lillooet, Highway 99 quickly starts climbing and soon gains panoramic views of dry limestone peaks, the Fraser River canyon and the town of Lillooet which is dwarfed by its surroundings. Fountain Ridge to the east is particularly striking in the late afternoon as the low-angled light highlights its buff-colored cliffs. In this first stretch, the highway curves around a big bend in the Fraser. Just before the highway doubles back, the gash of the Bridge River valley, the setting for the Carpenter Lake Road (Drive 19), can be seen far off to the northwest. On the opposite side of the Fraser, the West Pavillion Forest Service Road is seen switchbacking up a dry hillside. This road is the western side of a loop trip that could be completed from Lillooet back to Lillooet through the Fraser Canyon using the Big Bar ferry to cross the river (described later).

At 11.5 kilometers (6.9 miles), there is a fantastic view of the muddy Fraser being compressed through a narrow gorge of brown rock. Beyond here, the highway contours around a side canyon and has several tight corners before emerging and climbing once again to a terrace high above the river. At this point, the signed Fountain Valley Road takes off to the right. This backroad climbs steeply, accesses several ranches, and then descends to rejoin the Fraser on Highway 12, just south of Lillooet.

Just before the highway turns inland and away from the Fraser, look north toward where the drive will soon be traveling. For most drivers, this is their last glimpse of the river, but for those embarking on this drive, the best views of the Fraser are yet to come.

Pavillion, reached at 33 kilometers (19.8 miles), is hard to miss with its old buildings and prominent church. Just before the village is the oldest operating general store in the province, dating back to 1862. Turn left here and cross Pavillion Creek into the tiny native community. For a scenic side trip to this journey, travel east for about 20 minutes on Highway 99 to Marble Canyon and its 3,000-foot limestone walls that have become a popular climbing challenge. Pavillion Lake Provincial Park (located under the cliffs) is the best place to camp if you want to tackle the challenging parts of the drive in the morning.

Pavillion is the start of the exciting part of the drive. Although not the fastest way to Williams Lake, this route is one of the most scenic, adventurous, and historic backroad drives in the province. For the rest of the drive these roads twist and turn through dry canyons and sagebrush flats with the dark gorge of the Fraser almost constantly within sight. Even though the area is relatively close to Vancouver, it seems nearly as remote as BC's far north. Built and maintained to serve the few ranches and Indian settlements, these roads are quiet and little traveled. From here on, the route is on gravel roads, more suitable for trucks and four-wheel-drive vehicles than cars, although if the High Bar Road bypass is taken, its fine for almost any vehicle (except RVs of course).

*The soaring cliffs of Marble Canyon, a short distance east of Pavillion on Highway 99.*

This drive is more complicated than any other in this book so having the *BC Recreational Atlas* (new edition to be retitled *The BC Road and Recreational Atlas*) is a big aid in locating the various backroads. Refer to page 15, grid coordinates A-2 for the start of the drive. From here you can see the road running north over Pavillion Mountain and the prominent junction for the High Bar Road at A-1.3. The rest of the drive is on page 26.

Reset your odometer to zero at Pavillion (for those meeting this route description from the east), quickly pass through the settlement, and begin to climb steeply on the Pavillion Mountain Road which can be seen etched in the hillside behind the village. Although narrow, this road is in good condition and quickly gains excellent views southward. This portion is on the original Cariboo Road used to access the Cariboo gold rush in the late 1800s. In only 2 kilometers (1.2 miles), the tight switchbacks end and the road eases off and climbs out of the trees.

For the next several kilometers, the views of the Fraser to the east and the Coast Range to the south are breathtaking. Even in late summer, snowfields on the high peaks above Lillooet glisten in the distance. The open grassy slopes here are known for their flower display with Indian paintbrush being the most colorful and abundant. The road crests over 6,000-foot Pavillion Mountain and leaves the views behind just before passing through the gates of the Diamond S Ranch. In the next stretch, the road lazily traverses Pavillion Mountain through pleasant meadowlands. At 16.5 kilometers (9.9 miles) a T-junction is reached—stay left here.

Just past the junction, the road switchbacks down 2,000 feet on the north side of Pavillion Mountain through deep forest. In dry weather, this is no problem for standard cars but when wet, extra caution is required as the grades are steep and the corners tight. If you found this descent difficult, don't even think about taking the optional route down the High Bar Road ahead as it's *much* more exposed and challenging. Nearing the bottom of the switchbacks, Kelly Lake is visible ahead through the trees. Once at the valley floor, turn right at the intersection at 20.3 kilometers (12.2 miles) and proceed along the lake, a popular fishing spot for Clinton residents.

At 23 kilometers (13.8 miles) is a major intersection. Turn left here to proceed north on the Jesmond–Big Bar Road. Staying straight ahead on the paved road leads in about ten minutes to Clinton. If you are in need of gas or supplies, head to town to stock up and then backtrack to this point to continue the drive. For those wanting to avoid Pavillion Mountain or who are coming from the east, the drive can be accessed here via Highway 97 and Clinton. If coming that way, follow the signs for Downing Provincial Park (25 sites), located at Kelley Lake.

At the intersection is a ferry information sign, indicating whether or not the Big Bar ferry across the Fraser is operating. During peak flows on the river (usually late-spring to early summer), the ferry is almost always closed for several weeks.

Initially, the road is wide, well-traveled, and allows for near highway speeds. Passing though deep forest, there isn't much to see until the High Bar Road junction at 33.8 kilometers (20.3 miles). This junction is easily missed so slow down after about 30 kilometers and watch for the signed junction and fork in the road.

At the Y-junction, the High Bar Road forks to the left while the main road continues to the right. If you want to skip the High Bar Road with its exceptionally steep grades and sharp corners, stay straight and rejoin the route at Jesmond, located where the Big Bar ferry road turns off the main road to the left. Drivers traveling the High Bar Road also join the main route at Jesmond after seeing the High Bar ferry.

On the main road, the drive to Jesmond (a single ranch) is on a wide, easy road that passes beneath the new Marble Range Provincial Park which can be seen framing the eastern (right) skyline in a series of curious white peaks up to 7,400 feet high.

The High Bar Road is easily one of the wildest, most exciting back-roads in BC. The road drops in just a few kilometers from the 5,000-foot-high plateau at the junction to just over 1,000 feet in the depths of the Fraser Canyon. If you've got the right vehicle (four-wheel-drive only), back-road experience, and little fear of heights, driving this stretch of road is the most thrilling experience in the entire book. Be sure only to drive here when it's bone dry—if it's raining or threatening to rain, skip this drive as the road quickly turns slippery at the slightest hint of water. When you get to the top of the switchbacks decide if you want to attempt the descent. If not, turn around and head back to the junction and take the easier main road.

To tackle the High Bar Road, turn left at the signed Y-Junction. At first, the road drops steadily and narrowly through deep forest with little hint at what's to come. Six kilometers (3.6 miles) past the junction, the road suddenly curves a corner and the Fraser River is seen for the first time since south of Pavillion. The view is a heart-stopper; it's like looking into the Grand Canyon in Arizona. Park here and soak in the incredible scenery. From here to the river, the road is literally breathtaking, dropping over 3,500 feet in less than 5 kilometers (3 miles). A sign at the corner before the steep grades warns of the 23-percent grades ahead. Those highway signs on other roads that warn of 6-percent grades will lose all meaning after this descent!

This section of the road is maintained, although minimally, and is only one lane wide in most spots so pray that no one is coming up as you descend (unlikely to happen, but you never know). In several sections near the top, the crumbling cliffs to the left combined with the narrowness and steepness of the road make for a white knuckle experience. All the way down, your eyes will be riveted to the huge drop, mere feet away. Although forested, the mountainside has enough open spots to see the river far below as well as the consequences of going off the road. On several of the corners, pullouts exist where you can park and walk to the edge to admire the scenery, something you can't do while driving. These pullouts are also good places to let your brakes cool if you have been riding them on the descent. Once you start down, turning around will be very difficult but might be possible on a few of the corners if you're careful.

Near the bottom, you will see a ranch on a terrace above the river. Unlikely as it seems, the whole reason for the road seems to be to access this lonely ranch. At 44.5 kilometers (26.7 miles) the bottom of the switchbacks is reached where the road passes several historic barns that add a touch of human history to this vast land of sagebrush, canyons, and mountains. The peace and quiet here is refreshing, with the only noise coming from songbirds and the rustling of the wind.

From here, look back up the mountainside you just descended and wonder how you made it down. The road isn't even visible from this vantage point and the slope looks so steep that it would be hard to climb on foot.

The panorama of dry scenery here is unmatched in the province. Other than the road and a few buildings, the High Bar Road passes though an almost untouched landscape in the most remote sections of the Fraser River. Although BC for the most part is wet and lush, this area does one of the best impersonations of true desert in the whole province. The new Edge

*Driving along a bench above the Fraser in the middle sections of the High Bar Road.*

Hills Provincial Park straddles the road here but as of 1999, there is no signage or facilities.

Proceeding north, the road weaves in and out of side canyons and is often within sight of the Fraser which is deeply entrenched in a rocky gorge hundreds of feet below the road. For the most part, the High Bar Road traverses sagebrush benches with the river canyon to the left and high, dry peaks on both sides. In mid-summer, this area can be furnace-like with temperatures easily reaching 35 degrees C (95 degrees F). Early morning or late after-noon is the ideal time to drive this section as not only will the pastel-hued landscapes look better in the soft, low-

*Looking down into the Fraser River canyon from along the High Bar Road.*

angled light, but the temperatures will also be more bearable.

In many places, it's possible to hike from the road either up the dry hillsides to the right or over to the canyon rim to the left. One of the best places to stop is at 47.1 kilometers (28.3 miles), where you can park and walk about a hundred feet across the flat plateau to gain an incredible view of the Fraser pulsing through a sinister black-walled canyon (see photo this page). Although the distances along the High Bar Road are not great, it is a time-consuming drive, mostly due to the incredible scenery. Along the river in this stretch, there are a few steep, intimidating grades to contend with, but nothing like the descent to the river.

The opposite side of the river is a panorama of badlands and other ero-sional features. The higher up the canyon walls, the deeper the forest. This is due to the hot and dry microclimate along the banks of the Fraser easing off with altitude gain. At 55.9 kilometers (33.5 miles), a minor junction is reached.

Turning left here leads down to the Fraser in 2 kilometers (1.2 miles) along a narrow and treacherous side road. Scattered along the Fraser there are several old cars and buildings. Once at river level, the size and power of the river is easily appreciated as it swiftly flows by on its way to the ocean.

The next few kilometers are one beautiful scene after another with the view across the river to the colorful mountain slopes being the main attraction. Just beyond, the road curves into the Big Bar Valley and drops down to cross Big Bar Creek about 65 kilometers (39 miles) from Pavillion. Turning left here leads in several steep kilometers down to the Big Bar reaction ferry on the Fraser. This is a very scenic side trip (not included in the distance markers) but if you are pressed for time, turn right and head back to the main road at Jesmond.

Like the reaction ferry at Lytton, the Big Bar ferry utilizes the power of the river currents to speed it across the river. Used mostly to access the ranches along the west side of the Fraser, it is an interesting trip to take the ferry across and explore the other side. The ferry is free and crosses on a fixed schedule during daylight hours only. By crossing here, it is possible to head back to Lillooet on the West Pavillion Forest Service road which climbs into the dry mountains high above the river and slowly works its way back south to complete a scenic loop of the Fraser.

After exploring the area around the ferry, backtrack up to the junction where you turned left, and stay straight ahead. From the junction, the Big Bar Road climbs steadily on an easy gravel road to meet the main road at Jesmond in 14 kilometers (8.4 miles). Here the route rejoins the main road.

For those who skipped the High Bar Road, heading from Jesmond down to the ferry on the Big Bar Road will allow for a glimpse of this remote area. It is even possible to head south on the High Bar Road for several kilometers and then backtrack to Jesmond. This way the hair-raising sections of the road are bypassed while still seeing some of the scenery.

At the Jesmond T-junction, turn left to proceed north, following the sign pointing to Williams Lake and Gang Ranch. Both those who took the High Bar Road and those who bypassed it should reset their trip odometers to zero at the junction. The scenery for the next 30 kilometers (18 miles) or so is dominated by gentle plateau country, pleasant but with few views. The driving here is fast and easy on this main backroad past the occasional ranch. Much of the landscape is open with large, flower-filled meadows in midsummer.

At 14.8 kilometers (8.9 miles) a junction is reached—stay straight ahead. Turning right leads to Big Bar Lake Provincial Park (15 minutes away) and eventually back to Highway 97 north of Clinton.

At 18.8 kilometers (11.3 miles), another major T-junction is reached. Stay left here and onto the Canoe Creek Road, following the signs for Williams Lake. After traversing across a gentle plateau, the road begins to gradually descend, following Canoe Creek back into dry country. By 37 kilometers

(22.5 miles), the Fraser and its parched canyon walls are again within sight. The scenery in the next stretch is similar to what was seen along the High Bar Road, giving those who missed it a chance to see some of its highlights. The landscape along this lonely section of the Fraser is a beautiful combination of heavily eroded canyonlands backed by endless forests of the Chilcotin Plateau stretching off to the west.

At 51 kilometers (30.6 miles), the Canoe Creek Road reaches an important intersection. Turning left here leads down to and across the Fraser on a wooden one-lane bailey bridge. This bridge is the gateway to the historic Gang Ranch, one of the oldest and largest in North America, and a shortcut to Highway 20 (Drive 21) via Farwell Canyon. Immediately southwest is the newly-created Churn Creek Provincial Park which protects nearly pristine Churn Creek and its rare grasslands. It is a short but rewarding side trip to cross the river here and have a look at the heavily eroded desert scenery on the west side of the Fraser. The view north up the Fraser from the bridge deck is classic and makes for an excellent picture.

Back at the intersection, turn left (or stay straight if you skipped the side trip down to the bridge). The Alkali Lake Road starts a long and steep uphill climb for about 5 kilometers (3 miles) on the approach to Dog Creek that quickly grants panoramic views back down to the Fraser. At 60 kilometers (36 miles), the road curves into a side valley and drops down to the small Indian settlement of Dog Creek. Stay left at the intersection here to continue north on the drive to Williams Lake.

At 67 kilometers (40 miles) you see one of the best views along the whole drive, highlighted by the intricately folded and eroded cliffs flanking the river. Just past here, the road turns inland and starts to traverse a large flat plateau and loses all views. Historic Alkali Lake is reached at 95 kilometers (57 miles) and is notable for its old red-roofed buildings that date back to 1861.

In the last part of the drive, the road runs straight and fast and returns to pavement on the outskirts of Williams Lake. The end of the drive is reached at 144 kilometers (86.5 miles) (240 kilometers (144 miles) total) where the Alkali Lake Road intersects Highway 20. Turn left here for Bella Coola (Drive 21) or right for Williams Lake and its services.

# 21

# Freedom Highway

## Williams Lake to Bella Coola

**General description:** Highway 20 (the Freedom Highway) is a 460-kilometer (276-mile) drive across the vast Chilcotin Plateau from the interior to the coast, passing through one of the loneliest corners of the province. Along the way, the opportunities to go on scenic side trips are virtually endless. The second half of the drive, particularly from Tweedsmuir Provincial Park west, is one breathtaking vista after another as the highway descends the legendary "Hill" and passes beneath fierce summits on the way to the ocean at Bella Coola. Much of the drive is through ranch country with a tangible outback feel to it.

**Special attractions:** The list is endless and includes the greatest concentration of high peaks in BC, unparalleled opportunities for accessible wilderness exploration, numerous tour and guide outfitter companies, a real feeling of detachment from the modern world, working ranches, the descent down the "Hill," the roadside views of mountains and glaciers in the Bella Coola Valley, potential grizzly bear sightings in Tweedsmuir Park, and the opportunity to sail back to Vancouver Island on BC Ferries and see the majestic Pacific coast of BC on one of the three Land and Sea Circle Tours listed in the book.

**Location:** West Central BC due west of Williams Lake. Highway 20 is the only major route through this vast area.

**Drive route numbers:** Highway 20 the entire drive.

**Travel season:** Spring, summer, and fall. Winters are bitterly cold and many of the services shut down along the way. The decent into the Bella Coola Valley in winter is a potentially dangerous experience.

**Camping:** Dozens of possibilities from the designated campsites in the provincial parks (few) to the opportunities to camp just about anywhere (many). Remember that most of BC is Crown land, owned by everyone, and can be used to camp on as long as you're away from the highway. The *BC Recreational Atlas* (new edition to be retitled The *BC Road and Recreational Atlas*) marks all of the basic Forest Service campsites near or just off the highway.

**Services:** Few but regularly spaced out along the drive. Be sure to fill up at every opportunity and if you're doing long side trips off the main route, carry spare gas. Drivers need to be self-sufficient out here as the population is very sparse and widely dispersed. For anything major, be sure to pick it up in Williams Lake.

**Nearby attractions:** Seemingly endless wilderness both to the north and south of the highway—Farwell Canyon, Chilko Lake, the Coast Mountains near Mount Waddington, the BC midcoast.

 # The drive

This scenic and adventurous drive begins at Williams Lake, a town of 11,000 on the border between the Chilcotin (to the west) and the Cariboo (to the east). Williams Lake is the main commercial and supply center for the scattered residents and industrial operations of a huge area. The town is a typical BC resource community, basic but functional, and is best known for its popular rodeo held every summer. Be sure to gas up here and pick up anything you'll need for your journey west. Few services or supplies are available along Highway 20 other than the absolute basics.

The prominent turnoff to Bella Coola and Highway 20 is about halfway through town. This is the last traffic light you'll see in the nearly 1,000 kilometers (600 miles) to Bella Coola and back. While most drivers reach Williams Lake via the main north-south route of Highway 97, a far more scenic and interesting way to reach the start of this drive is to take the Chilcotin Backroads drive (Drive 20).

Once on Highway 20, the first 26 kilometers (15.6 miles) pass uneventfully until the Fraser River is spotted where the large bridge crosses its muddy waters. Here the Fraser Canyon, 500 kilometers (300 miles) from its mouth, is tame in comparison to the areas just to the south, being forested right down to the banks of the river. Once over the bridge, the highway climbs sharply away from the river and onto the Chilcotin Plateau proper.

Known as the "wild west" of BC, driving the Chilcotin is like a journey back in time. Laced with historic places, spectacular vistas, and outback communities, the Chilcotin is a world to itself. Seemingly untouched by modern civilization, this area is the place to go to escape the hustle and bustle of the modern world within a day's drive of Vancouver. Although not as utterly remote as BC's extreme northern areas, the Chilcotin has plenty of lonely and isolated country off the main routes.

The highway is a study in transition from the arid, sun-baked canyons in the east to the rainforests, glaciers, and waterfalls in the west. The final reward is to reach the ocean at one of only two places north of Vancouver Island where the BC's Pacific coast is accessed by road. This is big sky country and vast in scope, so large in fact that much of the highway across the plateau still isn't paved. Along this route you will be treated to some of the best scenery that BC has to offer, with the most beautiful part coming in the later half where the western end of the Chilcotin Plateau collides with the sky-splitting peaks of the central Coast Mountains.

# Drive 21: Freedom Highway

*Williams Lake to Bella Coola*

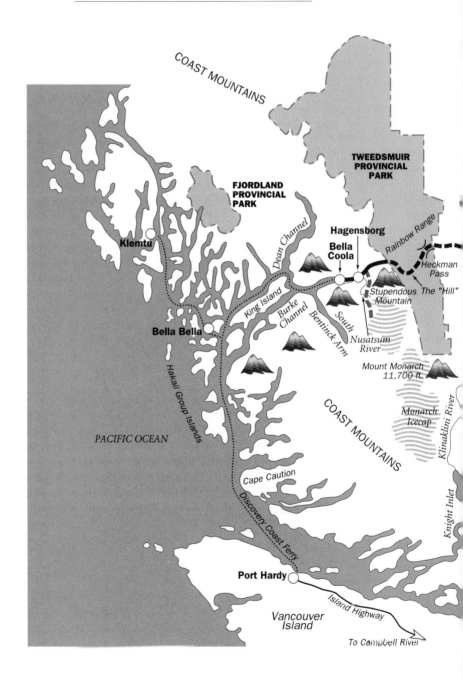

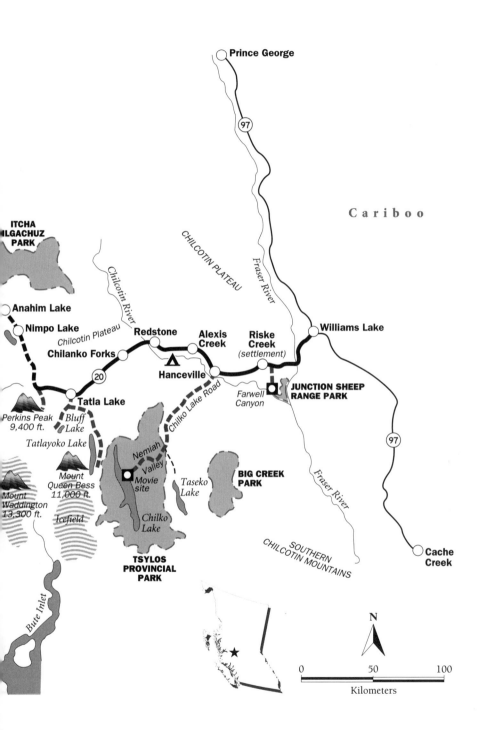

**Prince George**

(97)

C a r i b o o

**ITCHA ILGACHUZ PARK**

*Chilcotin River*

CHILCOTIN PLATEAU

*Fraser River*

**Anahim Lake**

**Nimpo Lake**

*Chilcotin Plateau* **Redstone**

**Chilanko Forks**

**Williams Lake**

**Alexis Creek**

**Riske Creek** *(settlement)*

(20)

**Hanceville**

*Farwell Canyon*

**JUNCTION SHEEP RANGE PARK**

**Tatla Lake**

*Perkins Peak 9,400 ft.*

*Bluff Lake*

*Chilko Lake Road*

*Tatlayoko Lake*

*Nemiah Valley*

**BIG CREEK PARK**

*Mount Queen Bess 11,000 ft.*

*Movie site*

*Taseko Lake*

*Fraser River*

*Mount Waddington 13,300 ft.*

*Icefield*

*Chilko Lake*

**TSYLOS PROVINCIAL PARK**

SOUTHERN CHILCOTIN MOUNTAINS

(97)

**Cache Creek**

*Bute Inlet*

N

0        50        100

Kilometers

On the drive from Williams Lake to Tatla Lake, press on through the endless forests and gentle landscapes of the plateau. Here the horizons are vast, with little to break up the skyline in the distance. Indeed in all of BC, this high plateau, averaging 4,000 or 5,000 feet in elevation, is some of the flattest land in the province. The Chilcotin is still authentic ranch and cowboy country and this initial stretch passes several large and long-operating ranches, lined by distinctive wooden fences.

There are two excellent side trips in the first half of the drive—Farwell Canyon and Chilko Lake. While the side trip to Farwell can be accomplished in a few hours, the trip to Chilko Lake will take at least a full day. Once there, the incredible beauty of Chilko might convince you to stay a few days.

The turnoff to Farwell Canyon is reached at 47.2 kilometers (28.3 miles), inconspicuously marked by a small wildlife viewing sign. The canyon is widely known for two reasons. It has the most spectacular desert scenery in BC and large numbers of California bighorn sheep. Now protected in Junction Sheep Range Provincial Park, the sheep roam in a great herd of 500 animals across the dry rolling hills of the area. The sheep have rebounded from disastrous overhunting in the early part of the century to today's healthy levels with this particular herd being used to restock other areas. Although the sheep may not be sighted, the arid, sun-baked, and grotesquely eroded Farwell Canyon is sure to deliver scenically.

The bridge over the Chilcotin River in Farwell Canyon is about 19 kilometers (11.4 miles) from Highway 20 with the road being steeply downhill for the last few kilometers. Surrounding the turquoise-hued river is a fantasyland of sand and rock pillars etched against the often deep blue sky. Nowhere else in BC does the land do such a good impersonation of the US desert southwest as right here. As an added attraction, just beyond the bridge on the banks of the river are the remains of a mining camp with several historic buildings well preserved in the dry desert air. The Chilcotin River is rated by many as one of the best whitewater rafting trips in North America.

Back on the highway traveling west, the land is consistently flat and unchanging. Hanceville, reached at 86 kilometers (51.6 miles), is a local supply point with gas and groceries as well as the turnoff for Chilko Lake and Tsylos Provincial Park. The drive to the so-called "movie site" on Chilko Lake is about 100 kilometers (60 miles) on good gravel roads. Expect to take about three hours to reach the lake. The way is not well-marked so be sure to stay on the main road and follow the signs for the Nemiah Valley and Tsylos Provincial Park. The route follows the Taseko Lake Road and then the Nemiah Valley Road to the park boundary. The *BC Recreational Atlas* (new edition to be retitled *The BC Road and Recreational Atlas*) is a big help here—consult pages 24 and 25 to see the road and the surrounding areas. Once in the native community of Nemiah Lake, the lake is just to the west. The last 2 kilometers (1.2 miles) down to the lakeshore are rough and bumpy.

*Chilko Lake from Duff Island.*

Chilko Lake, now fully protected parkland, is the largest high-elevation lake in North America, and stretches some 90 kilometers (54 miles) along the eastern spine of the Coast Range's highest peaks. The lake is a beautiful blue shade with 10,000-foot peaks lining its far western shore like a picket fence. Although the views from the campsite on the lake are magnificent enough, boating on the lake even a short distance from shore reveals the full length of the lake from the heavily glaciated peaks in the south to the desert-like peaks in the north. On a sunny, midsummer day there isn't a more beautiful place on earth. The lakeshore has excellent wilderness camping potential anywhere away from the launch point but the lake is known for its exceptionally cold, glacier-fed waters and sudden wind storms so try to stay close to the shoreline. Bears are also a hazard. Once done soaking up the scenery here, reluctantly head back to Highway 20 by retracing the same route.

Heading west on Highway 20, Alexis Creek (population 200) at 114 kilometers (68.2 miles) is the next place to stock up on gas and supplies before continuing the journey. A good place to pitch a tent for the night is Bull Canyon Provincial Park a few kilometers farther along the banks of the Chilcotin River.

Redstone, a rustic native community, is passed at 146 kilometers (87.6 miles) and is noted for its old cemetery alongside the highway. Chilanko Forks, reached at 169 kilometers (101.4 miles), has a much-needed gas station and small grocery store. Always fill up on this highway when you get the chance as there are no 24-hour gas stations along the way and you can never be sure that the next station will be open or have gas available.

The drive begins to get more scenic as the highway nears Tatla Lake at about the halfway point. In the far distance the faint outlines of giant Coast Range peaks begin to appear as if an illusion after the endless flatness of the plateau. Near Tatla Lake at 223 kilometers (134 miles), the highway travels due north of the Niut Range, a high and rugged cluster of peaks reaching 11,000 feet in places. The north faces of Whitesaddle and Razorback peaks, even from a distance, are stupendous. Tatla Lake, the local hub, has a gas station and well-stocked general store.

Just before the settlement is the well-signed turnoff to Tatlayoko Lake, a large wilderness lake nestled amongst soaring peaks. A side road leads to Bluff Lake, the local helicopter base serving both sightseers and climbers wanting to access the Waddington Range, which lies to the west of the Niut Range. So rugged are these peaks that Hollywood has used them to replicate the Himalayas and the Andes in several movies in the past few years. Mount Waddington, at 13,300 feet, is the highest peak fully in BC, and unlike Mount Robson in the Rockies, it can't be seen from any highway. The Coast Mountains have been discovered by the international climbing community who see them as a spectacular and untouched alpine playground of challenging climbs. Glaciers bury all but the tallest summits and tower sentinel-like above their surroundings. Except for a few places in Alaska and the Yukon, there are no more spectacular mountains in all of North America.

Just past Tatla Lake, the highway turns to gravel but still allows for near highway speeds, with more caution required on the corners. Beyond here, the highway slowly, almost imperceptibly, starts to climb toward Heckman Pass, the high point of the drive.

About a kilometer (0.6 mile) before One Eye Lake at 253 kilometers (152 miles), a wide gravel road takes off uphill to the left. Locate it on page 24 of the *BC Recreational Atlas*, new edition to be retitled *The BC Road and Recreational Atlas,* grid coordinates A-2.6. Occasionally this turnoff is marked with a sign pointing to Miners Lake Forest Service campsite. This seemingly insignificant road leads in 30 kilometers (18 miles) to one of the easiest places in BC to sample the high alpine world of the Coast Mountains. Built to service a small mine on the shoulder of 9,400-foot Perkins Peak, this road is easily passable to trucks and four-wheel-drive vehicles as well as many rugged cars.

Miners Lake Forest Service campsite is passed on the left about 15 kilometers (9 miles) up this road. Be wary of bears in this area as the campsite is often marked with bear warning signs. The road climbs beyond the campsite into new logging areas. Be sure to stay right on the old road at the main junction beyond the campsite. Toward the end at about 25 kilometers (15 miles), it roughens as it approaches treeline. The end of the road is located at a mine situated at the base of a high, colorful rock wall seen straight ahead.

To take in a splendid 360-degree view, walk up the switchbacks above the sometimes-working mine and be treated to a view of the endless expanse of the Chilcotin as well as a powerful view of the peaks along the eastern edge of the Coast Mountains. Just before the mine site, a side road branches left and curves around the prominent scree slope. This road is an easy walk into a beautiful alpine basin containing two lakes that mirror the surrounding mountains. Climbing the gentle arctic-like scree slopes above the lakes yields a great view of the peaks of the Niut Range to the south.

Past One Eye Lake, the highway begins to curve to the north on its way to Tweedsmuir Park, still traveling across the gentle Chilcotin Plateau. Most of the forest along the entire plateau is the spindly lodgepole pine. After years of pine beetle infestations, vast areas of these forests are dying, recognized as such by their red and black colors. An ambitious logging program is underway to try to stamp out the infected areas before the ravenous insects spread elsewhere.

Nimpo Lake, at 303 kilometers (182 miles), is known as the "floatplane capitol of BC." Numerous fly-in-only hunting, fishing, and wilderness lodges to the south on the western edge of the plateau are accessed through the busy floatplane base here. This is the land of the "guide-outfitters," the local all-knowing outdoorsmen who know the surrounding wilderness with the intimate knowledge gleaned from years of travel in this remote corner of the province. Call the Cariboo Tourism Association in Williams Lake for information on guide-outfitters in the Chilcotin (see Appendix).

Between here and Anahim Lake, the highway is paved, allowing for fast and easy travel. Just west of Nimpo Lake is the site of the Chilcotin War of 1861, a clash between Alfred Waddington (Mount Waddington) and the local native band. Waddington was attempting to build a road to Quesnel from the ocean at Bute Inlet when the natives, fearing a further smallpox outbreak and encroachment on their territorial lands, attacked the road building party, killing 18 of its workers. Government troops were dispatched and several of the natives where hung. The road never was built to the ocean and the intended route remains as wild today as it was in the 1800s.

Anahim Lake, at 317 kilometers (190.4 miles), is also an important floatplane base and is the bigger twin of Nimpo Lake with a population of just over 500. You will find all of the standard services here—food, lodging, supplies, and gas. Just beyond Anahim Lake, the road once again returns to gravel on its final approach to Tweedsmuir Provincial Park. Along this stretch of road in midsummer are splashes of color created by great swaths of Indian paintbrush, a bright red flower that graces many alpine meadows. Some of the flower displays alongside the road through here rival any wildflower meadow in the province for brilliance and extent of the bloom.

The eastern entrance of massive Tweedsmuir Provincial Park is a welcome sight at 357 kilometers (214 miles). Tweedsmuir is the largest and one of the oldest parks in the province with a vast majority of its almost one million hectares being utter and uncompromising wilderness. Roughly triangular shaped, Tweedsmuir is crossed at its narrow southern neck for just over 50 kilometers (30 miles) and encompasses the infamous "Hill," just ahead. The park covers a massive hunk of land on the boundary between the Chilcotin Plateau and the Coast Mountains, with the most rugged sections of the park being south of the highway in the area around 11,500-foot Mount Monarch. Through here, the snowy Coast Mountains are close at hand, giving drivers a preview of the scenery yet to come.

The trailhead to the volcanic Rainbow Range is reached at Heckman Pass, the 5,000-foot-high point of the highway at 363 kilometers (218 miles). A day hike up this mellow trail rewards hikers with dozens of exquisite alpine lakes and a mind-boggling view into the heart of the Coast Range to the south. The area is known as the Rainbow Range because of its colorful slopes and extinct volcanoes.

Hopefully by now you will have spotted some of the wildlife commonly seen alongside the highway. On one drive here several years ago I spotted a black bear, two moose, several deer, and over 25 mountain goats in a single day. The best times to see wildlife are near dawn and dusk when most animals are active.

At 365 kilometers (219 miles) is the beginning of the descent into the Bella Coola Valley. Several signs through this section warn of the steep 18 percent grades on the "Hill." Although work over the years has widened the road considerably, it can still be a scary initiation for those not used to tight, winding mountain roads.

This stretch of highway was actually built by the residents of valley themselves in the 1950s after giving up on the government who said it couldn't be done. Since its founding, Bella Coola was only reached by plane or boat and the residents of the valley wanted to be able to drive out to civilization. The road was completed up the Hill in 1953 after three years of work that connected the 60-kilometer (36-mile) gap between the valley and plateau roads. Highway 20 is nicknamed the Freedom Highway because the completion of this stretch of road allowed valley residents to drive to the outside world.

At 375 kilometers (225 miles), the gravel-surfaced highway reaches the very edge of the Chilcotin Plateau and starts its steep descent into the valley floor seen over 4,000 feet below. For first-time drivers of the Hill, the descent seems improbable. For the most part the way down is steep but wide enough for two vehicles to pass except in a few spots where the road narrows to barely over a lane wide. Popular stories tell of drivers who freeze up on the descent and refuse to go any farther, or other people who make it down but abandon their vehicles and fly out rather than face the Hill on their way home.

*Highway 20 at the top of the "Hill"—the steep 4,000-foot descent into the Bella Coola Valley.*

There are several wide pullouts along the way down where you can park and look over the edge to see the next switchback far below. As exciting as the drive down is on a dry, sunny summer day, just imagine what its like in winter! The bottom, and pavement, is reached at 383 kilometers (230 miles) at the turnoff to the Atnarko River and the trailhead for 1,200-foot-high Hunlen Falls, one of Canada's finest.

By now, you have reached the coastal zone and much of the time the sunny, dry weather of the plateau will have been exchanged for the grey, wet weather so common on the BC coast. If you are driving through the Bella Coola Valley on a blue-sky day, be thankful as the weather can be horrible for weeks on end.

The Atnarko River is well known as one of the easiest places in BC to see grizzly bears in the wild. In the fall months the bears are often seen fishing for salmon all along both the Atnarko and Bella Coola Rivers. The residents of the valley here are used to seeing bears; its a part of life in this remote place. Actually many residents would never think of camping as the tourists do for fear of bears, especially in the fall months.

Now that the highway is almost at sea level, the 9,000-foot peaks rising out of the valley floor seem all the more impressive. Aptly-named Stupendous Mountain is one of the signature peaks here as its rugged bulk rises to neck-stretching heights above the highway. Through this stretch, the peaks to the south (left) have an almost Disney-like quality about them. They are so steep and rugged that they appear to be the creation of some sculptor crafting the ultimate rugged mountains. The huge walls of rock that rise to the north (right) are frequented by mountain goats which can often be seen browsing beside the highway.

The headquarters for Tweedsmuir Park is passed on the left at 385 kilometers (231 miles) on the way west through grassy meadows created by old farmland. Just before exiting Tweedsmuir, the terminus of the Alexander Mackenzie Heritage Trail is seen on the right. This trail, tailor-made for modern day adventurers to follow, is a 300-kilometer (180-mile) wilderness trail that follows explorer Mackenzie's original path of 1793 across the Chilcotin Plateau to the ocean at Dean Channel, just west of Bella Coola.

Driving west through the pastoral Bella Coola Valley, the incredibly sharp spire of Nusatsum Mountain is an awesome sight as it towers almost 9,000 feet directly above the valley floor. At about 436 kilometers (262 miles), Highway 20 reaches the signed Nusatsum River Road (just before a substantial bridge over the Nusatsum River itself). This road, manageable by rugged cars, SUVs, and four-wheel-drive vehicles, leads to some of the best scenery in the entire Bella Coola Valley. It travels due south up this narrow valley for over 30 kilometers (18 miles) below heart-stopping peaks like Mount Nusatsum, Mount Saugstad, and the Matterhorn. Toward its far end, the road approaches dramatic Odegaard Falls, a great plume of whitewater gushing from a hanging valley.

*Stupendous Mountain as seen from Highway 20 near the bottom of the "Hill." The peak features well over 8,000 feet of vertical relief from the highway and is an outstanding sight*

All along this road, the peaks and glaciers are in full sight and near the end of the road the scenery is better than what's found along most trails. Emerald green avalanche slopes surround the road, giving way to great faces of rock and a multitude of glaciers. For the stretch beyond the falls a truck or four-wheel-drive vehicle is definitely required as the road steepens and grows rougher. Even by late July, the road is often blocked by avalanche snow. This is prime bear country so make a lot of noise if you are walking up the road.

Hagensborg, population 600, reached at 441 kilometers (265 miles), is considered to be the white settlement of the valley (Bella Coola is mostly native) and dates back to 1894 when Norwegians moved into the valley, attracted by the familiar mountain and fjord country. For those with the money and the inclination, the airport here has helicopters and airplanes that can be chartered to fly over the sea of peaks and glaciers that stretch away in all directions. From up in the air it becomes clear that the Bella Coola Valley is a thin ribbon of green in a world dominated by rock and ice.

While driving toward Bella Coola, slow down and take a look up each of the side valleys that intersect the highway. These V-shaped valleys all have massive summits anchoring their far ends but at highway speeds you won't see them as the valleys are passed by in a matter of seconds. The granite walls that rise on both sides of the highway are world-class and if this area was easier to reach, it would in time develop into a major rock-climbing center.

Bella Coola, finally reached at 459 kilometers (275 miles), is the thriving center of the Nuxalk Indian band. Around this compact town you will see symbols of the natives including several totems and a long house which serves as the cultural center. The Co-Op grocery store in the center of town seems also to serve as the unofficial gathering place for just about everyone. In the case of emergencies, there is also a small but modern hospital located here.

Recently the area has seen conflict between environmentalists and loggers. The forest companies are expanding their operations into what the environmentalists call the Great Bear Rainforest, the largest swath of temperate old-growth rainforest left in the world. Bella Coola is deep within a rugged coastal wilderness with most of the land in all directions being untouched. The rainforest valleys to the west will most likely become a battleground between those wanting to preserve the globally-significant forests here and the logging companies who are seeking to road and log the last of the commercially-viable forests on the coast.

Past Bella Coola, the highway continues several kilometers along the estuary of Dean Channel to the town's main harbor. This is classic west coast scenery with rustic canneries and fishing boats backed by high, snowy coastal peaks and the turquoise waters of the inlet. Dean Channel, at 70 kilometers (42 miles) long, is one of the longest fjords on BC's intricate

Pacific coast. The new Discovery Coast ferry runs from here down the inlet to the native community of Bella Bella on its way to Vancouver Island (see Land and Sea Circle Tours) and creates the potential to combine a trip down BC's Pacific coast with the Chilcotin to create an outstanding and exceptionally scenic loop trip.

Just beyond is Clayton Falls, a booming waterfall and recreation area on the shore of Dean Channel. It is reached by continuing on the gravel road along the water for another kilometer (0.6 mile). The trail to the roaring, multitiered falls is about ten minutes long and leads to an excellent viewing area. Also located at the parking area is a campground and picnic area on the shore of Dean Channel—a beautiful and relaxing place. At the mouth of Clayton Falls Creek, sea lions are commonly seen fishing for salmon and bald eagles are almost always seen drifting overhead.

Other than taking the ferry south to Vancouver Island, the only way back to the rest of BC is by retracing the route back to Williams Lake.

# North by Northwest

## 22

## Yellowhead Highway
### Smithers to Prince Rupert

**General description:** This, the western-most section of the Yellowhead Highway, is a long and varied 350-kilometer (210-mile) drive through the Coast Mountains, linking the interior with the coast. Although the drive passes through mountain-dominated landscapes the entire way, there's a lot else to see. The region has the best displays of northwest Indian culture in the whole province and the outdoor recreation possibilities are virtually unlimited. Prince Rupert, at the end of the drive, is the only access to the coast by road north of Bella Coola. The Yellowhead forms a key component of the Totem Land and Sea Circle Tour which covers a grand loop of BC by road and ferry.

**Special attractions:** Numerous distinctive peaks, northwest Indian culture, a full range of outdoor adventure possibilities, the Skeena River, distinctive north coast scenery, the Pacific coast.

**Location:** West-central BC almost due west of Prince George.

**Drive route numbers:** Highway 16, the Yellowhead Highway the entire distance.

**Travel season:** Any time of year. The drive travels from an interior-like climate near Smithers to the coastal rainforests in Prince Rupert so expect all types of weather. As is the case all over BC, most people travel here in mid-summer. Although the weather in Prince Rupert can be dismal any time of year, summer brings the best chance of sun.

**Camping:** The best camping is at Seeley Lake Provincial Park, just past New Hazelton; Kleanza Provincial Park, just east of Terrace; Exchamsisks Provincial Park, halfway between Terrace and Prince Rupert; and finally Prudhomme Provincial Park near the end of the drive.

**Services:** Other than in the towns and cities along the way, services are few and far between. Between Terrace and Prince Rupert there are no services at all.

**Nearby attractions:** Mountain wilderness in all directions; the Stewart-Cassiar Highway (Drive 23); the Great Bear Rainforest accessible by boat or plane from Kitimat; the Nass Valley and its lava beds; ferries to Vancouver Island, the Queen Charlotte Islands, and coastal Alaska.

# Drive 22: Yellowhead Highway
## Smithers to Prince Rupert

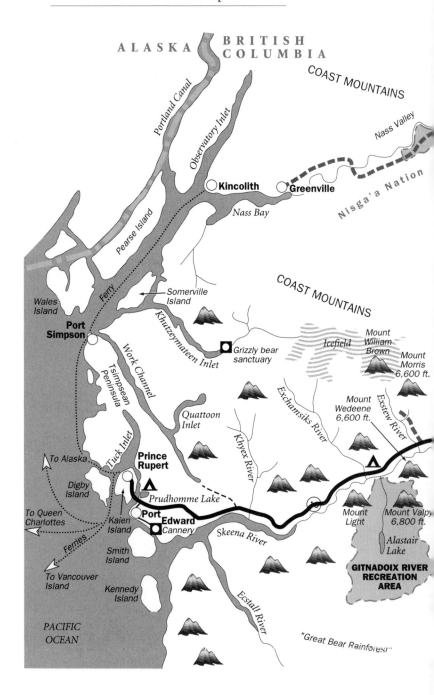

ALASKA

BRITISH COLUMBIA

COAST MOUNTAINS

Portland Canal

Nass Valley

Observatory Inlet

Kincolith

Greenville

Nass Bay

Nisga'a Nation

COAST MOUNTAINS

Pearse Island

Ferry

Somerville Island

Wales Island

Khutzeymateen Inlet

Icefield

Mount William Brown

Mount Morris 6,600 ft.

Port Simpson

Grizzly bear sanctuary

Exchamsiks River

Exstew River

Mount Wedeene 6,600 ft.

Work Channel

Tsimpsean Peninsula

Quattoon Inlet

Khyex River

To Alaska

Tuck Inlet

Prince Rupert

Digby Island

To Queen Charlottes

Kaien Island

Port Edward

Prudhomme Lake

Cannery

Skeena River

Mount Light

Mount Valpy 6,800 ft.

Alastair Lake

Ferries

Smith Island

GITNADOIX RIVER RECREATION AREA

To Vancouver Island

Kennedy Island

Ecstall River

PACIFIC OCEAN

"Great Bear Rainforest"

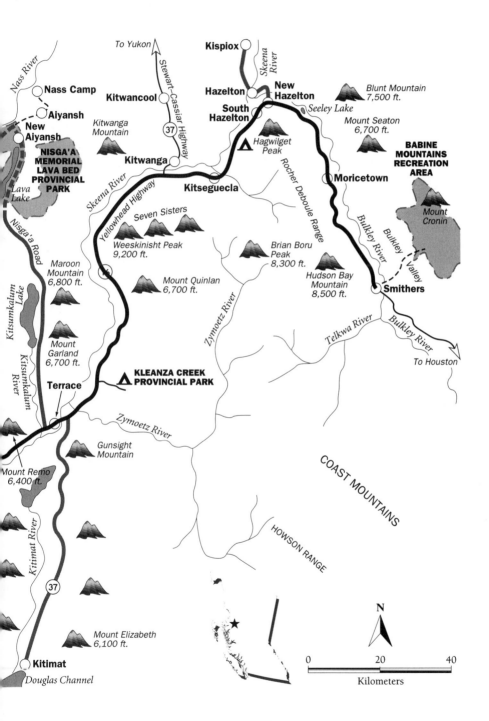

To Yukon

Kispiox

Nass River

Nass Camp

Aiyansh

New
Aiyansh

Kitwancool

Kitwanga
Mountain

Stewart–Cassiar Highway

37

Hazelton

South
Hazelton

New
Hazelton

Skeena River

Seeley Lake

Blunt Mountain
7,500 ft.

Mount Seaton
6,700 ft.

NISGA'A
MEMORIAL
LAVA BED
PROVINCIAL
PARK

Lava
Lake

Kitwanga

Hagwilget
Peak

Rocher Deboule Range

Moricetown

BABINE
MOUNTAINS
RECREATION
AREA

Mount
Cronin

Nisga'a Road

Skeena River

Yellowhead Highway

Kitseguecla

Seven Sisters

Weeskinisht Peak
9,200 ft.

Brian Boru
Peak
8,300 ft.

Hudson Bay
Mountain
8,500 ft.

Bulkley River

Bulkley Valley

Smithers

Kitsumkalum Lake

Maroon
Mountain
6,800 ft.

16

Mount Quinlan
6,700 ft.

Zymoetz River

Kitsumkalum River

Mount
Garland
6,700 ft.

Terrace

KLEANZA CREEK
PROVINCIAL PARK

Telkwa River

Bulkley River

To Houston

Zymoetz River

Gunsight
Mountain

COAST MOUNTAINS

Mount Remo
6,400 ft.

Kitimat River

37

HOWSON RANGE

Mount Elizabeth
6,100 ft.

N

Kitimat

Douglas Channel

0        20        40

Kilometers

215

 # The drive

This scenic drive follows the westernmost end of BC's 1,100-kilometer (660-mile) long section of the Yellowhead Highway from Smithers to Prince Rupert through a cross section of beautiful mountain, river, forest, and ocean scenery. In the cross-BC length of the Yellowhead, this section is by far the most rewarding both culturally and scenically. The end of the drive at Prince Rupert is only one of two places where the Pacific coast of BC can be reached in the entire stretch of mainland north of the Sunshine Coast. Not only are the views outstanding, this is one of the easiest drives in the entire book and is free of radical grades, tight corners, or treacherous sections.

The drive begins on the outskirts of Smithers where Highway 16 (the Yellowhead Highway) crosses the Bulkley River and enters town. Just past the bridge is the turnoff on the left for the Hudson Bay Mountain ski area which is about a half-hour drive up the access road. Downtown Smithers has a Bavarian theme, appropriate given its mountain backdrop. The distance markers for this drive include a detour into the small downtown area to see some of the unique architecture. Turn left at 2.8 kilometers (1.7 miles), pass through the downtown core, and then make two rights to get back to Highway 16 at 4 kilometers (2.4 miles).

Smithers was known as Aldermere when it was founded in 1900. People and supplies reached the area by steaming up the placid Skeena River to Hazelton and then packing overland to this point. The town grew rapidly with the Grand Trunk Railway (GTR) in 1913 when it was selected for the railway's headquarters. The GTR was to be the second trans-Canada railway and terminated in Prince Rupert, some 800 kilometers (480 miles) closer to the Orient than Vancouver.

Smithers is the gateway to the Coast Mountains and is nestled in the wide Bulkley Valley between the Bulkley Range to the west and the Babine Range to the east. The town is dominated by 8,500-foot Hudson Bay Mountain with its multipeaked summit and distinctive glaciers. Few places in BC have a more scenic backdrop. The Bulkley Valley at this point is wide and gentle but framed at every point on the compass by high peaks.

Smithers is a popular base for outdoor recreation with activities ranging from fishing to mountaineering. The Babine Mountains recreation area, whose reddish summits rise on the eastern skyline, is accessed from signed gravel roads branching off of Highway 16 near the town center. The Yellowhead makes a U-shaped arc from here to Terrace and between these two communities is a great concentration of seldom visited peaks in the Rocher Deboule and Howson Ranges. Several logging roads penetrate into this icy wilderness but most of it is unknown even to the local residents.

The Bulkley Valley, which the highway passes through, until the Hazeltons bears a resemblance to the Fraser Valley near Vancouver in that it is gentle and pastoral but ringed by mountain walls on both sides. The valley is much drier than any area to the west as it lies in the rainshadow of the extensive chain of the Coast Mountains. It is on the borderline between continental and maritime climates, with the day-to-day weather being influenced by both. The valley is used extensively for ranching and for agriculture so little of the original forest remains.

As the highway heads north from Smithers, even more dramatic views of Hudson Bay Mountain and its glaciers are soon reached. At 7.7 kilometers (4.6 miles) is the side road to the trailhead for Glacier Gulch and Twin Falls, both seen from a trail that climbs onto the eastern flanks of Hudson Bay Mountain. Twin Falls is easily reached but the trail to the glacier is a strenuous and difficult hike.

At 36 kilometers (21.6 miles), the Yellowhead enters the native settlement of Moricetown at the point where the wide and placid Bulkley River is pinched through a narrow rock chasm. This spot has been used by native fishermen for over 4,000 years, according to recent archaeological findings. Native fishermen are often seen here using traditional gaff hooks to catch salmon leaping through the rapids. Although the gorge can be seen from a viewing area beside the highway, the bridge just beyond leads to a closer viewpoint as well as to Moricetown itself which was named after a Christian missionary who resided here in the late 1800s.

North of here the mountains crowd in closer to the highway with the bright, highly mineralized northern Babine Range being particularly striking off to the east. The colors of the rocks were surely an attraction to early miners. The mountain views here are but a taste of what's to come later in the drive. Past 50 kilometers (30 miles), the highway starts to bend to the northwest as it curves around the northern ramparts of the Bulkley Range.

Just before New Hazelton is reached at 71 kilometers (42.6 miles), the turnoff for Ross Lake Park is passed on the right. No camping is allowed there but the lake is a popular boating spot in the shadow of the majestic Rocher Deboule Range. New Hazelton, Hazelton, and South Hazelton, all near the junction of the Skeena and Bulkley Rivers, are known collectively as the Hazeltons. Before pressing on, try to allow time to explore the fascinating aboriginal history of this area.

Although natives have lived here for hundreds of years, Hazelton (the oldest of the three) grew as a supply post at the furthest point that Skeena River steamships from the coast could make it upriver. A Hudson Bay Company trading post was established in Hazelton in 1868 to service the miners who wintered here before continuing north to the various gold rushes. New Hazelton (the biggest of the three) and South Hazelton have their roots in the Grand Trunk Railway which was built through here in 1911.

The Hazeltons are situated in the shadow of spirelike Hagwilget Peak, one of the most distinctive mountains seen from a BC highway. The sheer north face of the peak rises over 5,000 feet from its base on the gentle valley floor. The Gitxsan native peoples name for the peak means "stand alone" and it looms large in native mythology. Hagwilget is also the northernmost peak in the Rocher Deboule Range and its name means "fallen rocks" in French because it constantly plagued early settlers with rockfall.

At the main intersection in New Hazelton at 72.5 kilometers (43.5 miles), turn right at the signs for Kispiox and follow the road to Hazelton after passing over the exciting one-lane Hagwilget suspension bridge high above the Bulkley River. This is an optional but very rewarding side trip. Hazelton is reached in 8 kilometers (4.8 miles) from Highway 16. The main attraction in this native village is 'Ksan Village, an authentic reconstruction of a traditional Gitxsan settlement complete with totem poles and long houses. Also located here is the Northwestern National Exhibition Center and Museum which houses an extensive collection of displays and artifacts. In all of BC, this is one of the best places to experience northwest native culture. Kispiox, a little further north along the Skeena, has a collection of 15 totem poles, some original and some new.

Once back on Highway 16, tiny South Hazelton is passed where the route curves south and around the sheer western flanks of the orange-hued Rocher Deboule Range. On the southwestern horizon, the serrated Seven

*The top sections of the 5,000-foot north face of Hagwilget Peak as seen from the native village of Hazelton.*

Sisters peaks are seen far ahead and even from this distance positively dominate their surroundings. At 82 kilometers (49 miles) is the turnoff to Seeley Lake Provincial Park on the right which has 12 campsites complete with gorgeous mountain views. Kitseguecla Village, passed just a little further on, is a small Gitxsan community with several original totem poles.

Along here, the highway begins to run alongside the wide and placid Skeena River for the first time. The Skeena is one of the largest volume rivers in BC and one of only a handful that cut right through the barrier of the Coast Mountains from the interior to the coast. It drains a massive section of north-central BC and is known as one of the world's great salmon-producing rivers. Much of the commercial fishing fleet in Prince Rupert and southeast Alaska is based on the Skeena fishery.

The beginning of the Stewart-Cassiar Highway (Drive 23) is reached at the major intersection at 116 kilometers (69.6 miles). This long and lonely route to the Yukon slashes through the largest tracks of wilderness in BC as it passes though mountain and plateau country in the extreme northwestern corner of the province.

At 122 kilometers (73.2 miles) comes the best viewpoint for the Seven Sisters peaks, a famed massif that, more than any other, symbolizes the rugged beauty of northwestern BC. These seven peaks, all with native names, line up like a picket fence, each steep-sided and hung with glacial ice on their forbidding northern faces. What makes these peaks so impressive is that the viewing area is only a few hundred feet above sea level while the highest peak, Mount Weeskinisht, is 9,200 feet high. If you've been to Moraine Lake in Banff National Park, you will notice that these mountains bear a striking resemblance to the Valley of the Ten Peaks found there.

Once past the Seven Sisters, the highway curves around to the south and follows closely alongside the Skeena River. By looking steeply up to the left in this section, the westernmost Seven Sister and its glacier can be seen towering above the highway. From here all the way to Terrace, the Yellowhead passes through a glorious panorama of river, forest, and mountain scenery. As little logging has occurred through here, the scene looks as wild today as it would have hundreds of years ago. The mountains to the west are beginning to look more coastal with rounded, glacier-capped summits, great walls of exposed granite, and precipitous flanks that shoot straight out of the valley floor. By now the highway has also crossed the invisible line from continental to coastal; the change being witnessed in the lush forests and jungle-like undergrowth.

At 192 kilometers (115 miles), the Yellowhead passes the access road to Kleanza Creek Provincial Park, situated beside a river canyon several kilometers off the highway. This is one of the best places to camp (21 sites) along the drive, but try to arrive early as the park is popular with Terrace residents.

Terrace is reached at 204 kilometers (122 miles), located beside the Skeena in a wide bowl ringed by coastal peaks. The city, with a population of 14,000, is a vibrant, bustling place, now competing with Prince Rupert to be the commercial capital of northwestern BC. Like Smithers, Terrace and the immediate area feature dozens of possible recreational activities from mountain biking to hiking in the alpine. Be sure to follow the Highway 16 signs through downtown Terrace as the route makes a couple of turns before continuing on to Prince Rupert.

The Terrace area is well known for the population of rare kermode bears (also called spirit bears) that are occasionally seen in the surrounding valleys. These are a white subspecies of black bears that range throughout the north coast of BC. Princess Royal Island, south of Prince Rupert, is known as "Spirit Bear Island" for its population of kermode bears. In an attempt to preserve the habitat of these unique creatures, numerous major environmental organizations are battling both the forest industry and the provincial government over logging plans for the north coast.

This area is the hub of many recreational and scenic driving opportunities. Although this drive description continues along the Yellowhead to Prince Rupert, a couple of scenic side trips can be made from Terrace. The shortest is to drive south to Kitimat, situated at the head of Douglas Channel, one of the longest fjords on the BC coast. Kitimat is known for its aluminum smelter and is situated on the edge of pure coastal wilderness in all directions. Boats can be charted for fishing or sightseeing into some of the most spectacular fjord, island, and mountain scenery in the province. The area to the south is known as the Great Bear Rainforest by environmentalists for its healthy but threatened population of grizzlies. While most of the area is still untouched and totally wild, logging companies are planning to start extensive logging there. A large environmental conflict has been simmering for years and may erupt once logging begins on a large scale.

A longer and more rewarding side trip is to drive north from Terrace to the Nisga'a Memorial Lava Bed Provincial Park. The turnoff is 3 kilometers (1.8 miles) west of Terrace on Highway 16. This paved road leads through the mountain-lined Kitsumkalum River valley to the Nisga'a lava beds, the site of the most recent lava flows in Canada. The lava covers some 39 square kilometers of land and features cinder cones, lava tube caves, and other volcanic features. The lava originated in the 1775 eruption of nearby Tseax Cone which killed up to 2,000 natives living in the area at the time.

By following the main road further, the Nisga'a Nation and the Nass River are soon reached. The Nisga'a recently signed a treaty with the BC and Canadian governments to give it self-government and control over the natural resources in the entire Nass River valley. Just past the settlement of New Aiyansh, the main Nisga'a village, the road intersects the Nass with roads heading both up and downriver to other Nisga'a settlements. From

Terrace the drive to the Nisga'a area is about a 170-kilometer (102-mile) round trip and will take a full day to see.

Just west of Terrace, the Kitsumkalum Indian Reserve is passed with a few totems being seen from the highway. Signs warn of no gas or services for the 132-kilometer (79-mile) drive from here to Prince Rupert so be sure to fill up in Terrace. From this point on, the highway travels almost due west along the north side of the Skeena River through the outer Coast Mountains which rise in great leaps skyward. For many, the rest of the drive to Prince Rupert is the highlight of the trip even though the land here is rain-soaked and most often grey and gloomy. This area is as wet as any place in BC, so if you happen to drive this section on a clear sunny day, be thankful because it's rare to be able to actually see the mountains here. Even in poor weather, the scenery is still beautiful, having a hard-edged, moody feel to it. For some, the mystical north coast scenery is actually enhanced by the changing light and cloud formations of passing storms. As you drive along the Skeena, watch for the bald eagles that are commonly seen flying up and down the valley.

This outer coastal zone is characterized by jungle-like valleys being crowned by rounded granitic peaks that rise sheer from flat valley bottoms. Although most of the peaks along the river barely reach 6,000 feet, most rise right from sea level and are capped with permanent glacial ice. These mountains feature long and interconnecting ridge systems that mountaineers have recently used to do weeks-long alpine hiking traverses. Many of these peaks only received their first ascents in the past few years.

By 220 kilometers (132 miles), the Yellowhead runs within sight of the turquoise-hued Skeena River and the main views are across to the mountain walls and hanging valleys on the opposite side. Above the highway to the right, the peaks are often out of view but by pulling over and crossing the road, their lush green slopes, polished granite cliffs, and snowfields are easily seen.

At 246 kilometers (147.6 miles) is the turnoff to the optional side trip up the Exstew River valley. For those with four-wheel-drive vehicles or rugged cars, this trip is highly recommended. If you can't locate the turnoff, it's a half kilometer (0.3 mile) before the major bridge across the Exstew River. Although this road is not signed, it's easily located. It crosses the railroad tracks and heads north into a classic rainforest valley with a meandering river, extensive wetlands, and towering cliffs. The drive for the most part is gentle and easy but this changes year to year, depending upon maintenance. At the 10-kilometer (6-mile) mark, the road ends below an incredibly high and booming waterfall on the granite cliffs above—a very memorable sight. There's a large clearing here where people sometimes camp but be wary of bears should you decide to spend the night here.

Back on the highway, the twin summits of Mount Valpy and Mount Light on the opposite side of the Skeena in the remote Gitnadoix River

*A waterfall beside the Exstew River Road,*
*a beautiful side trip off the Yellowhead Highway near Terrace.*

recreation area are the two most distinctive summits along the Skeena, both having sheer, spire-like forms. Many of the stately peaks in the area sport granite walls that are among the finest on earth.

Near 260 kilometers (156 miles), the mountainsides plunge to the highway and the river is forced to weave around the base of several impressive crags. At 265 kilometers (159 miles) is the beautifully-situated Exchamsiks Provincial Park (18 campsites), nestled at the foot of a soaring cliff alongside the Exchamsiks River. Be sure to keep an eye out for the waterfalls that are easily seen on most of the mountainsides in this area.

At 298 kilometers (179 miles) is a rest area right on the banks of the Skeena that allows for the easiest access to the river on the entire drive. Not far past here, the river merges with the ocean and becomes wider, gentler, and tidally-influenced. Fishing boats are commonly seen on the river as they troll back and forth catching some of the plentiful salmon run.

Near where the highway turns inland and away from the ocean at 323 kilometers (194 miles), the forests break up and become bonsailike due to the severe outer-coastal weather. In the last section of the drive, the highway weaves though a landscape of exposed rock, stunted forests, and passes Prudhomme and Diana Lakes. Both of these small lakes are parkland and are popular for camping, fishing, swimming, and boating.

At 345 kilometers (207 miles), the highway crosses a bridge to Kaien Island on which Prince Rupert is situated. Just before the bridge, Port Edward Road turns off to the left and leads past a major pulp mill before reaching the well-groomed company town of Port Edward. A little further on is the well-preserved North Pacific Cannery Village Museum. The drive from the Highway 16 turnoff to the cannery is about 11 kilometers (6.6 miles). The cannery (open in the summer months), dating back to 1889, is the oldest remaining one in the province. The National Historic Site here protects the cannery and surrounding village which is the last of the 19 canneries that once lined the shores of the Skeena in the early part of the century.

Prince Rupert, at the end of the Yellowhead Highway at 356 kilometers (214.6 miles), is known as the "City of Rainbows" and is located on Kaien Island at the mouth of the Skeena River. It has Canada's deepest ice-free harbor and is a major link for trade to the Orient. A bustling city of 16,000, Prince Rupert is strung out along the waterfront and has numerous ocean-based attractions. The city features both BC and Alaska state ferry terminals, a large and busy commercial fishing fleet, and the Museum of Northern BC. This museum showcases the history of the Tsimshian Indians who have lived in the area for thousands of years. The numerous white shell middens and petroglyphs on the nearby islands prove that this area has always had one of the largest native populations on the entire BC coast.

The modern day discovery of the area belongs to Russians who explored and colonized southeastern Alaska in the early 1800s. Long before the founding of Prince Rupert, the nearby trading posts of Port Simpson and Port Essington served fur traders, explorers, and missionaries. Prince Rupert itself was founded when the Grand Trunk Railway built its Pacific terminus here in 1910. The town was only reached by water or air until the 1940s when the Canadian government built a road to the town to counter the Japanese invasion threat during World War II.

Once in Prince Rupert there's a lot to see and do, weather dependent of course. The tourist Infocenter at 1st and McBride in downtown is the best source for local information. Cow Bay at the north end of the city is the most picturesque section of waterfront with its well-preserved buildings, seafood restaurants, and gift shops.

Tours can be booked in the city to head out into the marine wilderness beyond. A new attraction in the area is Khutzeymateen Provincial Park, situated about 45 kilometers (27 miles) northeast of Prince Rupert in a fjord off Portland Canal. The park is one of the only designated grizzly bear reserves on earth and access to the park is strictly controlled. Up to 60 grizzlies call this small coastal valley home. Access is by boat only. For questions about the city and possible tours, call the Infocenter (see Appendix).

From Prince Rupert the options for further scenic driving are numerous. Either retrace the route back to Smithers or take the ferry down BC's spectacular Pacific coast to Vancouver Island (the Totem Land and Sea Circle Tour) or continue your coastal adventure northwards into southeast Alaska. Another option is to take the car ferry to the Queen Charlotte Islands. Although known for its beautiful seascapes and marine life, the driving opportunities on the islands are rather limited. With access to a boat however, either private or chartered, the opportunities for exploration are incredible, particularly in Gwaii Haanas National Park on the very southern tip of Moresby Island.

# 23

# Stewart-Cassiar Highway
## Meziadin Junction to Boya Lake

**General description:** The Stewart-Cassiar Highway (Highway 37) is the longest and most remote drive in the book, running nearly 500 kilometers (300 miles) through the vast wilderness of northwestern BC on its way to the Yukon. A more challenging drive than the famous Alaska Highway to the east, the Stewart-Cassiar is every bit as beautiful as it threads its way through endless forests, alongside wild rivers, and beneath the colorful Skeena and Cassiar Mountains. Long stretches of gravel and the lack of services along the way make for an adventurous drive.

**Special attractions:** Seeing deep wilderness from the security of a vehicle, excellent mountain scenery, potential wildlife sightings, the Iskut Lakes, the Stikine River, Dease Lake, the shortest route to the Yukon and Alaska from southern BC.

**Location:** The northwestern corner of BC, east of the Alaskan Panhandle.

**Drive route numbers:** Highway 37, the Stewart-Cassiar Highway, the entire distance.

**Travel season:** Late spring, summer, and early fall. Summer is pleasant but the insects are out in full force. The best time to come is late August and all of September for blazing fall color, clear skies, and a lack of bugs. In winter, the highway can be a survival test if you're unlucky enough to be here when the temperature drops way below zero and the highway is covered in snow and ice.

**Camping:** The best campsites are at Meziadin Lake Provincial Park at the start of the drive, at Kinaskan Lake Provincial Park at the midpoint, or Boya Lake Provincial Park at the end. Wherever you camp, be wary of bears. There are more basic Forest Service campsites along the highway at Bob Quinn Lake, Morcheau Lake, and the south end of Dease Lake.

**Services:** Services are few and far between in this vast wilderness. Gas stations are found often enough to keep from running out, but just barely! Always fill up when you can as you never know if the next one is open or even has gas. You will have to be more self-sufficient on this drive than anywhere else in BC. Although most of the settlements along the way have at least a cafe, the only place with a well-stocked grocery store is in Dease Lake.

**Nearby attractions:** The Glacier Highway (Drive 24) at the start of this drive, endless wilderness in all directions, fishing on the many lakes and rivers in the area, nature study in an untouched landscape, two of BC's most remote provincial parks—Mount Edziza and Spatzizi, the drive from Dease Lake to Telegraph Creek along the Grand Canyon of the Stikine (Drive 25), traveling north from the end of this drive description to the Yukon.

# Drive 23: Stewart-Cassiar Highway
*Meziadin Junction to Boya Lake*

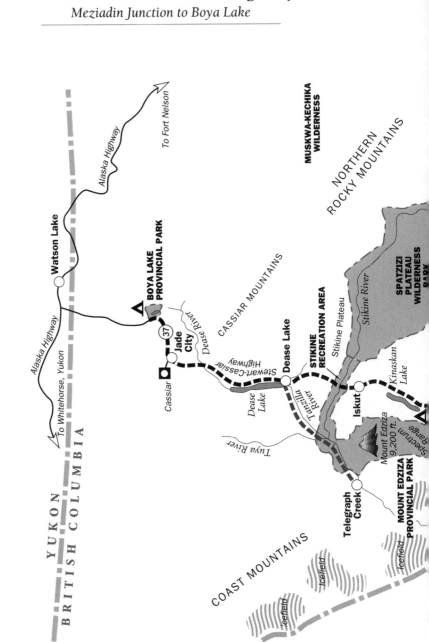

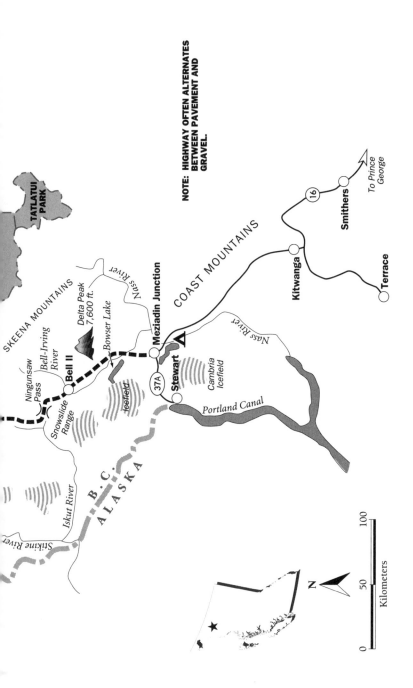

NOTE: **HIGHWAY OFTEN ALTERNATES BETWEEN PAVEMENT AND GRAVEL.**

TATLATUI PARK

SKEENA MOUNTAINS

Ningunsaw Pass

Bell-Irving River

Bell II

Snowslide Range

Iskut River

Stikine River

B. C.
ALASKA

Delta Peak
7,600 ft.

Bowser Lake

Nass River

Icefield

Meziadin Junction

37A

Stewart

Cambria Icefield

Nass River

Portland Canal

COAST MOUNTAINS

Kitwanga

16

Smithers

To Prince George

Terrace

N

0    50    100
Kilometers

227

 # The drive

The Stewart-Cassiar Highway is easily the most "out-there" drive in this book. While signs of modern civilization are few, the signs of true wilderness are many—untouched forests, range after range of wild mountains, gorgeous lakes, and free-flowing rivers. Up in the remote northwestern corner of BC is one of the remotest large areas of true wilderness left on earth. The highway is a thin corridor of human development with many areas nearby having probably never seen a human footprint. Although many people think of the Alaska Highway as remote, this lesser-used route to the north is even more so—less of it is paved, the traffic is lighter, and there are far fewer services along the way.

More than any other drive in BC, this one requires caution, good planning, and a reliable vehicle. Breaking down on this lonely highway will be an expensive and memorable experience you won't ever want to repeat. In summer, much of the traffic on the highway is recreational vehicles traveling to or from Alaska. Many visitors to Alaska and the Yukon travel up the Alaska Highway and then down the Stewart-Cassiar on the way back. Although much of the highway is paved or hard surfaced, a lot of its distance is still gravel with some sections alternating between pavement and gravel seemingly every 100 feet or so. The highway is in good condition for the most part but this can change year to year or even day to day. Slow down on the gravel and be sure to have a good spare tire ready.

The highway is a relatively new one, being completed in 1972 in order to carry ore from a new mine in Cassiar south to processing facilities. The population along the entire 721-kilometer (433-mile) route from Kitwanga to the Yukon is barely over 2,000, a good indicator of just how isolated the area is. In this great empty corner of BC, the population is actually expected to drop in the next 20 years, a startling fact in light of world population growth.

This description takes in the most spectacular 490-kilometer (294-mile) section of the highway between Meziadin Junction and Boya Lake Provincial Park. Although the entire Stewart-Cassiar Highway could be driven in a day, the side trips on the Glacier Highway (Drive 24) and the Telegraph Creek Road (Drive 25) are both excellent and deserve a few extra days to see. The early part of the drive north from Highway 16 to Meziadin Junction follows the path of the Kitwancool Grease Trail that natives once used to travel between the villages to the north and the Oouilcan fishery on the Nass River.

Start the drive at Meziadin Junction, about 160 kilometers (96 miles) up the Stewart-Cassiar from Kitwanga on Highway 16. Before heading north, the best supply base is either Smithers or Terrace. Meziadin Junction is hard to miss. The highway comes to a T-junction with Stewart to the left (Drive 24) and the Stewart-Cassiar continuing north to the right. Be sure to gas up here as well as pick up any needed supplies in the small general store.

The highway continues north, following a gentle plateau within sight of the looming, ice-clad Coast Mountains as it approaches the Bell-Irving River valley, one of the main tributaries of the Nass River. Although some logging has taken place through here to harvest beetle-killed trees it does not overly detract from the sense of wilderness. As the highway approaches the first crossing of the Bell-Irving River at 31 kilometers (19 miles), it comes alongside the Skeena Mountains which pinch in from the east. Through here, the land becomes more interiorlike as the hemlock trees give away to a typically northern forest of stunted lodgepole pine and subalpine fir.

Where the highway crosses the Bell-Irving River for the first time, a forestry road takes off to the left and leads to massive Bowser Lake. This lake is formed from meltwater originating from the Salmon Glacier area. The lake is a perfect setting for a wilderness trip by boat to its far end in untouched wilderness very near the eastern edge of the Coast Mountains in the Longview Range.

By 41 kilometers (24.6 miles), the highway is running alongside the Bell-Irving River on alternating paved and gravel sections. In addition to the few designated rest areas on the highway, numerous wide gravel pullouts along the way also serve as stopping areas. As the highway approaches Bell II, the second crossing of the Bell-Irving River, it runs near the base of glaciated Delta Peak, a rugged 7,600-foot peak of the Skeena Mountains. Although the mountains here in the far north are lower than those in the southern half of BC, many are just as impressive as the treeline is also lower and many have a barren, arctic-alpine look. These mineralized northern mountains are memorable for their colorful slopes streaked with snow, large green meadows, and wild setting. Although close to the highway, many peaks in this area have most likely never been climbed. Just before Bell II is the Hoder Lake rest area where drivers can take a break if tired.

The settlement of Bell II at 96 kilometers (57 miles) is located where the Bell-Irving River turns inland toward its source high in the Skeena Mountains. Be sure to gas up and have a bite to eat as the next services are several hours north. A pay phone is located here as well. Cell phones are useless in much of northern BC so you will have to rely on the phones located at the gas stations along the highway if you need to make a call.

Past Bell II, the highway climbs into Snowbank Creek valley and into one of the most picturesque sections of the entire drive. Along here majestic peaks of the Snowslide Range on both sides crowd in and tower over the emerald-green valley bottom dotted with tiny lakes and meandering streams. The colors in the Skeena Mountains are exceptionally vibrant, with the rust-hued peaks set above bright emerald meadows. In the fall, the colors are further enhanced when the tundra and heather turn golden. Although not seen from the highway, many of the peaks here are glaciated and are the source of the sediment that gives the lakes and rivers their distinctive turquoise color. The wetlands alongside the highway in this section are excellent habitat for a variety of wildlife including moose and beaver. Lucky drivers may see wildlife anywhere along the drive, including grizzly bears, deer, wolves, or stone sheep.

A highlight of the trip is Ningunsaw Pass (1,500 feet), 25 kilometers (15 miles) north of Bell II where the highway leaves the Nass River system and enters the vast and even more remote Stikine River system. From the pass, the highway begins a long descent into the Iskut River valley, one of the major tributaries of the Stikine River. Before encountering the Iskut, the highway runs alongside the rapids of the Ningunsaw River for many kilometers as it rushes downhill and toward the ocean. From the vicinity of the pass the views are panoramic and take in a huge sweep on the eastern edge of the Coast Mountains to the west. Although unseen, some of the largest glacial icecaps in all of BC lie on the mountains above the Iskut River.

By now the highway has entered an increasingly northern-type boreal forest made up of deciduous species such as aspen, birch, and willow. In late September and early October, the trees change with the onset of cooler weather and put on a showy display of color. Near Echo Lake, north of the pass, a historical marker tells the story of the efforts of workers to erect the Yukon telegraph line through this uncompromising wilderness. At 142 kilometers (85 miles) is Bob Quinn Lake, the site of a rest area and Forest Service campsite alongside the lake. Not far beyond, a small airport is located alongside the highway, built as a base for fire fighting, rescue, and to access mines in the Iskut drainage far to the west.

At 162 kilometers (97 miles), the Stewart-Cassiar enters an extensive open area known as the Iskut Burn where in 1958 a lightning strike ignited a forest fire that engulfed a huge swath of land. Today the forest is regenerating and serves as a good feeding area for local wildlife. Bears are commonly seen here in the fall months as they feed on berries to fatten themselves before their winter hibernation. It's almost a certainty that the bear population along the highway is larger than the human one. Luckily in the north, bears are most commonly seen from the security of a vehicle. Northern bears are less likely to have frequent human contact and will most often bolt off into the bush if spotted on the highway. This is in sharp contrast to bears in the Rockies which often are so used to people that they have little fear of contact.

Past the burn, the highway descends steeply to the Iskut River with panoramic views much of the way. The Iskut, which the highway follows for a great distance, leaves the highway here and flows southwest and passes through an almost unknown land of rock and ice before reaching the Stikine River not far from the ocean.

At 194 kilometers (116 miles), Eastman Creek rest area is located near the point where a little-used trail heads toward the Spectrum Range in Mount Edziza Provincial Park. Traveling north, the Stewart-Cassiar passes between Mount Edziza Provincial Park to the west (left) and Spatzizi Plateau Wilderness Park to the east (right). The vast wilderness area between here and the Alaska Highway far to the east has been called the "Serengeti of the North" for its variety and quantity of big game wildlife. The immense and newly-created Muskwa-Kechika Wilderness Area east of Spatzizi ensures that a great portion of the area forever stays in its wild state and serves as an important reminder of what all of BC was like less than 100 years ago.

Although not readily visible from the highway, Mount Edziza and Spatzizi are two of the most remote and beautiful parks in all the province. Mount Edziza has the highest concentration of major volcanic features in Canada and the colorful mountains of the Spectrum Range while Spatzizi preserves a massive chunk of the Spatzizi Plateau and Skeena Mountains and also forms the headwaters of the Stikine River. To access either park, most visitors fly in from floatplane bases in either Tatogga or Dease Lakes. Both parks are accessible by long trails but these are best done on horseback in the company of an experienced local guide. As both parks lie mostly above treeline, the opportunity to wander over the open alpine tundra is limitless and open to the imagination.

Most hikers head to Mount Edziza to either the famed Spectrum Range in the south or to the volcanic areas near Coffee Crater in the north. Spatzizi is well known as one of BC's best wilderness canoeing destinations. For experienced paddlers, the multiweek journey down the Stikine River from Tuaton Lake all the way to the ocean (with a portage of the Grand Canyon of the Stikine) is the trip of a lifetime. For information on either Mount Edziza or Spatzizi, call the BC Parks office in Dease Lake (see Appendix).

Heading north, the Stewart-Cassiar reaches the southern end of the Iskut Lakes chain at 214 kilometers (128 miles) when it reaches Kinaskan Lake Provincial Park. The park stretches from Natadesleen Lake to the south end of Kinaskan Lake. While the park serves as the access to both lakes, the actual campground is on Kinaskan Lake. There are excellent canoeing and camping opportunities on any of the lakes here but as is the case anywhere in the north, be wary of bears. Beyond the park, the highway travels on the east side of emerald Kinaskan Lake and its backdrop of the colorful peaks in the eastern Spectrum Range. East of the highway, Todagin Mountain has a year-round herd of stone sheep, the northern cousins of the Rocky Mountain and California bighorn sheep seen in the southern half of BC.

At 227 kilometers (136 miles), the Stewart-Cassiar crosses Todagin Creek and reaches Tatogga Lake at 239 kilometers (143 miles). Here you will find a gas station, resort, floatplane base, restaurant, and accommodation along the lakefront. Also located here is the signed turnoff to Spatzizi

Provincial Park and the start of a long and lonely backroad that heads east into the Klappen River system and intersects with several trails used by horsepackers to enter the park's core area.

Just north of Tatogga Lake is long Eddontenajon Lake which is set below craggy Mount Poelzer, the dominant peak in view. As the highway traverses steep hillsides through here, the narrow lake and its colorful backdrop are within constant view. Paddlers can launch at the rest area on the lake and paddle all the way south back to Natadesleen Lake if they are capable of running the creeks that connect the lakes. At the north end of Eddontenajon Lake is the native settlement of Iskut at 255 kilometers (153 miles). Although small, services are available including gas and limited groceries. Several guides based in Iskut take visitors into the surrounding wilderness areas either on foot or horseback tours. For more information on guiding services, call either BC Parks in Dease Lake or the Iskut band office (see Appendix).

Heading out of Iskut, the highway begins to climb up to the Stikine Plateau, a vast high-elevation area in the middle sections of the Stikine River. About 13 kilometers (8 miles) past Iskut is Forty Mile Flats, another small collection of services including gas and food. As the highway travels back into the wilds and elevation is gained, the forests become even more stunted and hardly resemble the giants found in the southern half of the province. From the plateau near Morcheau Lake (boat launch, camping), Mount Edziza, the highest volcano in Canada at 9,200 feet, can be seen on the southwestern horizon. This prominent mountain is covered with an extensive icefield and although heavily eroded and hardly recognizable as a volcano, several nearby vents are more recent and exhibit near-perfect cone shapes. Mount Edziza's last eruption was about 10,000 years ago when it covered hundreds of square kilometers with lava and cinder.

Just after the narrow Stikine River recreation area is entered, the gravel-surfaced highway begins to sharply descend to the Stikine. From the descent, the views open up a huge swath of forested plateau in all directions. By now the mountain views have been left behind and the land is gentler but still just as remote. At 287 kilometers (172 miles), the river is crossed on a large metal bridge. The Stikine, one of the great rivers in BC, is only one of several that cut cross the entire Coast Mountain chain and provide access from the coast to the interior. The river, 640-kilometers (384 miles) long and draining a huge area of 50,000 square kilometers, is only crossed by a road once (here) in its entire distance. Virtually all of the river lies in true wilderness from its start in the high tundra of Spatzizi Park, all the way to its end in the Pacific near Wrangell, Alaska.

To the coastal Tlingit Indians the Stikine was known as the "great river"—a place of awe. When famous wilderness explorer John Muir explored the icy, glacier-shrouded world of the lower Stikine in 1889, he referred to it as "A Yosemite 100 miles long." To see more of the Stikine, including sections of the famed Grand Canyon, be sure to drive out to Telegraph Creek from Dease Lake (Drive 25). Paddlers who are traveling the entire river must take out at the bridge here and drive to Telegraph Creek before continuing their journey to the ocean as the Grand Canyon section, starting just west of the bridge, is unrunnable and extremely dangerous.

Although still wild, the Stikine has had the threat of a BC Hydro dam hanging over its head for decades. Local environmental groups have been lobbying the Canadian government for years to create a national park to protect its natural wonders. The Stikine River recreation area protects only a small band around the river from Spatzizi Park to near Telegraph Creek and does nothing to protect the surrounding landscapes.

Once past the Stikine, the highway begins to climb toward Gnat Pass through a landscape of stunted forest, open meadows, and rocky slopes. The pass, at 4,100 feet, is an important dividing line between waters flowing north to the Arctic via the Dease River and west to the Pacific via the Stikine. Traveling ever north, the highway next descends into the Tanzilla River system with sinuous Dease Lake being visible far up ahead.

Dease Lake, reached at 338 kilometers (203 miles), is the largest community along the entire length of the Stewart-Cassiar with a population of about 700 hardy souls brave enough to face the remoteness of the area and the bitterly cold winters. Here you will find all the essential services for travelers including food, gas, accommodation, and mechanical repair. The town also has both a BC Parks and Forest Service offices, making this an important stop if venturing out into the surrounding parks. The town is located on the southern end of long Dease Lake and has always had its roots as a supply center for the outlying regions. During the period from 1838 to 1841, the town served as an important Hudson Bay Company fort and trading post, supplying the trappers who scoured the land looking for valuable furs. Twenty-five years later, the town served as the center of supply for a gold rush on nearby Dease and Thilbert Creeks. Dease Lake serves as the starting point of the thrilling Telegraph Creek Road (Drive 25).

Past the town, the highway once again enters deep wilderness as it traverses above Dease Lake. For almost the next 20 kilometers (12 miles), the lake is in full view of the highway, making for a beautiful drive through this section. Just before Joe Irwin Lake at 406 kilometers (244 miles), the Stewart-Cassiar crosses to the west side of the Dease River and begins to enter the magnificent realm of the Cassiar Mountains, a subrange of the northern Rocky Mountains. From here to the end of the drive description at Boya Lake is the most beautiful part of the entire trip as the highway passes through wide, sweeping valleys with high colorful peaks standing over exquisite forests, rivers, wetlands, and lakes. Numerous peaks along here are heavily mineralized, as noted by the bright colors of the exposed slopes. Before bending around a prominent corner at about 428 kilometers (257

*An old building in tiny Jade City on the Stewart-Cassiar Highway just south of Boya Lake Provincial Park.*

miles), the highway enters a large burn area which is the result of a wildfire that engulfed over 9,000 hectares in 1982.

At the big curve west, the highway turns away from the Dease River and enters the Cottonwood River valley. The entire area is one picture-perfect scene after another and every bit as beautiful as anything found along the Alaska Highway far to the east. After passing by Simmons Lake at 441 kilometers (265 miles), the highway passes directly beneath multihued peaks which loom above in a grand sweep of forest, meadow, and bare rock. In this high stretch, many of the alpine slopes are a short hike away, tempting a hike up through the thin band of forest toward the summits of the gentler peaks.

The tiny settlement of Jade City is reached at 453 kilometers (272 miles), set in a wide valley ringed with pale colored mountains. The town, a supply outpost, has its roots in the mining industry, serving both the now-defunct Cassiar mine as well as Princess Jade Mine far to the east. Be sure to fill up on gas here before pressing on northwards. The nearby town of Cassiar, built to serve an asbestos mine, died in 1992, a victim of a dwindling supply of easy-to-mine asbestos and increasing costs. Once home to 1,500 people, the town has been dismantled and the site is currently being reclaimed so access to it is no longer allowed.

The excellent views of the Cassiar Mountains climax at Good Hope Lake, 21 kilometers (13 miles) past Jade City. This pretty turquoise lake is set amongst a gorgeous setting of mineralized peaks and makes for an excellent stop. If you take only one picture of the highway along the way, this is the spot to do it.

The end of the drive is reached at the turnoff to Boya Lake Provincial Park at 490 kilometers (294 miles). Boya Lake, found just over 3 kilometers (1.8 miles) down the access road, is a perfect study in the effects of glaciation. Here eskers, drumlins, moraines, and lakes all show the effects of the last ice age when the area was crushed and ground under a vast icecap. Although the mountains are left behind past here, the Horseranch Range, the most northerly outrider of the Cassiar Mountains, is seen to the east. The lake with its intricate shorelines and warm shallow waters makes it an excellent place to explore by small boat or canoe.

Although the drive description ends here, the Stewart-Cassiar Highway continues north for another 85 kilometers (51 miles) before reaching the Alaska Highway and the Yukon just west of Watson Lake. Most drivers will want to head back south via the Alaska Highway (Drive 26) from Watson Lake in order to be treated to the scenic wonders along its length and to be able to complete a grand loop of northern BC.

# 24

# Glacier Highway
## *Meziadin Junction to Salmon Glacier*

**General description:** Known as the Glacier Highway, this 110-kilometer (66-mile) drive is easily the best place to see glaciers up-close in all of North America. After traveling through a wealth of beautiful scenery ranging from soaring peaks to wild rivers, the drive reaches the historic towns of Steward and Hyder on the way to its thrilling climax in the last 15 kilometers (9 miles) where the Salmon Glacier Road climbs and traverses above a massive sea of ice. Drivers also have a chance to see bears fishing for salmon at the Fish Creek bear viewing area along the way.

**Special attractions:** Meziadin Lake, the Blue Bear Glacier, the semi-ghost town of Hyder, the Fish Creek bear viewing area, old mines, the Salmon and Berenden Glaciers, the adventurous nature of the last part of the drive.

**Location:** Northwestern BC on the eastern edge of the Alaskan Panhandle.

**Drive route numbers:** Highway 37A from Meziadin Junction to Stewart and then the Salmon Glacier Road the rest of the way.

**Travel season:** All year for the paved portion of the road from Meziadin to Hyder and summer only for the Salmon Glacier. Mid to late summer is the best time for the drive to see both the bears and the Salmon Glacier.

**Camping:** At either Meziadin Lake Provincial Park or at the Forest Service campsite on the Bear River north of Stewart. There is also commercial camping in Hyder and informal camping at the end of the drive by the Berenden Glacier.

**Services:** Gas at Meziadin Junction, all other services in Stewart or Hyder. Overall there are few services in this remote area.

**Nearby attractions:** Mountain and marine wilderness stretching away in every direction, incredible outdoor adventure opportunities, the chance to take an Alaska state ferry to Ketchikan and see the long Portland Canal fjord.

 The drive

The Glacier Highway begins at Meziadin Junction, 160 kilometers (96 miles) up the Stewart-Cassiar Highway from its start at Kitwana. From the T-junction, turn left to head west on Highway 37A following the signs for Stewart. The Stewart-Cassiar Highway (to the right) leads from this point north to the Yukon and travels through a vast wilderness landscape of mountains, forests, and lakes. If you are low on gas, fill up at the junction as there are no

# Drive 24: Glacier Highway
*Meziadin to Salmon Glacier*

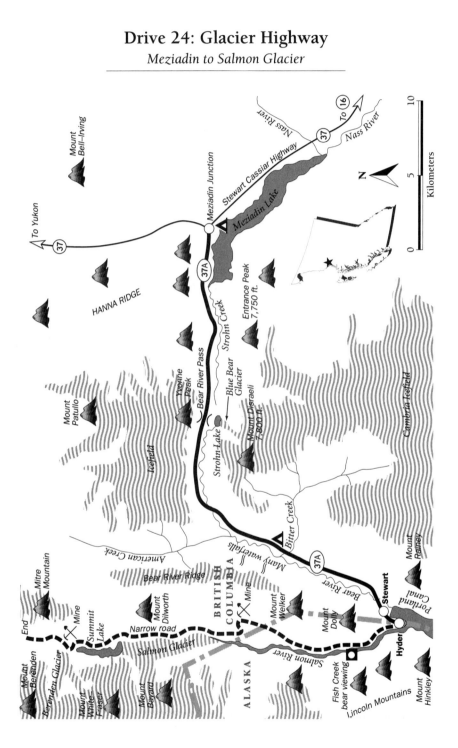

more services until Stewart is reached. Anywhere in the more remote parts of BC it's wise to fill up at every opportunity as the gas stations are few and far between and often have limited hours of operation. Just south of the junction on the Stewart-Cassiar is the turnoff on the left for Meziadin Lake Provincial Park and its 42 scenic campsites.

Driving due west on the Glacier Highway, turquoise Meziadin Lake and its backdrop of steep, dark peaks hanging with glacial ice comes quickly into view. Several pullouts along this initial stretch allow for peak and lake gazing. By the time the highway nears the western end of the lake, you approach the first of the rugged summits that line the highway for the rest of the drive.

This highway doesn't pass below the peaks, it travels right through them, giving the average driver a mountaineer's view of this rugged landscape. More often than not, the scenery will have a moody look with clouds and mist drifting in and out over the peaks and allowing only for quick glimpses of the wild backdrop to this drive. Rarely in this rainforest climate will the weather be clear enough to see the mountains in all their glory. If you do hit a stretch of good weather, thank the weather gods and don't expect it to be the same the next day. In this area, and indeed all of the coast, the weather can change rapidly and unfortunately, too often for the worse!

By 14 kilometers (8.4 miles), 7,750-foot Entrance Peak, one of the most dramatic sights along the drive, is in full view so look for a place to pull out and admire its high-angle slopes of hanging glaciers, emerald-green avalanche chutes, and thin bands of rainforest. Although foreshadowed, the 6,500-foot rise of the peak above the highway is breathtaking. In several places the broken edges of the hanging glaciers display an almost shocking blue color, quite a revelation for those who thought glaciers were white. The blue color is from the compression of the snow into ice over decades and even centuries. The colors of the glacial ice are actually enhanced by cool, cloudy weather.

Even in midsummer, cold, wet rainstorms can dust these coastal peaks with snow. Despite the glacial ice and their rugged character, the summits along the drive are not high. Most of the mountains rise to only 5,000 or 6,000 feet, the elevation of a typical valley bottom in the Rockies. What gives them their rugged look is the climate, which is often stormy and wet, as well as the fact that the vertical relief is outstanding. The highest point along the highway is just over 2,000 feet, making for some very impressive looking mountains.

Industrial traffic is common on the highway so caution is required, especially around the blind corners. You are almost sure to see both logging trucks and mining trucks carrying ore to a shipping facility on Portland Canal. In addition, RVs regularly ply this route so patience is required if caught behind one on an uphill stretch. Slowing down to enjoy the breathtaking scenery is the best policy for a safe and memorable trip on the Glacier Highway.

On the approach to the highway's summit, the mountain slopes to the left are a kaleidoscope of typical coastal mountain scenery with sharp peaks, glacial ice, and prominent avalanche paths choked with brilliant green bush. Any trees trying to establish themselves in this narrow valley are mercilessly crushed by tons of avalanching snow sloughing off the mountains during vigorous winter storms.

At 24 kilometers (14.3 miles), there is a scenic rest area on the left with picnic tables right across from a thundering waterfall and the first glimpses of the Blue Bear Glacier. The next 2 kilometers (1.2 miles) of highway have several large viewing areas for Strohn Lake and the Blue Bear Glacier tongue which occasionally calves huge chunks of ice into the lake's silty waters. This, the only roadside glacier in the province, is a memorable sight for those who have never seen a major glacier this close before.

Although the tongue of the glacier is almost always visible, its mountain source is usually buried in fog and cloud. On a cloudy day, one can only wonder about the unseen source of this river of ice, flowing from its cold and stormy mountain world in the Cambria Icefield to the south. The 7,800-foot Mount Disraeli, seen on the right, is the highest mountain visible from the pass. With the aid of binoculars you can study the glacier in detail and notice details unseen to the naked eye, like the deeper blue shades of the ice deep within the crevasses. Even in midsummer, the winds off the glacier can be bone-chilling so be prepared if you want to walk around. Unfortunately, the

*The sheer face of the Blue Bear glacier*
*where it descends to Strohn Lake near the Glacier Highway.*

glacier face is hard to approach due to the lake's steep banks and the impassable barrier of the outlet of the Bear River.

Once past the glacier, the highway is downhill all the way to Stewart and is accompanied by the roaring torrent of the Bear River for much of the way. Along the rest of the highway, dozens of waterfalls are seen pouring out of the mountains, many small and delicate but several large and booming. Six kilometers (3.6 miles) past the glacier is a great example of a fan-shaped avalanche cone, formed by snow pouring out of narrow gullies above. In most places, the avalanche fans melt out in summer, but here it has accumulated year after year to form a permanent hunk of ice.

The further the highway travels and descends from the pass, the thicker the forests become and the taller the mountains appear. The Bear River is crossed to the south side for the first time at 40 kilometers (24 miles) and a few kilometers later the highway passes through a sheer, rock-walled gorge. Through this section, numerous parallel waterfalls are seen to the north (right) on the precipitous slopes of Bear River Ridge which rises out of low footings in American Creek. Past here, the Glacier Highway bends to the south and the rows of peaks stretching away toward Portland Canal are revealed. Slowly but steadily, the Bear River steadily changes its character from a canyonous mountain torrent to a wide and braided coastal river as the ocean is approached. Despite its short length, the large number of feeder streams has significantly increased its volume by now.

At 48.5 kilometers (29.1 miles) is a primitive BC Forest Service campsite, the only designated campsite along the highway. These campsites were once free but as of the summer 1999, the BC government has imposed a nightly fee of $8 per night for their use.

At 59 kilometers (35.4 miles), the highway enters the outskirts of Stewart, the most northerly ice-free port in Canada. Stewart is one of the most remote communities in BC and has a definite feeling of isolation. It wasn't until 1903 that a firm boundary between Canada and the US was established through here along the Alaskan Panhandle. A gold rush soon followed and the population of Stewart swelled to over 10,000 people in its heyday. To view some of the artifacts of Stewart's mining past, be sure to check out the Stewart Museum at Sixth and Columbia in the former fire hall. Both Stewart and Hyder now depend on tourism and scattered industrial activities like fishing, logging, and mining for their economic health. With its cold and severe climate, Stewart has also been the location of four major Hollywood movies including *The Iceman* and *The Thing*.

At 62.6 kilometers (37.6 miles) a T-junction is reached. To continue with the drive turn right and enter downtown Stewart, home to about 1,100 people. At the junction, it is a good idea to fill up on gas and gather any needed supplies before continuing the trip deeper into the backcountry In downtown Stewart there is a tourist infocenter, a good source for information on the town and the Salmon Glacier Road.

In addition to the Glacier Highway, both Stewart and Hyder can be accessed by Alaska state ferry which runs once every other week between Ketchikan and Hyder (see Appendix for phone number). This stunning journey travels all the way up mountain-lined Portland Canal for hours on end and grants nonstop views of quintessential coastal fjord scenery.

Stewart is situated at the end of 150-kilometer (90-mile) Portland Canal, one of the longest fjords in the world which stretches from the open ocean at Dixon Entrance to far into the Coast Mountains. The BC/Alaskan border runs right down the middle of this narrow fjord for its entire length. Peaks tower over the head of the canal to neck-stretching heights, rising in great walls of forest, rock, and ice right out of their barnacle-encrusted bases.

Past the intersection, the highway (now a narrow road) curves around and hugs the mountain wall that falls away into the ocean. At the head of the canal is a green, grassy river estuary with orderly pilings still marking the site of long-gone canneries. Passing dilapidated waterfront docks and more modern industrial buildings, Hyder, Alaska, is reached at 67 kilometers (40 miles).

The border arrangement between these two towns is fascinating. The stores in Hyder all use Canadian money (except the post office) as the only bank is in Stewart. Both towns celebrate a joint Canada Day/Fourth of July with festivities lasting from July 1 to 4. When passing into Alaska there is no border stop, although on the way back into BC you may be stopped at the small Canada Customs building on the waterfront.

Hyder is funky, outback Alaska at its best with ramshackle buildings mixed in with newer structures modified to suit the tastes of the owners in this remote place. Antlers are commonly tacked above doors and a spare car or two lies around waiting for long-needed repairs. Hyder is pleasantly set in deep forest and has several gift shops, a campground, and three drinking establishments in which to get "Hyderized," a local drinking tradition that is only for the adventurous.

Past Hyder the road curves back north, turns to gravel, and starts to enter the Salmon River drainage, marked by an imposing rock wall on the left. At 69 kilometers (41.4 miles) there is a Tongass National Forest information board on your right with current information about the Fish Creek bear viewing area. Within minutes the road begins running alongside the braided and silty Salmon River backed by lush, coastal peaks. This stretch of the road is wide, flat, and easy and is plied by dozens of RVs daily in the summer. If you are pulling a trailer and planning on tackling the rest of the Salmon Glacier Road, be sure to drop it off in Hyder.

At 73 kilometers (44 miles) is the Fish Creek bear viewing area, the only roadside bear viewing area in Alaska. A bridge crosses Fish Creek here and there is a large parking area on the left. On summer days, dozens of people patiently wait around for the bears to appear. The best time of year to see the bears is midsummer to early fall, but a few weeks either way might bring out the bears, depending upon the salmon runs. The best chance of seeing either black or grizzly bears (called brown bears in Alaska) is near dawn and dusk, although in peak season, bears are often readily seen in the day. Binoculars are very helpful as the bears might be up the river and are hard to watch in dim light.

A couple of days' stay here is almost surely to be rewarded with a bear sighting. Once a bear is spotted, the crowds rush over to see it. At this point you'll realize that, as was put to me by a Forest Service ranger, "the people are the wild animals, not the bears." With the area growing in popularity, the Forest Service has plans in the works to restrict viewing to several areas, build guard fences, and generally lessen the impact of people on the bears. Like a scene right out of a nature documentary, it's fascinating to watch the different behavior of the bears as they fish for salmon. Some pounce right in and chase the salmon up and down the creek while others timidly dip a paw in the waters to test the temperature and approach the hunt in a passive way. Bald eagles are a constant companion in the skies above as they circle around looking for an easy dinner.

Past the bear viewing area, the road follows the wide Salmon River for several kilometers before climbing gradually to gain elevation. Clearly, the next part of the road is not for people with a fear of heights as it is etched into exposed mountainsides for most of its remaining distance. Although it is a good, well-maintained road passable to almost any car, truck, and four-wheel-drive vehicle, it's not a place for the careless or inattentive as there are no guard rails and it's a long drop to the glacier. In several places, the road narrows to one lane due to rockfall or precipitous slopes. For the experienced backroad driver, the road is an easy cruise but for those who are not used to mountain driving, it will be both thrilling and memorable. The road ahead is one of the most spectacular places to drive in the world. The Salmon Glacier Road grants the mere driver access into the high mountain world of rock and ice that is usually reserved for hardcore mountaineers.

At 78 kilometers (47 miles), the remains of an old mine site is marked by a pile of rusting junk on the right side of the road. Along the remainder of the drive you will be frequently reminded of the industrial origins of this road as it passes numerous mine shafts and buildings. Just after passing back into BC, the road sweeps around a prominent corner, climbs, and a modern mine is seen just below.

By 91 kilometers (54.6 miles), the road curves around and back into the Salmon River valley, except that now the river is over 1,000 feet below in a deep, sinister-looking gorge. Beyond this point the road gets more exposed. There are several pullouts on the left here where you can look down

*The end of the Salmon Glacier Road where it overlooks the massive Berenden Glacier. The abandoned Granduc Mine is just out of view to the left.*

the length of the Salmon River toward the ocean and marvel at the steeply-pitched coastal peaks that envelop the river. From the same viewpoint, the terminus of the Salmon Glacier and its striking blue ice tongue surrounded by brown scree slopes can be seen far below. Curiously, several glacial lakes lie alongside the silty brown river and range in color from near black to turquoise blue.

The next section is narrow and exposed so caution is required through here. The first view of the massive Salmon Glacier is an astonishing sight. Flowing off a massive but unnamed coastal icecap, it descends toward the ocean in a blinding river of ice. The glacier spills off the icecap in two directions. One tongue flows left toward the sea and is the source of the Salmon River and the other tongue turns hard right and descends into Summit Lake, an iceberg-choked body of water 2 kilometers (1.2 miles) long. The rest of the drive to the end of the road is one unforgettable sight after another. Be sure to drive this stretch on a clear day so the glacier will be in full sight. By now the road has climbed to 4,300 feet and is solidly in the subalpine zone. The forest has been left behind and steep mountain slopes of snow, rock, and stunted trees climb to the skyline on the right. There are numerous wide shoulders where you can park and marvel at the glacier through this stretch.

At 102 kilometers (61 miles) is the high point in the road. Past here it begins to gradually descend and pass above Summit Lake. The view down to the chaotic lake from the road is spectacular. Where the Salmon Glacier enters the lake, it is crazily broken up into wild seracs and pillars of fractured blue ice. Above the lake, the road becomes more gentle as it passes scattered mine shafts and buildings that lie on a bench above the lake's southern shores.

Once past the newer mine buildings, the road curves around a corner and the heavily crevassed Berenden Glacier comes into view. This glacier is much closer to the road and also flows into an iceberg-strewn lake. When looking at the glacier, it's easy to see the medial moraine piles—the stripes of dark rock—that indicate where two glaciers join together.

The prominent grey Granduc Mine sits abandoned and silent facing the rubble-covered glacier snout. Be extremely cautious if prowling around the mine as all sorts of hidden dangers lurk about. There is a large parking area in front of the main building where fire rings mark the places where people have camped in the past.

The road continues to about the 110-kilometer (66-mile) mark in the desolate Bowser River valley before coming to an abrupt end at a washed-out bridge. There are numerous places for rough camping throughout this section but be careful with the weather which is rapidly changing and often vile in this icy mountain world. Once you are done admiring the scenery here, cautiously retrace the same route to Hyder and then back out to the Stewart-Cassiar Highway

# 25

# Telegraph Creek Road
### *Dease Lake to Telegraph Creek*

**General description:** This scenic and exciting 120-kilometer (72-mile) drive in BC's far northwestern corner leads to one of the most historic and isolated towns in the province and features thrilling views into the Grand Canyon of the Stikine, one of BC's most infamous river canyons. Those with a fear of heights might want to skip this drive as it is etched into exposed canyons for much of its last half.

**Special attractions:** Some of the most remote towns in BC, the Grand Canyon of the Stikine, the northern boreal forests, one of the most exhilarating drives in the province, wildlife viewing, the historic community of Telegraph Creek.

**Location:** The northwestern corner of BC just southwest of Dease Lake.

**Drive route numbers:** Not an official highway, simply known as the Telegraph Creek Road.

**Travel season:** Late spring, summer, and fall. No one but locals are around in the bitterly cold winter months.

**Camping:** No formal camping along the way. Accommodation in Telegraph Creek at the Stikine Riversong. There is a Forest Service campsite at Dease Lake at the start of the drive.

**Services:** There are no services between Dease Lake and Telegraph Creek. Limited services at end of drive.

**Nearby attractions:** Mount Edziza Provincial Park to the south, the ghost town of Glenora, the Stikine River downstream of Telegraph Creek where it flows through the heavily glaciated Coast Mountains.

 The drive

Dease Lake, the start of the drive, is approximately 490 kilometers (294 miles) north of Kitwanga on the Stewart-Cassiar Highway (Drive 23). Like so many towns in BC, Dease Lake was founded after gold was found in Dease Creek in 1873. Mining and tourism are the mainstays of the economy in this area. Today this small outpost, with a population of 800, is the only substantial community along the entire 721-kilometer (433-mile) length of the Stewart-Cassiar Highway. A lonely and isolated place, this area also is known for its distinctly northern climate. In winter, temperatures can drop as low as -40 degrees C (-58 degrees F), but few tourists venture this far

# Drive 25: Telegraph Creek Road
## Dease Lake to Telegraph Creek

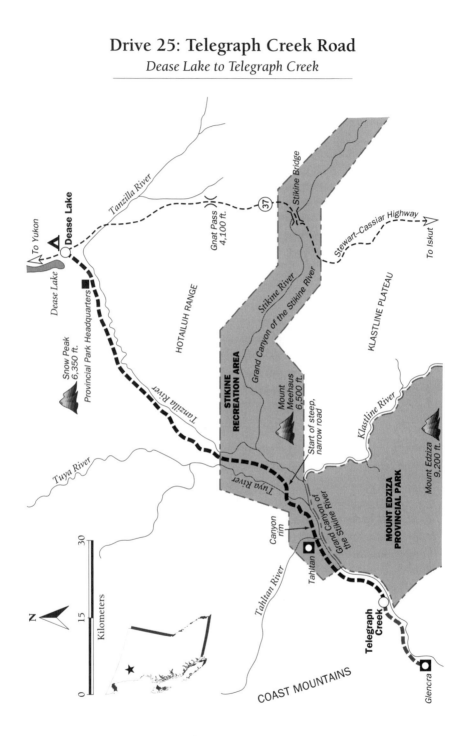

north at that time of the year. September and October are the nicest time to do the drive with the cool, sunny weather combined with beautiful fall colors as the aspen forests and tundra change color in anticipation of winter.

This drive is suitable for all vehicles except RVs and those pulling trailers. In the second half of the drive the road is steep and intimidating with grades up to 20 percent in three places, so skip this drive if you have a fear of exposure and heights. That said, the road is usually in very good condition and graded annually. In fact the road is in far better shape than the road along Carpenter Lake (Drive 19), a similar type of drive along the rim of a deep gorge. Before heading out to Telegraph Creek, be sure to pick up anything you need as there are no services along the way until Telegraph Creek is reached, and even there, they are obviously limited.

In downtown Dease Lake, turn left at the main gas station and grocery store and follow the road through town heading west. When the major T-junction is reached, turn left and follow the signs for Telegraph Creek. The airport is soon passed on the left with the BC Parks office on the right. This is the administrative center for both Mount Edziza and Spatzizi Provincial Parks, two of BC's most remote and most spectacular wilderness areas. If you are planning a trip to these parks, the main access is from floatplane bases at Dease Lake or from Tatogga Lake to the south.

Mount Edziza Provincial Park, the closest of the two to this drive, has two breathtaking areas—the Mount Edziza area in the north of the park with Canada's highest volcano and the perfectly shaped volcanic cones of Coffee and Cocoa Craters in the south of the park; and the Spectrum Range, famous for its brilliant rock colors, open alpine, and views to the jagged Coast Mountain crest to the west. Spatzizi is even more remote and less visited and forms the headwaters of the Stikine River, the setting for this drive, and one of the few rivers that cuts right across the full width of the Coast Mountains. Both parks are totally isolated with no facilities and are visited by only a few experienced adventurers each summer. See *Adventuring in British Columbia* or call BC Parks in Dease Lake for details (see Appendix for phone numbers).

The first 60 kilometers (36 miles) of the drive are on a wide and easy gravel road through thick forests in the Tanzilla River valley, one of the main tributaries of the Stikine. With the tight, closed-in scenery, there is little to see through this section so press on toward the climax of the drive in the last 50 kilometers (30 miles) where the dramatic views and thrilling stretches of road more than make up for this mellow start. After 60 kilometers (36 miles), the road begins to run in a straight shot for several kilometers before the first of the steep grades begin. From this long stretch, wide panoramas are revealed and include the volcanic and alpine areas near Mount Edziza just across the Stikine.

247

By 67 kilometers (40.2 miles), the road begins to descend and at 71 kilometers (42.6 miles) a sign warns of the more than 18 percent grades on the next section. From here on in, this drive is one of the most memorable in the province. The road switchbacks down steeply into the Tuya River canyon with its layered brown walls and open aspen forests. Beyond here, the land grows ever drier and the thick forests are left behind for open meadows and exposed rock outcrops as the maximum rainshadow of the Coast Mountains is approached. Most likely the weather will be improving as you drive west since the Telegraph Creek area exists in a sunny, dry climate not unlike Okanagan, far to the south. At the bottom of the descent, the Tuya River is crossed on a one-lane bridge and then the road quickly curves out of the canyon and toward the Stikine itself.

The Tuya River system, like most of the rivers in the area, is virtually untouched and one can only wonder about the deep wilderness in its headwaters to the north. Other than the few roads in this area, this lonely corner of BC is as wild as almost any place on earth. It has vast tracts of virtually unknown land along the Alaskan Panhandle, great concentrations of wildlife, and literally hundreds of magical places waiting to be discovered. Despite the fact that only a few hundred people live here in an area bigger than many US states, the population of the northwest corner of BC is actually expected to drop in the next 20 years as the traditional resource industries continue to suffer.

Once out of the Tuya River, the Stikine is seen for the first time up ahead after staying left at the prominent Y-junction. A sign here warns of the 20-percent grades on the descent to the river. At the top of the switchbacks, pull out and enjoy the panoramic views of the Stikine Plateau and its alpine backdrop before continuing down into the Grand Canyon itself. From this high vantage point, 9,200-foot Mount Edziza can be seen in the far distance to the south while the leading edge of the Coast Mountains can also be seen on the far western horizon.

The next stretch is thrilling as the road descends sharply several hundred feet to a small ranch on a nearly flat plateau above the Stikine. Take care on the descent and keep an eye on both the road and the views. Once at the bottom, take a deep breath and then continue driving southwest on a bench high above the river. Be sure to stop and enjoy the views from the Windy Point rest area at 89 kilometers (53 miles), perched right on the edge of the sheer drop into the Grand Canyon. Anywhere along the canyon's rim, be careful as you approach the edge to look over as it's often loose, unstable, and lacks guardrails.

Traveling past here, the road is etched into steep, barren hillsides with cliffs to the right and a sheer drop into the river, mere feet from the edge of the road, on the left. It goes without saying that the next section calls for slow speeds and a careful approach. Try to drive the road early in the morning or late in the afternoon if possible. Not only will the light be better for photography, you will hopefully avoid the locals who often drive through here at dangerous speeds. In many places the road is just over a lane wide so passing is often difficult and nerve-wracking, especially on the return when you'll be driving on the outside.

While hardly as dramatic as the Grand Canyon in Arizona, this canyon is still a magical place. The entire Stikine River, 640 kilometers (384 miles) long and free-flowing, is one of North America's great wilderness rivers. The Grand Canyon section is about 100 kilometers (60 miles) long and about 1,000 kilometers deep in most places. From the air, it resembles a giant black gash through an otherwise flat, forested plateau. The Stikine flows from its source high in the Skeena Mountains in Spatzizi Provincial Park through the Grand Canyon and then on to its end on the Pacific coast of southeast Alaska. In its last few kilometers, the river flows through an icy mountain landscape with several valley glaciers descending right into the river. In all, there is no more scenic and ecologically diverse river in Canada.

For many years, experienced paddlers have traveled down the entire length of the Stikine, except for the Grand Canyon, which was long thought to be too dangerous to navigate through. In several places, the entire river is pinched though sinister dark gorges with the rock walls mere feet apart. Despite the canyon's menacing reputation, several years ago the grade six (maximum difficulty) rapids of the canyon were kayaked for the first time. A recent television production, filmed by helicopter flying through the inner depths of the canyon, introduced the scenic wonders of the Stikine to a wide audience.

In many spots along the road you can pull off and walk to the sheer edge of the canyon and peer into its depths hundreds of feet below. Signs of volcanic activity such as basaltic columns and lava fields are strewn throughout the area and are easy to spot, as is the 360-strong mountain goat herd that lives in the canyon. Numerous published photographs of the goats show them as they move along the cliffs with the grace of world-class rock climbers. Grizzly bears, mountain goats, wolves, stone sheep, caribou, moose, and bald eagles are just a few of the wildlife also found in the vast and untouched land surrounding the river.

Several environmental organizations have been pushing the Canadian government to create a national park around the Stikine before resource industries begin to chip away at its wild heart. For many years, the main threat to the Stikine was a proposed dam in the Grand Canyon that would have forever altered the river by flooding it and creating a huge lake. Thankfully, these plans have been shelved, but several mines in the Stikine area continue to be a source of concern because of toxic runoff and damage to the river's salmon runs.

At 93 kilometers (56 miles) comes a hair-raising stretch where the road runs along the top of a narrow rim with the Stikine River on one side and the Tahltan River on the other. This is the most spectacular spot on the entire drive so pull out here and walk around. The distinctive rim the road travels up and over was created where an ancient lava flow was quickly cut through by the two rivers, leaving the top of the flow exposed here. On the crest the land is so dry that sagebrush grows in profusion. Be sure to look into both river systems but be careful near the edges. By walking just a few feet off the road to the right, you will be treated to a dizzying view 400 feet down into the Tahltan River canyon with its perfectly sheer walls and white-water rapids (see photo next page).

From the rim, the road curves around a tight corner and drops steeply to the Tahltan River right where it meets the Stikine. From the top of the descent, look upriver and spot the next stretch of road as it climbs away from river level to resume its high traverse of the canyon. Tahltan, at the junction of the Stikine and Tahltan Rivers, is a tiny native settlement and the home of the Tahltan First Nation. These natives are fighting hard to preserve the Stikine as it has been their homeland for hundreds, if not thousands, of years. The sandy beach located at the river junction is a popular native fishing spot but is off-limits to non-natives.

The final portion of the drive from Tahltan to Telegraph Creek is memorable for its frequent views of the Grand Canyon as well as for the magnificent fall color (if you're here in September or October). By now the road is solidly within the northern boreal forests zone and is dominated by quaking aspen, birch, and poplar. The road is often narrow and plagued by rockfall so take the corners especially slowly. Most people will be nervously gripping the wheel through here and ignoring the heart-stopping views.

Between 95 and 98 kilometers (57 and 59 miles), there are continuous views into the Grand Canyon from the road which is blasted right into the upper part of the canyon walls. Although much of the land in all directions is gentle and rolling plateau country, the views grow to include the glaciers and towering peaks far to the west above the lower Stikine. Be sure to be on the lookout for mountain goats in this section, as they are easily spotted against the dark rock with binoculars.

The outskirts of Telegraph Creek are reached at 115 kilometers (69 miles). The upper part of town is made up primarily of natives from the Tahltan Nation. Just past, a Y-junction is reached with left leading down to the Stikine and the main area of town and right heading uphill to the area's services (gas and food) and on to the ghost town of Glenora, 16 kilometers (9.6 miles) beyond.

To reach the town center, follow the signs and descend steeply through a rocky gorge to reach the banks of the Stikine and the end of the drive at 117 kilometers (70 miles). Telegraph Creek, likely BC's remotest town, is reminiscent of the more "out-there" communities in the deserts of Nevada. With about 300 people in the entire area, the population is way down from

*The Tahltan River gorge as seen from the canyon rim above the native settlement of Tahltan.*

*A home in the village of Tahltan, not far from the end of the drive at Telegraph Creek.*

the level of 100 years ago when it swelled into the thousands during the various gold rushes. Although "ghost town" comes to mind when visiting here, Telegraph is a small but vibrant community deeply connected to the surrounding wilderness.

The town has its roots as the end of the line for steamships navigating up the Stikine River from Wrangell, Alaska. It has been continuously settled since 1861 when gold was found in the surrounding hills. A few years later it was further built up as a transit point for the Cassiar and Klondike gold rushes. For miners heading north, it was a lot easier to access the mines from here than via long trails from the south. The settlement was named after the telegraph line that was laid through here in the late 1800s as part of the newly emerging communications grid that linked the scattered northern towns with the rest of North America.

In town, old buildings dating back to the early 1900s are found in abundance. Although many are abandoned, some are fixed up and house families in this lonely place. Telegraph is so isolated that a telecommunications company picked it as a prime spot to perfect satellite-based Internet connections. As of 1999, the residents here are linked to the information superhighway even if the phone service is still substandard.

The Stikine Riversong, on the banks of the river, is the social center of town and its most famous landmark, dating back to the 1800s when it was a Hudson Bay Company post. Today it serves as a small hotel, restaurant, and gift shop. The Riversong is also the best place for area information or to be put in touch with the various wilderness guides working in the area. For boat trips down the Stikine, the launch point is just a few feet away in front of the unique police station with its hand-painted police sign on a moose antler!

After enjoying one of the most interesting places in BC, carefully retrace the route back to Dease Lake and continue the journey north to the Yukon or south back to Kitwanga and Highway 16.

# Peace River/ Alaska Highway
## 26

## Alaska Highway
### *Fort Nelson to Liard Hot Springs*

**General description:** This drive description takes in the most spectacular 300-kilometer (180-mile) portion of the legendary Alaska Highway from Fort Nelson to Liard Hot Springs. The highway passes though some of the deepest wilderness left on earth in northern BC where the combination of alpine peaks, turquoise lakes, vast forests, and abundant wildlife makes for a memorable driving experience. The highlight of the drive is the stretch from Stone Mountain to Muncho Lake in the northern Rockies, considered by many to be the most scenic stretch on the entire Alaska Highway.

**Special attractions:** Extensive views of wilderness, the opportunity to see wildlife, the vistas in the northern Rockies, the "out-there" feel of the drive, Liard Hot Springs, and the bragging rights associated with driving one of the world's most famous highways.

**Location:** In the extreme northeastern corner of BC, generally west of Fort Nelson.

**Drive route numbers:** Highway 97 (the Alaska Highway) the entire distance.

**Travel season:** April to October. In the winter months, the temperatures drop far below zero and snow and ice make the road surface hazardous. In this remote area, help is never very close so avoid the winter months. Mid to late fall brings gorgeous fall color but the temperatures by then are hovering around zero even during the day.

**Camping:** Any of the provincial parks along the route, particularly Stone Mountain, Muncho Lake, and Liard Hot Springs.

**Services:** Be sure to get everything you need in Fort Nelson, or more preferably, in Prince George way to the south. Supplies are very limited along the highway other than the basic essentials. Be sure to fill up with gas at every opportunity along the way.

**Nearby attractions:** As this is virtually untouched wilderness, most of the attractions are natural—the scenery, the wildlife, the adventure possibilities in the mountains and on the rivers and lakes.

 # The drive

This spectacular section of the Alaska Highway begins in Fort Nelson, 450 kilometers (270 miles) from the start of the highway in Dawson Creek. The Alaska Highway was built during World War II in nine short months in order to fortify and supply the Aleutian Islands off the Alaskan coast. After the Japanese invaded several islands there, the urgency to build a land route to Alaska was dramatically increased as prior to that time, Alaska was only reached by air or sea. The original highway was built by US Army engineers with the help of Canadian contractors who worked day and night to push nearly 2,300 kilometers (1,380 miles) of road through total wilderness in order to meet the threat.

After the war, the highway was improved and passed over to Canadian control and has over time become the main gateway to northern BC, northern Canada, and Alaska. It wasn't until 1948, however, that civilians were allowed to drive the highway for the first time. For years afterwards, driving the entirely dirt and gravel highway was an epic of blown tires, smashed windshields, jerry cans of spare gas, and run-ins with wildlife. For drivers back then having completed the highway was a major accomplishment and a source of pride.

Although the adventure quotient of the drive has dropped significantly, the magnificent scenery remains the same. In this northern landscape the signs of civilization are few and far between and are mostly limited to a narrow strip along the highway. The distant vistas are as wild today as they were hundreds of years ago when the explorers first encountered them. Although the highway is open year round, this drive is most feasible from April to October. At other times, snow, incredible cold, and closed services mean that the trip is best reserved for locals or the extremely adventurous.

Of the entire length of the Alaska Highway, a little less than half is in BC. The section described rivals the Icefields Parkway in the Rockies as the most scenic drive in Canada as it weaves through the remote northern Rocky Mountains. Not only is the scenery breathtaking and untouched, the opportunities for wildlife viewing and wilderness exploration are unmatched in North America. Although the Alaska Highway has a reputation as a challenging drive, in reality it's fairly easy overall with the main concerns relating to the scarcity of services and the remoteness. In many ways, the Alaska Highway is easier (but far longer) than most of the drives in this book because it travels through a mostly gentle landscape and doesn't have the mountain-hugging stretches of other BC highways. Compared to the more remote and less-used Stewart-Cassiar Highway (Drive 23), this drive is more relaxing with services found more often along its course. Additionally, most (all but a few kilometers) of it is paved and the long gravel stretches encountered on the Stewart-Cassiar are not found here.

# Drive 26: Alaska Highway
*Fort Nelson to Liard Hot Springs*

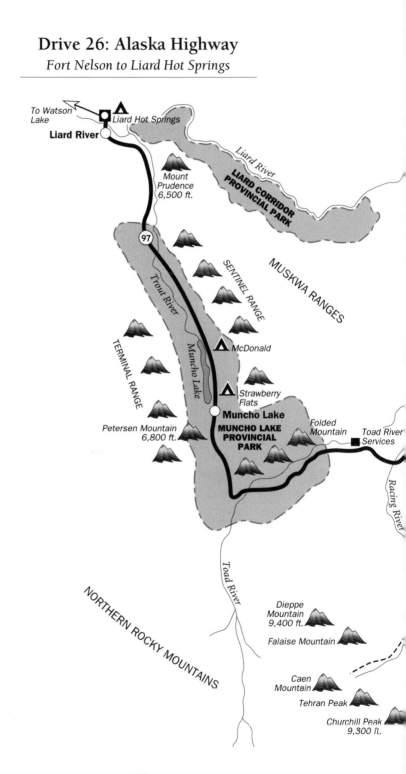

To Watson Lake

Liard Hot Springs

**Liard River**

Liard River

Mount Prudence 6,500 ft.

**LIARD CORRIDOR PROVINCIAL PARK**

97

Trout River

SENTINEL RANGE

MUSKWA RANGES

McDonald

Muncho Lake

TERMINAL RANGE

Strawberry Flats

**Muncho Lake**

**MUNCHO LAKE PROVINCIAL PARK**

Petersen Mountain 6,800 ft.

Folded Mountain

Toad River Services

Racing River

Toad River

NORTHERN ROCKY MOUNTAINS

Dieppe Mountain 9,400 ft.

Falaise Mountain

Caen Mountain

Tehran Peak

Churchill Peak 9,300 ft.

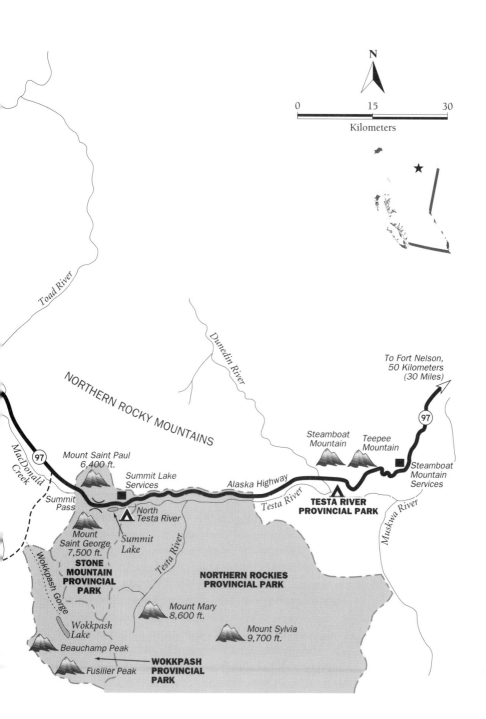

N

0   15   30
Kilometers

*Toad River*

*Dunedin River*

NORTHERN ROCKY MOUNTAINS

To Fort Nelson,
50 Kilometers
(30 Miles)

97

*MacDonald Creek*

97

Mount Saint Paul
6,400 ft.

Summit Lake
Services

Summit
Pass

North
Testa River

Alaska Highway

*Testa River*

Steamboat
Mountain

Teepee
Mountain

Steamboat
Mountain
Services

TESTA RIVER
PROVINCIAL PARK

Mount
Saint George
7,500 ft.

Summit
Lake

*Testa River*

*Muskwa River*

STONE
MOUNTAIN
PROVINCIAL
PARK

NORTHERN ROCKIES
PROVINCIAL PARK

*Wokkpash Gorge*

Mount Mary
8,600 ft.

Mount Sylvia
9,700 ft.

*Wokkpash
Lake*

Beauchamp Peak

Fusilier Peak

WOKKPASH
PROVINCIAL
PARK

The start of the drive is in Fort Nelson, a northern outpost of 4,000. Fort Nelson exists largely to service Alaska Highway travelers and the booming natural gas industry in the surrounding region. Fort Nelson was established in 1805 as a fur trading post and was named after Lord Nelson, the British admiral who won the naval battle of Trafalgar. For the remainder of the century, the site of the town was relocated several times due to attacks from natives and flooding, and today sits on its fifth site. To put its remoteness in perspective, Fort Nelson is the only incorporated town in the Fort Nelson/Liard Land District, covering over 10 percent of BC (bigger than some US states).

Before venturing north out of Fort Nelson, stock up on all the supplies that you will need since there's little more than gas and basic groceries at the tiny roadside communities along the way. Restaurants are easier to find than well-stocked food stores. Keep in mind that the population between Fort Nelson and Watson Lake is less than 1,000 people, a startling fact when you consider just how much land there is between these two towns. With that in mind, don't come here expecting services every few miles!

Once past Fort Nelson, the highway traverses due west through deep lodgepole pine forests with closed-in views for the first section. The most notable feature early on is the turnoff at 29 kilometers (17 miles) for the Liard Highway, an exceptionally remote dirt road that heads due north 137 kilometers (82 miles) to the BC/Northwest Territories border before connecting with the road to Yellowknife, the capital of the Northwest Territories. This lonely road is very much like the old Alaska Highway—few services and an almost total lack of civilization along the way.

Beyond the junction, the highway begins its long ascent of Steamboat Mountain. In places the highway climbs at a 10-percent grade toward the 3,500-foot-high point at 79 kilometers (48 miles) where the views from this mountain ridge are breathtaking. High above the Testa River valley, the views of the northern Rockies in the far distance are a mere taste of the scenery to come later in the drive. Just before the crest, the tiny settlement of Steamboat is passed, home to a gas station and cafe.

This area, called "Steamboat Country" by the locals, was named by a Scottish pioneer who thought the mountain resembled a steamboat when viewing it from below. To the south, the views encompass a great deal of the Muskwa (which means "bear") River, a major tributary of the Liard, as well as Indian Head Mountain, a local landmark above the highway. At 97 kilometers (58 miles) is a designated viewpoint for Teetering Rock, a prominent rock on the horizon.

To the west and south, the edges of one of the largest protected areas in the world can be seen. The newly created 10.8-million-acre Muskwa-Kechika Wilderness Area preserves a major part of the vast tract (700 kilometers wide by 1,200 high) of northern Rockies between the Alaska and

Stewart-Cassiar Highways. The area is called by many prominent biologists "the Serengeti of the north" as it is has a virtually intact predator-prey system and is one of the richest wildlife environments in the world; a place where life functions much as it has for thousands of years without the interference of humans. Although much of the new wilderness area is within "special management zones" that still allow for limited hunting and mining, several massive new "Class A" (the highest level of protection) parks have been created. The largest one, Northern Rockies Provincial Park, which lies to the east and south of Stone Mountain, is now BC's third largest park at 665,700 hectares.

Before dropping to the Testa River valley in a series of long curves, the highway continues to traverse high above the gentle, rolling landscape and has panoramic views to the west for several more kilometers. At the bottom of the descent, Testa River Provincial Park is reached at 100 kilometers (60 miles) and has 25 grassy campsites alongside the river. About 20 minutes beyond the park entrance is a small group of services including gas, food, and accommodation. Through here, the highway heads due west through deep forests in the North Testa River valley before beginning to climb into the eastern edge of the northern Rockies at Summit Lake.

After traveling well to the east of the northern Rockies for hundreds of kilometers, the Alaska Highway finally meets the range at the southern entrance of Stone Mountain Provincial Park at 140 kilometers (84 miles). The park is a dramatic combination of desolate peaks, jewel-like turquoise rivers, high alpine lakes, hoodoos, and glacier-carved U-shaped valleys. As much of Stone Mountain lies above treeline, the wilderness hiking opportunities across the tundra are virtually endless and open to the imagination.

The stretch of highway from here to the north end of Muncho Lake Provincial Park is one glorious panorama after another. After climbing steeply past stark mountain and canyon scenery, the highway reaches the high point for the entire Alaska Highway just past Summit Lake at 143 kilometers (86 miles). At 4,250 feet, the highway here is nearly in the alpine, with only a thin band of forest separating the highway from the barren tundra and rock slopes of the mountains lining the route. With the short summers this far north, come prepared for any weather in the pass area as it has been known to snow here in every month of the year. The gentle peaks in the area are strikingly similar in color with light greys and oranges being the main colors. Although unseen, the highest summits have small glaciers that supply the "rock flour" that gives the lakes and rivers in the area their distinctive aquamarine color.

Summit Lake is a beauty, with its pale blue waters mirroring the rounded summits that cradle it on both sides. At the 28-site campground near the lake is a boat launch for paddling the frigid waters. Located near the eastern tip of the lake is a cluster of services which include a lodge, restaurant, and gas station.

From the summit area, several short trails allow for a sampling of the unique landscapes of the park. The easy and rewarding Erosion Pillars Trail passes through some of the many interesting geological features of the park. The access road to the longer Flower Springs Lake Trail branches off to the left at the park's services. This 6-kilometer (3.6-mile) round-trip trail is an easy way to hike into the alpine and ends at a beautiful turquoise lake set below 7,400-foot Mount Saint George, the highest peak in the immediate vicinity. For those driving four-wheel-drive vehicles, the Microwave Tower Viewpoint Road, accessed off the same road as for the Flower Springs Lake Trail, can be driven to a high vista above the pass.

While in the area, be sure to be on the lookout for the Stone sheep the park was named after. These sheep are closely related to both the Dall sheep of the Yukon as well as being more distant cousins to the California and Rocky Mountain bighorn sheep found in southern BC. The sheep are protected from hunting and have little fear of people so are commonly seen grazing or looking for salt licks alongside the highway. Mountain caribou and grizzlies are also seen alongside the highway near the summit on occasion.

Beyond the pass, the highway descends into the MacDonald Creek valley and wanders through a scenic limestone gorge and quickly out of the park at the bottom of the descent. After leaving the park, the access road to Wokkpash Provincial Park (attached to the south end of Stone Mountain) is reached at 158 kilometers (95 miles). This gravel access road is the jumping-off point for the long, multiday trek into the Wokkpash Gorge, a stunning hoodoo-lined canyon famous for its wild erosional formations. The trail ends at the gorgeous turquoise expanse of Wokkpash Lake, set below a series of high peaks named after Canadian battles and war heroes of World War II.

Past MacDonald Creek, the highway curves around into the Racing River, another main tributary of the Toad River. Through here the Alaska Highway runs between the Stone Range to the east and the Muskwa Range to the west. Toad River, a small settlement with services, is reached at 193 kilometers (116 miles), just before the southern entrance to Muncho Lake Provincial Park. Another service center, the Poplars, is found 5 kilometers (3 miles) farther. As stone sheep and other wildlife often come to unfortunate ends on the highways in collisions with vehicles, several warning signs along here tell drivers to keep a sharp eye open for wildlife and to slow down, especially at night.

Muncho Lake Provincial Park is reached at 200 kilometers (120 miles) where the highway begins to wind through a series of gorge-like valleys set along the base of desolate limestone peaks. Considered by many to be one of BC's most beautiful parks, Muncho Lake protects the alpine and tundra country on both sides of the Alaska Highway for its 90-kilometer (54-mile) stretch through the park. Through the park, the highway travels near or at treeline, allowing adventuresome hikers to wander across the tundra and strike out for the peaks. Driving here is easily the highlight of the entire BC section of the Alaska Highway. The highway was built through this mountainous stretch after it was decided that construction through the Grand Canyon of the Liard, just north, would be too expensive and time-consuming.

Muncho Lake encompasses a landscape typical of the northern Rockies with features such as limestone peaks, thrust faults, rolling alpine meadows, alluvial fans, and hoodoos. The park is drained by two major river systems, the Trout and the Toad, both of which eventually empty into the Liard River. Although part of the Rockies, these mountains are unlike the main chain of the Rockies protected in the national parks. These mountains are much more eroded and rounded by the elements of time, weathering, and glaciation. In many ways the area bears a striking resemblance to the front ranges of the Rockies near Calgary.

The mountains in the area are sedimentary in nature (as is most of the Rockies) and are wildly contorted in several areas along this initial section. Folded Mountain, a few kilometers into the park, is a result of the pressure of plate tectonics over millions of years as the land is compressed, folded, and uplifted. Most of the park's mountains are a uniform grey color that contrasts starkly with the dark greens of the forests.

At Centennial Falls, found just after crossing the Toad River, the highway is squeezed between towering peaks with cliffs descending down to roadside. Centennial Peak, which stands above the falls, is one of the most distinctive mountains in the park and is noted for its massive summit cliffs. After following right alongside the swift rapids of the Toad River, the highway then bends around a prominent corner and climbs into Muncho Creek and for the first time in the drive, begins to travel due north. From the curve, the views into the rugged headwaters of the Toad River are outstanding.

Wildlife is commonly seen in the park, especially at dawn and dusk. The natural salt licks within the park attract several species including stone sheep and mountain caribou. The salt that accumulates in the course of the winter's road maintenance is also a draw for the animals.

If you haven't already noticed, insects can be bad anywhere along the Alaska Highway, particularly in early summer. With Muncho Lake providing a good breeding ground, mosquitoes in particular can be bothersome along here. The worst time to be on the Alaska Highway is in late spring or early summer when all sorts of nasty insects can make being outside an unpleasant experience.

From where the highway bends back to the north, the mountains that line the eastern side of the highway all the way to the end of the park form an almost continuous ridge system of scree slopes and alpine tundra. At even intervals, narrow V-shaped gorges slice into the peaks where alluvial fans descend to the highway. By hiking away from the highway and up any of these side canyons, interesting and desolately beautiful gorges can be entered at the base of the peaks.

Just before reaching Muncho Lake, a collection of businesses including four lodges, several restaurants, a campground, and a gas station is found. This is one of the few settlements within a park in the entire province. In addition to boat launches for those with their own boats, several companies based here offer lake tours in the summer months. Also located on the lake is Liard Air, a charter floatplane company that can arrange scenic flights over the endless mountains and landings on remote lakes. The distinctive red-roofed Northern Rockies Lodge, found beside the highway and fronting the lake, is one of the largest log buildings in BC and is a luxurious way to enjoy the park.

The southern end of 11-kilometer (6.6-mile) Muncho Lake (which means "big lake" in the native language) is reached at 245 kilometers (147 miles) where the highway begins to run along the shores of the lake below blasted-out cliffs. In the entire length of the Alaska Highway, this area gave the builders the most problems and was the most expensive stretch to build. At one time, the highway ran above the present location but the unstable slopes made it necessary to relocate the road alongside the lake.

Muncho Lake is yet another of the aquamarine-colored lakes found in the Rockies and is actually one of the biggest lakes in the entire chain. The lake is situated between the Sentinel Range to the east and the Terminal Range to the west. The Terminal Range is considered the very northernmost extension of the Rocky Mountain chain that stretches 3,000 kilometers (1,800 miles) from New Mexico in the southern United States to northern BC.

Although only at an elevation of 2,700 feet, Muncho Lake feels much higher. With the surrounding peaks rising as high as 7,000 feet, the vertical relief (especially to the east) is impressive. Strawberry Flats campground with its 15 sites is reached at 246 kilometers (148 miles) while MacDonald campground, also with 15 sites, is found 9 kilometers (5.4 miles) farther north. Both campgrounds are alongside the lake and offer excellent views.

The best pictures of Muncho Lake are taken from the well-signed viewpoint high above the lake's northern tip. Here the sweeping view includes the lake, its mountain rim, and peaks in the far distance above the Toad River.

The scenery continues to be exciting as the highway travels north and down into the Trout River system. As the mountain views begin to fade, the highway passes out of the park at 283 kilometers (170 miles) and into an area of lower hills on the outer edge of the Rockies where the landscape fades back into plateau. After a curvy section at 292 kilometers (175 miles), the highway passes the first view of the mighty Liard River to the east at 300 kilometers (180 miles).

The Liard is one of BC's great rivers and drains the whole northeastern corner of the province before merging with the even larger Mackenzie River

*Looking south down the length of Muncho Lake from the viewpoint
at the north end of the lake.*

in the Northwest Territories. From there, the Liard's waters are spilled into the cold depths of the Arctic Ocean in Canada's far north. The river was named by French-Canadian explorers. They used the French word for the poplar tree ("liard") because the poplar often lines the riverbanks. From the bridge across the river at 309 kilometers (185 miles), the Alaska Highway follows the Liard all the way to Watson Lake in the Yukon. As the highway travels north through deep forest, the mountain views are exchanged for frequent views of the Liard River for much of the remaining way to the Yukon. During construction, the Liard Valley was seen as the easiest way to punch the highway through to Alaska. The Grand Canyon of the Liard, the most dramatic part of the entire river, is just east of here but not visible from the highway. As part of the new Muskwa-Kechika Wilderness Area, a long section of the Grand Canyon of the Liard has been protected in a new provincial park.

The small community of Liard River is reached just north of the bridge where basic tourist services, including a gas station and a restaurant, are found. Just north of here was BC's lowest-ever recorded temperature, a bone-chilling -59 degrees C (-74 degrees F), recorded in 1947. The gas station is a taste of the outback style so famous in the north with its antlers and rustic appearance. Just a kilometer (0.6 mile) past the community is the famous Liard Hot Springs and the end of the drive description.

Liard Hot Springs is an almost mandatory stop before proceeding north. The two pools here, Alpha and Beta, have water temperatures between 38 and 49 degrees C (100 F to 120 degrees F). The moist and warm microclimate of the immediate area hosts a variety of rare plant life found nowhere else in BC. Although the hot springs were known by a few pioneers prior to the building of the highway, the discovery of their waters was a welcome sight for weary construction crews in 1942. In addition to the hot springs, the park here features interpretive programs in the summer and a well-groomed campground with 53 sites.

The hot springs gained international exposure in 1997 when two people where killed when a hungry black bear attacked bathers on the boardwalk to the hot springs. Anywhere in the north, be aware that the bear population outnumbers the human population and act accordingly. This means keeping your senses tuned to what's happening around you, making noise when walking through the forest, and traveling in pairs at the minimum. Most northern hikers come equipped with both bear bells and bear spray.

After relaxing in the hot springs, head north on the final leg of this unforgettable journey toward the Yukon. Watson Lake, the next major settlement, is 256 kilometers (154 miles) northwest and will take another three or four hours of steady driving to reach. To complete a massive loop trip of northern BC, head south on the Stewart-Cassiar Highway (Drive 23) from just west of Watson Lake to Kitwanga and Highway 16 (Drive 22, Yellowhead Highway). From there, drive east on the Yellowhead Highway back to Prince George.

# Appendix: Sources of More Information

## Recommended resources

### BC Accommodations Guide
Call 1-800-663-6000 to obtain a copy. This free publication lists almost every accommodation in the province, ranging from campgrounds to five-star hotels. It covers all of BC and is broken down by region for easy reference.

### Beautiful British Columbia Travel Guide
Published by *Beautiful British Columbia Magazine*. The bible of travel information on BC, this volume is very comprehensive and is a must-have resource. It can be ordered directly from the publisher at 1-800-663-7611.

### The BC Recreational Atlas (new edition to be retitled *The BC Road and Recreation Atlas*)
Published by PTC Phototype Composting Ltd, 1989. This atlas contains the best series of road maps for BC and shows the locations of all the major backroads, campsites, and parks. For adventuring off the beaten track, this book is a must. It can be ordered on-line through the Adventurous Traveler Bookstore (http://www.adventuroustraveler.com) or from Whitecap Books at 604-980-9852, ext. 226.

### The Canadian Rockies Trail Guide, 6th Edition
Brian Patton and Bart Robinson
Summerthought Publishers, Banff, Alberta, 1994

### Classic Hikes in the Canadian Rockies
Graeme Pole
Altitude Publishing, Canmore, Alberta, 1994

### Inside Out British Columbia: A Best Places Guide to the Outdoors
Jack Christie
Raincoast Books, Vancouver, 1998
This is a new, thoroughly complete, and detailed guide to outdoor adventures from easy to extreme, covering activities ranging from fishing to climbing. It is an excellent resource.

### Adventuring in British Columbia
Isabel Nanton and Mary Simpson
Douglas & McIntyre Publishers, Vancouver, 1991
This is the bible for outdoor recreation for BC. It is very comprehensive and covers a full range of activities and all regions.

## Important phone numbers

1. **Super Natural British Columbia**
   1-800-663-6000 for accommodation reservations
   1-800-667-3306 for travel information
   (from anywhere in North America)
   Super Natural British Columbia is run by the Ministry of Tourism. Call for information and maps, to book accommodations, and to obtain general travel information. They also can be contacted at:
   Tourism British Columbia
   Parliament Buildings
   Victoria, BC
   Canada, V8V 1X4

2. **BC Parks Headquarters**
   250-387-5002
   They also can be contacted at:
   BC Parks
   800 Johnson Street
   Victoria, BC
   Canada, V8V 1X4

3. **BC Ministry of Highways**
   250-387-7788
   They also can be contacted at:
   Ministry of Transportation and Highways
   P.O. Box 9850
   Stn. Prov Govt
   Victoria, BC
   Canada, V8W 9T5

4. **BC Ferries**
   250-386-3431 (see website in next section)

## Recommended BC websites for BC travel

1. **Discover British Columbia**
   http://www.discoverbc.com/
   A good general information source including vacation planners, maps, weather forecasts, on-line accommodation booking, and lists of attractions.

2. **Travel BC**
   http://travel.bc.ca/
   The premier travel and tourism planning site for BC. Excellent source for information. This is the place to start your search.

3. **BC Online Highways**
   http://www.ohwy.com/bc/homepage.htm
   Put together by a travel magazine. Has key word searches and links to many of BC's communities. Not slick but very comprehensive.

4. **BC Ministry of Highways Route Information**
   http://www.th.gov.bc.ca/bchighways/routeinfo.htm
   Highway descriptions and suggested routes and links to other highway sites.

5. **BC Ministry of Highways Road Reports**
   http://www.th.gov.bc.ca/bchighways/roadreports/roadreports.htm
   The best source for up-to-date highway conditions.

6. **Environment Canada Weather Reports**
   http://weather.ec.gc.ca/bc_e.shtml
   Excellent site with forecasts for all the major communities in BC. The best source for weather information. Gives current conditions and 4-day forecasts.

7. **BC Ferries**
   http://www.bcferries.bc.ca/index.html
   Official BC Ferries website. Very comprehenisve.

8. **BC Adventure Network**
   http://www.bcadventure.com/
   Excellent site for BC's regions and outdoor recreation opportunities.

9. BC Ministry of Parks
   http://www.env.gov.bc.ca/
   Official BC government site. A gold mine of information on every park in the province with contact information for each.

10. BC Forest Service
    http://www.for.gov.bc.ca/
    Official government site of the BC Forest Service.

11. BC Forest Service Districts
    http://www.for.gov.bc.ca/mof/regdis.htm
    Links to the various BC Forest District offices throughout BC. The best source for information on current backroad conditions in the various regions.

12. The British Columbia Outdoors
    http://bcadventure.com/adventure/wilderness/
    A good source of information on outdoor recreation and nature of BC.

13. Outdoor Recreation Council of BC
    http://www.orcbc.bc.ca/
    Links to all of the province's outdoor clubs.

14. Super Camping BC
    http://www.camping.bc.ca/
    An excellent source for campsite locations.

15. Lodging BC
    http://www.lodging.bc.ca/
    A source for links to commercial accommodations.

16. Travel BC.com
    http://www.vacationsbc.com/index.html
    A good general reference on traveling in BC.

17. Tourism BC
    http://www.tbc.gov.bc.ca/tourism/tourismhome.html
    Official Tourism BC site.

18. Bivouac Mountaineering Directory
    http://www.bivouac.com/

    Excellent source of information on the mountains and climbing opportunities in BC. Has mountain-club trip schedules, contact information, and links to other mountain-oriented sites.

19. Mountain Equipment Co-op
    http://www.mec.ca/

    The premier outdoor equipment store in Vancouver. The place to gear up before your trip.

20. Adventurous Traveler Bookstore
    http://shop.gorp.com:80/atbook/bookloc.asp?location_id=CAN
    The best selection on BC guidebooks on the web.

Note: Internet sites are as of October 1999. Addresses may change. If the address listed here doesn't work, an Internet search should find the new address.

# More information for specific drives

## Drive 1: West Coast Highway

**BC Parks**
South Vancouver Island District
2930 Trans Canada Highway
Victoria, BC, V9E 1K3
250-391-2300

**BC Ministry of Highways**
South Island District
103-4475 Viewmont Ave.
Victoria, BC, V8Z 5K8
250-952-4515

**Tourism Association of Vancouver Island**
Victoria, BC
250-382-3551

**Port Renfrew Parks Canada Information Centre**
West Coast Trail (seasonal)
250-647-5434

*The Islands*
Published by Tourism Vancouver Island
#302-45 Bastion Square
Victoria, BC, V8W 1J1
250-382-3551
> An excellent, free publication for all of Vancouver Island and the Gulf Islands.

**BC Parks**
http:/www.env.gov.bc.ca.bcparks/
http://www.elp.gov.bc.ca/bcparks/explore/svidis.htm

*Pacific Rim National Park Official Site*
http://www.harbour.com/parkscan/pacrim/

*Sooke Website*
http://www.sookenet.com/sooke.html

*Juan De Fuca Marine Trail*
http://www.sookenet.com/sooke/activity/trails/jdftrail.html

*BC Parks*
http://www.env.gov.bc.ca/bcparks/

*The Islands*
http://bcadventure.com/adventure/explore/island.html

*Victoria and Vancouver Island Travel Guide*
http://victoriabc.com/

## Drive 2: Pacific Rim Highway

**BC Ministry of Highways**
Central Island District
6475 Metral Dr.
Nanaimo, BC, V9T 2L9
250-390-6100

**BC Parks**
Strathcona District
P.O. Box 1479
Parksville, BC, V9P 2H4
250-954-4600

**M.V. Lady Rose ship**
250-723-8313

**Tourism Association of Vancouver Island**
Victoria, BC
250-382-3551

**Pacific Rim National Park Reserve**
Box 280
2185 Ocean Terrace Rd.
Ucuelet, BC, VOR 3A0
250-726-7721

**Tofino Infocenter**
Campbell Street
Tofino, BC
250-725-3414

*The Islands*
Published by Tourism Vancouver Island
#302-45 Bastion Square
Victoria, BC, V8W 1J1
250-382-3551
> An excellent, free publication for all of Vancouver Island and the Gulf Islands.

*Kayak Routes of the Pacific Northwest Coast*
Peter McGee
Greystone Books, 1998
> The premier sea kayaking guide to BC's long and rugged coast. Useful for anyone exploring by boat. Covers the Broken Islands and Clayoquot Sound.

*Pacific Rim National Park Official Site*
http://www.harbour.com/parkscan/pacrim/

*BC Parks*
http://www.elp.gov.bc.ca/bcparks/explore/stradis.htm

*The Islands*
http://bcadventure.com/adventure/explore/island.html

*Victoria and Vancouver Island Travel Guide*
http://victoriabc.com/

*Tofino Guide*
http://www.tofino-bc.com/

*Alberni Chamber of Commerce*
http://www.alberni.net/~avcoc/index.html

## Drive 3: Old Island Highway

**BC Ferries**
250-386-3431

**BC Parks**
Strathcona District
P.O. Box 1479
Parksville, BC, V9P 2H4
250-954-4600

**BC Ministry of Highways**
Central Island District
6475 Metral Dr.
Nanaimo, BC, V9T 2L9
250-390-6100

**Tourism Association of Vancouver Island**
Victoria, BC
250-382-3551

**Parksville Infocenter**
Highway 19
Parksville, BC, V9P 263
250-248-3613

**Courtenay-Comox Infocenter**
2040 Cliffe Avenue
Courtenay, BC, V9N 2L3
250-334-3234

**Campbell River Infocenter**
1235 Shoppers Row in Tyee Plaza
Campbell River, BC, V9W 5B6
250-287-4636

*The Islands*
Published by Tourism Vancouver Island
#302-45 Bastion Square
Victoria, BC, V8W 1J1
250-382-3551
> An excellent, free publication for all of Vancouver Island and the Gulf Islands.

*Kayak Routes of the Pacific Northwest Coast*
Peter McGee
Greystone Books, 1998
> The premier sea kayaking guide to BC's long and rugged coast. Useful for anyone exploring by boat. Covers Georgia Strait.

*BC Parks*
http://www.elp.gov.bc.ca/bcparks/explore/stradis.htm

*The Islands*
http://bcadventure.com/adventure/explore/island.html

*Victoria and Vancouver Island Travel Guide*
http://victoriabc.com/

*Campbell River Tourism*
http://www.vquest.com/crtourism/

*City of Parksville*
http://city.parksville.bc.ca/

## Drive 4: Gulf Islands

**BC Parks**
South Vancouver Island District
2930 Trans Canada Highway
Victoria, BC, V9E 1K3
250-391-2300

**Tourism Association of Vancouver Island**
Victoria, BC
250-382-3551

**Saltspring Island Infocenter**
121 Lower Ganges Road
Saltspring Island, BC, V0S IV0
250-537-4223

*The Islands*
Published by Tourism Vancouver Island
#302-45 Bastion Square
Victoria, BC, V8W 1J1
250-382-3551
> An excellent, free publication for all of Vancouver Island and the Gulf Islands.

*The Gulf Islander*
Published by Driftwood Publishing
328 Lower Ganges Road
Saltspring Island, BC, V8K 2V3
250-537-9933
> A comprehenive, free publication covering the main Gulf Islands.

*Island Paddling*
Mary Ann Snowden
Orca Book Publishers, 1993
> A sea kayaking guide that covers the shorelines of the Gulf Islands extensively.

*Hiking the Gulf Islands*
Charles Kahn
Orca Book Publishers, 1995
> The bible for hiking trails in the Gulf Islands.

*BC Parks*
http://www.elp.gov.bc.ca/bcparks/explore/svidis.htm

*The Islands*
http://bcadventure.com/adventure/explore/island.html

*Gulf Islands Online*
http://www.gulfislands.net/

*Victoria and Vancouver Island Travel Guide*
http://victoriabc.com/

## Drive 5: Strathcona Provincial Park

**BC Parks**
Strathcona District
P.O. Box 1479
Parksville, BC, V9P 2H4
250-954-4600

**BC Ministry of Highways**
North Island District
550 Comox Rd.
Courtenay, BC, V9N 3P6
250-334-6951

**Campbell River Infocenter**
1235 Shoppers Row in Tyee Plaza
Campbell River, BC, V9W 586
250-287-4636

*Hiking Trails III—Central and Northern Vancouver Island*
Jane Waddell
Outdoor Club of Victoria, 1986.
> This small guide covers the hikes in the mountains of Strathcona Park as well as those on Cape Scott on the northern tip of Vancouver Island.

*The Islands*
Published by Tourism Vancouver Island
#302-45 Bastion Square
Victoria, BC, V8W 1J1
250-382-3551
> An excellent, free publication for all of Vancouver Island and the Gulf Islands.

**Strathcona Park Lodge**
250-286-3122

**Uchuck III ferry**
250-283-2325

*BC Parks*
http://www.elp.gov.bc.ca/bcparks/explore/stradis.htm

*Strathcona Park Lodge*
http://www.strathcona.bc.ca/colt_location.htm

*The Islands*
http://bcadventure.com/adventure/explore/island.html

*Victoria and Vancouver Island Travel Guide*
http://victoriabc.com/

## Drive 6: Sunshine Coast Highway

**BC Parks**
Garibaldi/Sunshine Coast District
Alice Lake Park
P.O. Box 220
Brackendale, BC, V0N 1H0
604-898-3678

**Ministry of Highways**
1975 Field Rd.
Sechelt, BC
250-740-5040

**Sechelt Infocenter**
5755 Cowrie Street
Sechelt, BC, V0N 3A0
604-885-0662

**Powell River Infocenter**
4690 Marine Avenue
Powell River, BC, V8A 2L1
604-485-4701

**Savary Island water taxi**
604-483-9749

*Vancouver, Coast & Mountains*
Published by Vancouver, Coast &
    Mountains Tourism Region
204-1755 West Broadway
Vancouver, BC, V6J 4S5
604-739-9011
    An excellent, free publication for
    Vancouver and southwestern BC.

*Sunshine & Salt Air*
Bryan Carson and Karen Southern
Harbour Publishing, 1991
    The bible for outdoor recreation on
    the Sunshine Coast.

*Kayak Routes of the Pacific Northwest*
    *Coast*
Peter McGee
Greystone Books, 1998
    The premier sea kayaking guide to
    BC's long and rugged coast. Useful for
    anyone exploring by boat. Covers all
    of the fjords off the Sunshine Coast.

*Secrets of Cruising: The New Frontier, British*
    *Columbia Coast & Undiscovered Inlets*
Hugo Anderson
Anderson Publishing Company, 1995
ISBN: 0-945989-25-3
    The guide to the magical BC coast. Very
    comprehensive. Best suited to sailors.

*Sunshine Coast Tourism Information*
http://www.bigpacific.com/

*Gibsons Chamber of Commerce*
http://www.sunshine.net/www/200/
    sn0213/default.html

*Sechelt Chamber of Commerce*
http://www.sunshine.net/www/200/
    sn0257/default.html

## Drive 7: Sea to Sky Highway

**BC Parks**
Garibaldi/Sunshine Coast District
Alice Lake Park
P.O. Box 220
Brackendale, BC, V0N 1H0
604-898-3678

**BC Ministry of Highways**
Howe Sound District
1690 Main St.
North Vancouver, BC, V7J 1E3
604-981-0042

*Vancouver, Coast & Mountains*
Published by Vancouver, Coast &
    Mountains Tourism Region
204-1755 West Broadway
Vancouver, BC, V6J 4S5
604-739-9011
    An excellent, free publication for
    Vancouver and southwestern BC.

**Squamish Infocenter**
37950 Cleveland Avenue
Squamish, BC, V0N 3G0
604-892-9244

**Whistler Infocenter**
Highway 99 & Lake Placid Road
Whistler Creekside
Box 181
Whistler, BC V0N 2B0
604-932-5528

*A Guide to Climbing and Hiking in Southwestern British Columbia*
Bruce Fairley
Gordon Shoules Book Publishers, 1986
The bible for hikers and climbers in SW BC. Lists hundreds of peaks.

*103 Hikes in Southwestern British Columbia*
Mary and David Macaree
Douglas & McIntyre, 1987
The best guide for hiking trails in the lower Coast Mountains. Covers Garibaldi Park and the whole Whistler area well.

*Sea to Sky.com*
http://www.sea2sky.com/

*Whistler Resort Guide*
http://www.whistler.net/

## Drive 8: Duffey Lake Road

**BC Ministry of Highways**
Howe Sound District
1690 Main St.
North Vancouver, BC, V7J 1E3
604-981-0042

*Vancouver, Coast & Mountains*
Published by Vancouver, Coast & Mountains Tourism Region
204-1755 West Broadway
Vancouver, BC, V6J 4S5
604-739-9011
An excellent, free publication for Vancouver and southwestern BC.

*A Guide to Climbing and Hiking in Southwestern British Columbia*
Bruce Fairley
Gordon Shoules Book Publishers, 1986
The bible for hikers and climbers in SW BC. Lists hundreds of peaks.

*103 Hikes in Southwestern British Columbia*
Mary and David Macaree
Douglas & McIntyre, 1987
The best guide for hiking trails in the lower Coast Mountains. Lists the hikes off the Duffey Lake Road.

## Drive 9: Chilliwack River Valley

**BC Forest Service** (for road information)
Chilliwack Forest District
Box 159, 9880 South McGrath Road
Rosedale, BC, V0X 1X0
604-794-2100

**BC Parks**
Lower Mainland District
1610 Mt. Seymour Road
North Vancouver, BC, V7G 1L3
604-924-2200

**Chilliwack River Hatchery tours**
604-858-7227

**Chilliwack Infocenter**
44150 Luckakuck Way
Sardis, BC, V2R 4A7
604-858-8121

*A Guide to Climbing and Hiking in Southwestern British Columbia*
Bruce Fairley
Gordon Shoules Book Publishers, 1986
The bible for hikers and climbers in SW BC. Lists hundreds of peaks.

*103 Hikes in Southwestern British Columbia*
Mary and David Macaree
Douglas & McIntyre, 1987
The best guide for hiking trails in the lower Coast Mountains. Lists the hikes off the Duffey Lake Road.

## Drive 10: The Okanagan

**BC Parks**
Okanagan District
Box 399
Summerland, BC, V0H 1Z0
250-494-6500

**BC Ministry of Highways**
South Okanagan District
254 Haynes St.
Penticton, BC, V2A 5R9
250-492-1300

**Dominion Radio Astrophysical Observatory**
250-490-4355

Okanagan Similkameen Tourism Association
Kelowna, BC
250-860-5999

**Kelowna Infocenter**
544 Harvey Avenue (Hwy. 97)
Kelowna, BC, V1Y 6C9
250-861-1515

**Penticton Infocenter**
185 Lakeshore Drive
Penticton, BC, V2A 1B7
250-493-4055

**Osoyoos Infocenter**
Junction Highways 3 & 97
Osoyoos, BC, V0H 1V0
250-495-7142

**Thompson/Okanagan Tourism Association**
1332 Water Street
Kelowna, BC, V1Y 9P4
250-860-5999

*BC Parks*
http://www.elp.gov.bc.ca/bcparks/explore/
    okandis.htm

*Thompson/Okanagan*
http://bcadventure.com/adventure/
    explore/thompsonok.html

*Visit the Okanagan*
http://www.travelall.com/

*Kelowna Chamber of Commerce*
http://www.kelownachamber.org/

## Drive 11: Crowsnest Highway

**Manning Park Visitors Center**
250-840-8836

**BC Parks**
Okanagan District
Box 399
Summerland, BC, V0H 1Z0
250-494-6500

**Cathedral Lakes Lodge**
250-226-7560

**Ministry of Highways**
Fraser Valley District
45474 Luckakuck Way
Chilliwack, BC V2R 3S9
604-795-8363

**Okanagan Similkameen Tourism Association**
Kelowna, BC
250-860-5999

**Hope Infocenter**
919 Water Street
Hope, BC, V0X 1L0
604-869-2021

*BC Parks*
http://www.elp.gov.bc.ca/bcparks/explore/
    okandis.htm

*Thompson/Okanagan*
http://bcadventure.com/adventure/
    explore/thompsonok.html

## Drive 12: Silvery Slocan Loop

**BC Parks**
Kootenay District
Box 118
Wasa, BC, V0B 2K0
250-422-4200
250-825-3500 (Cody Caves)

**Ministry of Highways**
Central Kootenay District
2nd Floor, 310 Ward Street
Nelson, BC, V1L 5S4
800-665-2515

**Kootenay Country Tourist Association**
Nelson, BC
250-352-6033

**Nelson Infocenter**
225 Hall Street
Nelson, BC, V1L 5X4
250-352-3433

*BC Rockies Vacation Planner*
Published by Tourism Rockies
Box 10, 1905 Warren Avenue
Kimberly, BC, V1A 2Y5
250-427-3344
    An excellent free publication on the
    BC Rockies.

*Go & Do: The West Kootenay Visitor's*
  *Guide*
Box 430
Kaslo, BC, V0G 1M0
800-663-4619
  A free and informative guide.

*100 Hikes in the Inland Northwest*
Rich Landers
The Mountaineers, 1987.
  Covers the hikes in Valhalla and
  Kokanee Provincial Parks.

*BC Parks*
http://www.elp.gov.bc.ca/bcparks/explore/
  kootney.htm

*City of Nelson*
http://www.city.nelson.bc.ca/

## Drive 13: Kootenay Parkway

**Kootenay National Park**
P.O. Box 220
Radium Hot Springs, BC, V0A 1M0
250-347-9615
E-mail: Kootenay_reception@pch.gc.ca

**BC Parks**
Kootenay District
Box 118
Wasa, BC, V0B 2K0
250-422-4200

**Ministry of Highways**
East Kootenay District
129 10th Ave. South
Cranbrook, BC, V1C 2N1
250-426-1500

**Radium Hot Springs Infocenter**
7585 Main Street W.
Radium Hot Springs, BC, V0A 1M0
250-347-9331

**BC Rockies Vacation Planner**
Published by Tourism Rockies
Box 10, 1905 Warren Avenue
Kimberly, BC, V1A 2Y5
250-427-3344
  An excellent free publication on the
  BC Rockies.

*BC Parks*
http://www.elp.gov.bc.ca/bcparks/explore/
  kootney.htm

*British Columbia Rocky Mountains*
http://www.bctravel.com/se/index.html

*Visitor Information Guide to the Canadian*
  *Rockies*
http://canadianrockies.net/index.html

*BC Rockies Guide*
http://www.bcrockies.com/

*Official Kootenay National Park Site*
http://parkscanada.pch.gc.ca/kootenay/

*Radium Hot Springs*
http://www.radiumhotsprings.com/village/

## Drive 14: Icefields Parkway

**Banff National Park**
P.O. Box 900
Banff
Alberta, Canada, T0L 0C0
403-762-1550
E-mail: banff_vrc@pch.gc.ca

**Jasper National Park**
P.O. Box 10
Jasper, Alberta, T0E 1E0
780-852-6176

*Visitor Information Guide to the Canadian*
  *Rockies*
http://canadianrockies.net/index.html

*Official Banff National Park Site*
http://parkscanada.pch.gc.ca/banff/

*Official Jasper National Park Site*
http://parkscanada.pch.gc.ca/jasper/

## Drive 15: Trans Canada Highway—
## Golden to Lake Louise

**Yoho National Park**
P.O. Box 99
Field, BC, V0A 1G0
250-343-6783
E-mail: yoho_info@pch.gc.ca

**Ministry of Highways**
Selkirk District
555 Victoria Rd.
Revelstoke, BC, V0E 2S0
250-837-7646

**Golden Infocenter**
500-10th Avenue N.
Golden, BC, V0A 1H0
250-344-7125

*BC Rockies Vacation Planner*
Published by Tourism Rockies
Box 10, 1905 Warren Avenue
Kimberly, BC, V1A 2Y5
250-427-3344
    An excellent free publication on the
    BC Rockies.

**Yoho Burgess Shale Foundation**
800-343-3006

*British Columbia Rocky Mountains*
http://www.bctravel.com/se/index.html

*Visitor Information Guide to the Canadian Rockies*
http://canadianrockies.net/index.html

*BC Rockies Guide*
http://www.bcrockies.com/

*Golden Chamber of Commerce*
http://www.rockies.net/~goldcham/

*Official Yoho National Park Site*
http://parkscanada.pch.gc.ca/yoho/

## Drive 16: Fraser Canyon

**BC Parks**
Thompson River District
1210 McGill Road
Kamloops, BC, V2C 6N6
250-851-3000

**Cattermole Timber**
604-823-6525

**Ministry of Highways**
Fraser Valley District
45474 Luckakuck Way
Chilliwack, BC, V2R 3S9
604-795-8363

**Hope Infocenter**
919 Water Street
Hope, BC, V0X 1L0
604-869-2021

*A Guide to Climbing and Hiking in Southwestern British Columbia*
Bruce Fairley
Gordon Shoules Book Publishers, 1986
    The bible for hikers and climbers in
    SW BC. Lists hundreds of peaks.

*BC Parks—Stein Valley*
http://www.elp.gov.bc.ca/bcparks/explore/parkpgs/steinvly.htm

*Hope Area*
http://www.rainbowcountry.bc.ca/

## Drive 17: Trans Canada Highway— Revelstoke to Golden

**Glacier Park Lodge**
250-837-2126

**Mount Revelstoke and Glacier National Parks**
P.O. Box 350
Revelstoke, BC, V0E 2S0
250-837-7500
E-mail: revglacier_reception@pch.gc.ca

**Ministry of Highways**
Selkirk District
555 Victoria Rd.
Revelstoke, BC, V0E 2S0
250-837-7646

**Revelstoke Infocenter**
Junction Highways 1 & 23
Revelstoke, BC, V0E 2S0
250-837-5345

*BC Rockies Vacation Planner*
Published by: Tourism Rockies
Box 10, 1905 Warren Avenue
Kimberly, BC, V1A 2Y5
250-427-3344
    An excellent free publication on the
    BC Rockies.

*Official Mt. Revelstoke National Park Site*
http://parkscanada.pch.gc.ca/revelstoke/

*Official Glacier National Park Site*
http://parkscanada.pch.gc.ca/glacier/

*BC Parks*
http://www.elp.gov.bc.ca/bcparks/explore/
    kootney.htm

*Revelstoke Chamber of Commerce*
http://www.revelstokecc.bc.ca/

## Drive 18: Mt. Robson Provincial Park

**Mt. Robson Visitors Center**
Box 579
Valemount, BC, V0E 1Z0
250-566-4325

**Ministry of Highways**
Robson District
300 Robson Ctr.
McBride, BC, V0J 2E0
250-569-3750

**Valemount Infocenter**
Highway 5
Valemount, BC, V0E 2Z0
250-566-4846

*BC Parks*
http://www.elp.gov.bc.ca/bcparks/explore/
    parkpgs/mtrobson.htm

*Visitor Information Guide to the Canadian
    Rockies*
http://canadianrockies.net/index.html

*BC Rockies Guide*
http://www.bcrockies.com/

*British Columbia Rocky Mountains*
http://www.bctravel.com/se/index.html

## Drive 19: Carpenter Lake Road

**BC Parks**
Cariboo District Office
281-1st Avenue North
Williams Lake, BC, V2G 1Y7
250-398-4414

**Forest Service in Lillooet**
250-256-1200

**Ministry of Highways**
Cariboo District
209-540 Borland St.
Williams Lake, BC, V2G 1R8
250-398-4510

**Ministry of Forests: Squamish**
604-898-2100

**Lillooet Travel Infocenter**
790 Main Street
Lillooet, BC, V0K 1V0
250-256-4308

*A Guide to Climbing and Hiking in
    Southwestern British Columbia*
Bruce Fairley
Gordon Shoules Book Publishers, 1986
    The bible for hikers and climbers in
    SW BC. Lists hundreds of peaks.

*BC Parks*
http://www.elp.gov.bc.ca/bcparks/explore/
    cariboo.htm

*Cariboo, Chilcotin, Coast*
http://bcadventure.com/adventure/
    explore/cariboo.html

## Drive 20: Chilcotin Backroads

**BC Parks**
Cariboo District Office
281-1st Avenue North
Williams Lake, BC, V2G 1Y7
250-398-4414

**BC Forest Service** (for backroad info)
Cariboo Forest Region
200-640 Borland Street
Williams Lake, BC, V2G 4T1
250-398-4345

**Ministry of Highways**
Cariboo District
209-540 Borland St.
Williams Lake, BC, V2G 1R8
250-398-4510

*Cariboo, Chilcotin, Coast*
http://bcadventure.com/adventure/
    explore/cariboo.html

## Drive 21: Freedom Highway

**BC Parks**
Cariboo District Office
281-1st Avenue North
Williams Lake, BC, V2G 1Y7
250-398-4414

**BC Forest Service** (for backroad info)
Cariboo Forest Region
200-640 Borland Street
Williams Lake, BC, V2G 4T1
250-398-4345

**Ministry of Highways**
Cariboo District
209-540 Borland St.
Williams Lake, BC, V2G 1R8
250-398-4510

**Cariboo Tourism Association**
Williams Lake, BC
250-392-2226

*Secrets of Cruising: The New Frontier,*
*British Columbia Coast & Undiscovered*
*Inlets*
Hugo Anderson
Anderson Publishing Company, 1995
ISBN: 0-945989-25-3
The guide to the magical BC coast.
Very comprehensive. Suited for
sailors. Covers the midcoast accessible
from Bella Coola.

*BC Parks*
http://www.env.gov.bc.ca/bcparks/

*Cariboo, Chilcotin, Coast*
http://bcadventure.com/adventure/
explore/cariboo.html

*Chilcotin Guide*
http://www.chilcotin.bc.ca/

## Drive 22: Yellowhead Highway

**BC Parks**
Skeena District
3790 Alfred Avenue, Bag 5000
Smithers, BC, V0J 2N0
250-847-7320

**Ministry of Highways**
Skeena District
4825 Keith Ave.
Terrace, BC, V8G 1K7
250-638-6440

*Northern British Columbia Travel Guide*
Published on behalf of the Northern Bitish
Columbia Tourism Assocation by OP
Publishing
780 Beatty Street, Suite 300
Vancouver, BC, V6M 2M1
604-606-4644
An excellent free publication on the
north.

**Prince Rupert Infocenter**
250-624-5637

*Secrets of Cruising: The New Frontier,*
*British Columbia Coast & Undiscovered*
*Inlets*
Hugo Anderson
Anderson Publishing Company, 1995
ISBN: 0-945989-25-3
The guide to the magical BC coast.
Very comprehensive.

**Smithers Infocenter**
250-847-9854

*BC Parks (descriptions of parks)*
http://www.elp.gov.bc.ca/bcparks/explore/
skeendis.htm

*Smithers On-line*
http://www.hiway16.com/a/index.htm

*Prince Rupert Virtual City*
http://www.rupert.net/

*North by Northwest*
http://bcadventure.com/adventure/
explore/north.html

## Drive 23: Stewart-Cassiar Highway

**BC Parks**
Skeena District
3790 Alfred Avenue, Bag 5000
Smithers, BC, V0J 2N0
250-847-7320
250-771-4591 (Dease Lake)

Iskut band office
250-234-3331

**Ministry of Highways**
Stikine District
Bag 2000, Stikine Rd., Hwy 37
Dease Lake, BC, V0C 1L0
250-771-4511

*Northern British Columbia Travel Guide*
Published on behalf of the Northern
    British Columbia Tourism Assocation
    by OP Publishing
780 Beatty Street, Suite 300
Vancouver, BC, V6M 2M1
604-606-4644
    An excellent free publication on the
    north.

*North by Northwest*
http://bcadventure.com/adventure/
    explore/north.html

## Drive 24: Glacier Highway

**Alaska State Ferry**
800-642-0066

**Ministry of Highways**
Skeena District
4825 Keith Ave.
Terrace, BC, V8G 1K7
250-638-6440

**Stewart Infocenter**
222 5th Avenue
Stewart, BC, V0T 1W0
250-636-9224 (June to September)

*Tourism Stewart*
http://www.stewart.cmsd.bc.ca/commerce/
    tourism-map.html

*North by Northwest*
http://bcadventure.com/adventure/
    explore/north.html

## Drive 25: Telegraph Creek Road

**BC Parks in Dease Lake**
250-771-4591

**Ministry of Highways**
Stikine District
Bag 2000, Stikine Rd., Hwy 37
Dease Lake, BC, V0C 1L0
250-771-4511

*North by Northwest*
http://bcadventure.com/adventure/
    explore/north.html

## Drive 26: Alaska Highway

**BC Parks**
Peace-Liard District Office
#250-10003 110th Avenue
Fort St. John, BC, V1J 6M7
250-787-3407

**Ministry of Highways**
North Peace District
10003-110th Ave.
Fort St. John, BC, V1J 6M7
250-787-3237

*Northern British Columbia Travel Guide*
Published on behalf of the Northern
    British Columbia Tourism Assocation
    by OP Publishing
780 Beatty Street, Suite 300
Vancouver, BC, V6M 2M1
604-606-4644
    An excellent free publication on the
    north.

**Peace River Alaska Highway Tourist
    Association**
Fort St. John, BC
250-785-2544

**Fort Nelson Travel Infocenter**
250-774-6400 (summer only)

*BC Parks (descriptions of parks)*
http://www.elp.gov.bc.ca/bcparks/explore/
    pldis.htm

Peace River/Alaska Highway
http://bcadventure.com/adventure/
    explore/peace.html

# Index

Page numbers in **bold** refer to maps.
Page numbers in *Italics* refer to photos.

279

# About the Author

Scott Pick was born and raised in the Vancouver area and from an early age had a deep love of the outdoors. For ten years now he has been spending every free minute on adventures in the Pacific Northwest ranging from surfing in Oregon, to climbing in the BC Coast Range, to sea kayaking in Alaska. When not away on an adventure he is often found plotting new trips by poring over his huge map and guidebook collection. After graduating with a business administration degree from Simon Fraser University in 1995, he has dedicated himself to capturing as much of the spectacular beauty of BC on film as possible and now runs a stock photo business based on his images of wilderness landscapes and adventure sports. This is his first book.